Alexander Macfarlane

Elementary mathematical Tables

Alexander Macfarlane

Elementary mathematical Tables

ISBN/EAN: 9783743330146

Manufactured in Europe, USA, Canada, Australia, Japa

Cover: Foto ©Thomas Meinert / pixelio.de

Manufactured and distributed by brebook publishing software
(www.brebook.com)

Alexander Macfarlane

Elementary mathematical Tables

MATHEMATICAL TABLES.

BY

ALEXANDER MACFARLANE, D.Sc., LL.D.,

PROFESSOR OF PHYSICS IN THE UNIVERSITY OF TEXAS.

———•o⟩o⟨o•———

BOSTON, U.S.A., AND LONDON:

GINN & COMPANY, PUBLISHERS.

1890.

TYPOGRAPHY BY J. S. CUSHING & CO., BOSTON, U.S.A.

PRESSWORK BY GINN & CO., BOSTON, U.S.A.

PREFACE.

THESE tables are designed to be useful not only in computing and in the graphic method, but also in the teaching of arithmetic and in the illustration of the theorems of algebra.

I have arranged the several tables on a uniform decimal plan, so that the entries for a particular number are generally found in the same position on the page. The arrangement is that of double entry, so that in general the order of reading is the same as for ordinary print. The argument and entry are so expressed that it is easy to find the entry corresponding to any other position of the decimal point in the argument. In most cases the whole of a table is seen at one opening of the pages, and the tenth compartment, when not required for the main table, is filled with a short table which is in general auxiliary to the main table.

Special acknowledgments are due to Prof. Hastings of Yale University, and Prof. Halsted of this University. In the proof-reading and independent computation, I have received aid from D. W. Spence and J. C. Nagle, science students of this University.

ALEXANDER MACFARLANE.

UNIVERSITY OF TEXAS,
  April, 1889.

CONTENTS.

————•◦•————

* A caption in Italics indicates a small table appended to the main table.

CONTENTS.

V

n	0	1	2	3	4	5	6	7	8	9	d
10	0000	0043	0086	0128	0170	0212	0253	0294	0334	0374	40
11	0414	0453	0492	0531	0569	0607	0645	0682	0719	0755	37
12	0792	0828	0864	0899	0934	0969	1004	1038	1072	1106	33
13	1139	1173	1206	1239	1271	1303	1335	1367	1399	1430	31
14	1461	1492	1523	1553	1584	1614	1644	1673	1703	1732	29
15	1761	1790	1818	1847	1875	1903	1931	1959	1987	2014	27
16	2041	2068	2095	2122	2148	2175	2201	2227	2253	2279	25
17	2304	2330	2355	2380	2405	2430	2455	2480	2504	2529	24
18	2553	2577	2601	2625	2648	2672	2695	2718	2742	2765	23
19	2788	2810	2833	2856	2878	2900	2923	2945	2967	2989	21
20	3010	3032	3054	3075	3096	3118	3139	3160	3181	3201	21
21	3222	3243	3263	3284	3304	3324	3345	3365	3385	3404	20
22	3424	3444	3464	3483	3502	3522	3541	3560	3579	3598	19
23	3617	3636	3655	3674	3692	3711	3729	3747	3766	3784	18
24	3802	3820	3838	3856	3874	3892	3909	3927	3945	3962	17
25	3979	3997	4014	4031	4048	4065	4082	4099	4116	4133	17
26	4150	4166	4183	4200	4216	4232	4249	4265	4281	4298	16
27	4314	4330	4346	4362	4378	4393	4409	4425	4440	4456	16
28	4472	4487	4502	4518	4533	4548	4564	4579	4594	4609	15
29	4624	4639	4654	4669	4683	4698	4713	4728	4742	4757	14
30	4771	4786	4800	4814	4829	4843	4857	4871	4886	4900	14
31	4914	4928	4942	4955	4969	4983	4997	5011	5024	5038	13
32	5051	5065	5079	5092	5105	5119	5132	5145	5159	5172	13
33	5185	5198	5211	5224	5237	5250	5263	5276	5289	5302	13
34	5315	5328	5340	5353	5366	5378	5391	5403	5416	5428	13
35	5441	5453	5465	5478	5490	5502	5514	5527	5539	5551	12
36	5563	5575	5587	5599	5611	5623	5635	5647	5658	5670	12
37	5682	5694	5705	5717	5729	5740	5752	5763	5775	5786	12
38	5798	5809	5821	5832	5843	5855	5866	5877	5888	5899	12
39	5911	5922	5933	5944	5955	5966	5977	5988	5999	6010	11
40	6021	6031	6042	6053	6064	6075	6085	6096	6107	6117	11
41	6128	6138	6149	6160	6170	6180	6191	6201	6212	6222	10
42	6232	6243	6253	6263	6274	6284	6294	6304	6314	6325	10
43	6335	6345	6355	6365	6375	6385	6395	6405	6415	6425	10
44	6435	6444	6454	6464	6474	6484	6493	6503	6513	6522	10
45	6532	6542	6551	6561	6571	6580	6590	6599	6609	6618	10
46	6628	6637	6646	6656	6665	6675	6684	6693	6702	6712	9
47	6721	6730	6739	6749	6758	6767	6776	6785	6794	6803	9
48	6812	6821	6830	6839	6848	6857	6866	6875	6884	6893	9
49	6902	6911	6920	6928	6937	6946	6955	6964	6972	6981	9
50	6990	6998	7007	7016	7024	7033	7042	7050	7059	7067	9
51	7076	7084	7093	7101	7110	7118	7126	7135	7143	7152	8
52	7160	7168	7177	7185	7193	7202	7210	7218	7226	7235	8
53	7243	7251	7259	7267	7275	7284	7292	7300	7308	7316	8
54	7324	7332	7340	7348	7356	7364	7372	7380	7388	7396	8
55	7404	7412	7419	7427	7435	7443	7451	7459	7466	7474	8
56	7482	7490	7497	7505	7513	7520	7528	7536	7543	7551	8
57	7559	7566	7574	7582	7589	7597	7604	7612	7619	7627	7
58	7634	7642	7649	7657	7664	7672	7679	7686	7694	7701	8
59	7709	7716	7723	7731	7738	7745	7752	7760	7767	7774	8

n	0	1	2	3	4	5	6	7	8	9	d
60	7782	7789	7796	7803	7810	7818	7825	7832	7839	7846	7
61	7853	7860	7868	7875	7882	7889	7896	7903	7910	7917	7
62	7924	7931	7938	7945	7952	7959	7966	7973	7980	7987	6
63	7993	8000	8007	8014	8021	8028	8035	8041	8048	8055	7
64	8062	8069	8075	8082	8089	8096	8102	8109	8116	8122	7
65	8129	8136	8142	8149	8156	8162	8169	8176	8182	8189	6
66	8195	8202	8209	8215	8222	8228	8235	8241	8248	8254	7
67	8261	8267	8□	□80	8287	8293	8299	8306	8312	8319	6
68	8325	8331	833□	□4	8351	8357	8363	8370	8376	8382	6
69	8388	8395	8401	□7	8414	8420	8426	8432	8439	8445	6
70	8451	8457	8463	8470	8476	8482	8488	8494	8500	8506	7
71	8513	8519	8525	8531	8537	8543	8549	8555	8561	8567	6
72	8573	8579	8585	8591	8597	8603	8609	8615	8621	8627	6
73	8633	8639	8645	8651	8657	8663	8669	8675	8681	8686	6
74	8692	8698	8704	8710	8716	8722	8727	8733	8739	8745	6
75	8751	8756	8762	8768	8774	8779	8785	8791	8797	8802	6
76	8808	8814	8820	8825	8831	8837	8842	8848	8854	8859	6
77	8865	8871	8876	8882	8887	8893	8899	8904	8910	8915	6
78	8921	8927	8932	8938	8943	8949	8954	8960	8965	8971	5
79	8976	8982	8987	8993	8998	9004	9009	9015	9020	9025	6
80	9031	9036	9042	9047	9053	9058	9063	9069	9074	9079	6
81	9085	9090	9096	9101	9106	9112	9117	9122	9128	9133	5
82	9138	9143	9149	9154	9159	9165	9170	9175	9180	9186	5
83	9191	9196	9201	9206	9212	9217	9222	9227	9232	9238	5
84	9243	9248	9253	9258	9263	9269	9274	9279	9284	9289	5
85	9294	9299	9304	9309	9315	9320	9325	9330	9335	9340	5
86	9345	9350	9355	9360	9365	9370	9375	9380	9385	9390	5
87	9395	9400	9405	9410	9415	9420	9425	9430	9435	9440	5
88	9445	9450	9455	9460	9465	9469	9474	9479	9484	9489	5
89	9494	9499	9504	9509	9513	9518	9523	9528	9533	9538	4
90	9542	9547	9552	9557	9562	9566	9571	9576	9581	9586	4
91	9590	9595	9600	9605	9609	9614	9619	9624	9628	9633	5
92	9638	9643	9647	9652	9657	9661	9666	9671	9675	9680	5
93	9685	9689	9694	9699	9703	9708	9713	9717	9722	9727	4
94	9731	9736	9741	9745	9750	9754	9759	9763	9768	9773	4
95	9777	9782	9786	9791	9795	9800	9805	9809	9814	9818	5
96	9823	9827	9832	9836	9841	9845	9850	9854	9859	9863	5
97	9868	9872	9877	9881	9886	9890	9894	9899	9903	9908	4
98	9912	9917	9921	9926	9930	9934	9939	9943	9948	9952	4
99	9956	9961	9965	9969	9974	9978	9983	9987	9991	9996	4

pp.	4	5	6	7	8	9	10	11	12	13	14	15	16	17	18	19	20	21	22	23
1	0	1	1	1	1	1	1	1	1	1	1	2	2	2	2	2	2	2	2	2
2	1	1	1	1	2	2	2	2	2	3	3	3	3	3	4	4	4	4	4	5
3	1	2	2	2	2	3	3	3	4	4	4	5	5	5	5	6	6	6	7	7
4	2	2	2	3	3	4	4	4	5	5	6	6	6	7	7	8	8	8	9	9
5	2	3	3	4	4	5	5	6	6	7	7	8	8	9	9	10	10	11	11	12
6	2	3	4	4	5	5	6	7	7	8	8	9	10	10	11	11	12	13	13	14
7	3	4	4	5	6	6	7	8	8	9	10	11	11	12	13	13	14	15	15	16
8	3	4	5	6	6	7	8	9	10	10	11	12	13	14	14	15	16	17	18	18
9	4	5	5	6	7	8	9	10	11	12	13	14	14	15	16	17	18	19	20	21

n	0	1	2	3	4	5	6	7	8	9	d	pp.
100	0000	0004	0009	0013	0017	0022	0026	0030	0035	0039	4	5
101	0043	0048	0052	0056	0060	0065	0069	0073	0077	0082	4	1
102	0086	0090	0095	0099	0103	0107	0111	0116	0120	0124	4	1
103	0128	0133	0137	0141	0145	0149	0154	0158	0162	0166	4	2
104	0170	0175	0179	0183	0187	0191	0195	0199	0204	0208	4	2
105	0212	0216	0220	0224	0228	0233	0237	0241	0245	0249	4	3
106	0253	0257	0261	0265	0269	0273	0278	0282	0286	0290	4	3
107	0294	0298	0302	0306	0310	0314	0318	0322	0326	0330	4	4
108	0334	0338	0342	0346	0350	0354	0358	0362	0366	0370	4	4
109	0374	0378	0382	0386	0390	0394	0398	0402	0406	0410	4	5
110	0414	0418	0422	0426	0430	0434	0438	0441	0445	0449	4	
111	0453	0457	0461	0465	0469	0473	0477	0481	0484	0488	4	
112	0492	0496	0500	0504	0508	0512	0515	0519	0523	0527	4	
113	0531	0535	0538	0542	0546	0550	0554	0558	0561	0565	4	
114	0569	0573	0577	0580	0584	0588	0592	0596	0599	0603	4	
115	0607	0611	0615	0618	0622	0626	0630	0633	0637	0641	4	
116	0645	0648	0652	0656	0660	0663	0667	0671	0674	0678	4	
117	0682	0686	0689	0693	0697	0700	0704	0708	0711	0715	4	
118	0719	0722	0726	0730	0734	0737	0741	0745	0748	0752	3	
119	0755	0759	0763	0766	0770	0774	0777	0781	0785	0788	4	
120	0792	0795	0799	0803	0806	0810	0813	0817	0821	0824	4	4
121	0828	0831	0835	0839	0842	0846	0849	0853	0856	0860	4	0
122	0864	0867	0871	0874	0878	0881	0885	0888	0892	0896	3	1
123	0899	0903	0906	0910	0913	0917	0920	0924	0927	0931	3	1
124	0934	0938	0941	0945	0948	0952	0955	0959	0962	0966	3	2
125	0969	0973	0976	0980	0983	0986	0990	0993	0997	1000	4	2
126	1004	1007	1011	1014	1017	1021	1024	1028	1031	1035	3	2
127	1038	1041	1045	1048	1052	1055	1059	1062	1065	1069	3	3
128	1072	1075	1079	1082	1086	1089	1092	1096	1099	1103	3	3
129	1106	1109	1113	1116	1119	1123	1126	1129	1133	1136	3	4
130	1139	1143	1146	1149	1153	1156	1159	1163	1166	1169	4	
131	1173	1176	1179	1183	1186	1189	1193	1196	1199	1202	4	
132	1206	1209	1212	1216	1219	1222	1225	1229	1232	1235	4	
133	1239	1242	1245	1248	1252	1255	1258	1261	1265	1268	3	
134	1271	1274	1278	1281	1284	1287	1290	1294	1297	1300	3	
135	1303	1307	1310	1313	1316	1319	1323	1326	1329	1332	3	
136	1335	1339	1342	1345	1348	1351	1355	1358	1361	1364	3	
137	1367	1370	1374	1377	1380	1383	1386	1389	1392	1396	3	
138	1399	1402	1405	1408	1411	1414	1418	1421	1424	1427	3	
139	1430	1433	1436	1440	1443	1446	1449	1452	1455	1458	3	
140	1461	1464	1467	1471	1474	1477	1480	1483	1486	1489	3	3
141	1492	1495	1498	1501	1504	1508	1511	1514	1517	1520	3	0
142	1523	1526	1529	1532	1535	1538	1541	1544	1547	1550	3	1
143	1553	1556	1559	1562	1565	1569	1572	1575	1578	1581	3	1
144	1584	1587	1590	1593	1596	1599	1602	1605	1608	1611	3	1
145	1614	1617	1620	1623	1626	1629	1632	1635	1638	1641	3	2
146	1644	1647	1649	1652	1655	1658	1661	1664	1667	1670	3	2
147	1673	1676	1679	1682	1685	1688	1691	1694	1697	1700	3	2
148	1703	1706	1708	1711	1714	1717	1720	1723	1726	1729	3	2
149	1732	1735	1738	1741	1744	1746	1749	1752	1755	1758	3	3

n	0	1	2	3	4	5	6	7	8	9	d	pp.
150	1761	1764	1767	1770	1772	1775	1778	1781	1784	1787	3	3
151	1790	1793	1796	1798	1801	1804	1807	1810	1813	1816	2	0
152	1818	1821	1824	1827	1830	1833	1836	1838	1841	1844	3	1
153	1847	1850	1853	1855	1858	1861	1864	1867	1870	1872	3	1
154	1875	1878	1881	1884	1886	1889	1892	1895	1898	1901	2	1
155	1903	1906	1909	1912	1915	1917	1920	1923	1926	1928	3	2
156	1931	1934	1937	1940	1942	1945	1948	1951	1953	1956	3	2
157	1959	1962	1965	1967	1970	1973	1976	1978	1981	1984	3	2
158	1987	1989	1992	1995	1998	2000	2003	2006	2009	2011	3	2
159	2014	2017	2019	2022	2025	2028	2030	2033	2036	2038	3	3
160	2041	2044	2047	2049	2052	2055	2057	2060	2063	2066	2	
161	2068	2071	2074	2076	2079	2082	2084	2087	2090	2092	3	
162	2095	2098	2101	2103	2106	2109	2111	2114	2117	2119	3	
163	2122	2125	2127	2130	2133	2135	2138	2140	2143	2146	2	
164	2148	2151	2154	2156	2159	2162	2164	2167	2170	2172	3	
165	2175	2177	2180	2183	2185	2188	2191	2193	2196	2198	3	
166	2201	2204	2206	2209	2212	2214	2217	2219	2222	2225	2	
167	2227	2230	2232	2235	2238	2240	2243	2245	2248	2251	2	
168	2253	2256	2258	2261	2263	2266	2269	2271	2274	2276	3	
169	2279	2281	2284	2287	2289	2292	2294	2297	2299	2302	2	
170	2304	2307	2310	2312	2315	2317	2320	2322	2325	2327	3	2
171	2330	2333	2335	2338	2340	2343	2345	2348	2350	2353	2	0
172	2355	2358	2360	2363	2365	2368	2370	2373	2375	2378	2	0
173	2380	2383	2385	2388	2390	2393	2395	2398	2400	2403	2	1
174	2405	2408	2410	2413	2415	2418	2420	2423	2425	2428	2	1
175	2430	2433	2435	2438	2440	2443	2445	2448	2450	2453	2	1
176	2455	2458	2460	2463	2465	2467	2470	2472	2475	2477	3	1
177	2480	2482	2485	2487	2490	2492	2494	2497	2499	2502	2	1
178	2504	2507	2509	2512	2514	2516	2519	2521	2524	2526	3	2
179	2529	2531	2533	2536	2538	2541	2543	2545	2548	2550	3	2
180	2553	2555	2558	2560	2562	2565	2567	2570	2572	2574	3	
181	2577	2579	2582	2584	2586	2589	2591	2594	2596	2598	3	
182	2601	2603	2605	2608	2610	2613	2615	2617	2620	2622	3	
183	2625	2627	2629	2632	2634	2636	2639	2641	2643	2646	2	
184	2648	2651	2653	2655	2658	2660	2662	2665	2667	2669	3	
185	2672	2674	2676	2679	2681	2683	2686	2688	2690	2693	3	
186	2695	2697	2700	2702	2704	2707	2709	2711	2714	2716	2	
187	2718	2721	2723	2725	2728	2730	2732	2735	2737	2739	2	
188	2742	2744	2746	2749	2751	2753	2755	2758	2760	2762	3	
189	2765	2767	2769	2772	2774	2776	2778	2781	2783	2785	3	

n	0	1	2	3	4	5	6	7	8	9	d
1.00	.00 0000	0434	0868	1301	1734	2166	2598	3029	3461	3891	430
1.01	.00 4321	4751	5181	5609	6038	6466	6894	7321	7748	8174	426
1.02	.00 8600	9026	9451	9876	*0300	*0724	*1147	*1570	*1993	*2415	422
1.03	.01 2837	3259	3680	4100	4521	4940	5360	5779	6197	6616	417
1.04	.01 7033	7451	7868	8284	8700	9116	9532	9947	*0361	*0775	414
1.05	.02 1189	1603	2016	2428	2841	3252	3664	4075	4486	4896	410
1.06	.02 5306	5715	6125	6533	6942	7350	7757	8164	8571	8978	406
1.07	.02 9384	9789	*0195	*0600	*1004	*1408	*1812	*2216	*2619	*3021	403
1.08	.03 3424	3826	4227	4628	5029	5430	5830	6230	6629	7028	398
1.09	.03 7426	7825	8223	8620	9017	9414	9811	*0207	*0602	*0998	395

n	0	1	2	3	4	5	6	7	8	9	d	pp.
00	1000	1002	1005	1007	1009	1012	1014	1016	1019	1021	2	2 3 4
01	1023	1026	1028	1030	1033	1035	1038	1040	1042	1045	2	0 0 0
02	1047	1050	1052	1054	1057	1059	1062	1064	1067	1069	3	0 1 1
03	1072	1074	1076	1079	1081	1084	1086	1089	1091	1094	2	1 1 1
04	1096	1099	1102	1104	1107	1109	1112	1114	1117	1119	3	1 1 2
05	1122	1125	1127	1130	1132	1135	1138	1140	1143	1146	2	1 2 2
06	1148	1151	1153	1156	1159	1161	1164	1167	1169	1172	3	1 2 2
07	1175	1178	1180	1183	1186	1189	1191	1194	1197	1199	3	1 2 3
08	1202	1205	1208	1211	1213	1216	1219	1222	1225	1227	3	2 2 3
09	1230	1233	1236	1239	1242	1245	1247	1250	1253	1256	3	2 3 4
10	1259	1262	1265	1268	1271	1274	1276	1279	1282	1285	3	5 6 7
11	1288	1291	1294	1297	1300	1303	1306	1309	1312	1315	3	1 1 1
12	1318	1321	1324	1327	1330	1334	1337	1340	1343	1346	3	1 1 1
13	1349	1352	1355	1358	1361	1365	1368	1371	1374	1377	3	2 2 2
14	1380	1384	1387	1390	1393	1396	1400	1403	1406	1409	4	2 2 3
15	1413	1416	1419	1422	1426	1429	1432	1435	1439	1442	4	3 3 4
16	1445	1449	1452	1455	1459	1462	1466	1469	1472	1476	3	3 4 4
17	1479	1483	1486	1489	1493	1496	1500	1503	1507	1510	4	4 4 5
18	1514	1517	1521	1524	1528	1531	1535	1538	1542	1545	4	4 5 6
19	1549	1552	1556	1560	1563	1567	1570	1574	1578	1581	4	5 5 6
20	1585	1589	1592	1596	1600	1603	1607	1611	1614	1618	4	8 9
21	1622	1626	1629	1633	1637	1641	1644	1648	1652	1656	4	1 1
22	1660	1663	1667	1671	1675	1679	1683	1687	1690	1694	4	2 2
23	1698	1702	1706	1710	1714	1718	1722	1726	1730	1734	4	2 3
24	1738	1742	1746	1750	1754	1758	1762	1766	1770	1774	4	3 4
25	1778	1782	1786	1791	1795	1799	1803	1807	1811	1816	4	4 5
26	1820	1824	1828	1832	1837	1841	1845	1849	1854	1858	4	5 5
27	1862	1866	1871	1875	1879	1884	1888	1892	1897	1901	4	6 6
28	1905	1910	1914	1919	1923	1928	1932	1936	1941	1945	5	6 7
29	1950	1954	1959	1963	1968	1972	1977	1982	1986	1991	4	7 8
30	1995	2000	2004	2009	2014	2018	2023	2028	2032	2037	5	10 11
31	2042	2046	2051	2056	2061	2065	2070	2075	2080	2084	5	1 1
32	2089	2094	2099	2104	2109	2113	2118	2123	2128	2133	5	2 2
33	2138	2143	2148	2153	2158	2163	2168	2173	2178	2183	5	3 3
34	2188	2193	2198	2203	2208	2213	2218	2223	2228	2234	5	4 4
35	2239	2244	2249	2254	2259	2265	2270	2275	2280	2286	5	5 6
36	2291	2296	2301	2307	2312	2317	2323	2328	2333	2339	5	6 7
37	2344	2350	2355	2360	2366	2371	2377	2382	2388	2393	6	7 8
38	2399	2404	2410	2415	2421	2427	2432	2438	2443	2449	6	8 9
39	2455	2460	2466	2472	2477	2483	2489	2495	2500	2506	6	9 10
40	2512	2518	2523	2529	2535	2541	2547	2553	2559	2564	6	12 13
41	2570	2576	2582	2588	2594	2600	2606	2612	2618	2624	6	1 1
42	2630	2636	2642	2649	2655	2661	2667	2673	2679	2685	7	2 3
43	2692	2698	2704	2710	2716	2723	2729	2735	2742	2748	6	4 4
44	2754	2761	2767	2773	2780	2786	2793	2799	2805	2812	6	5 5
45	2818	2825	2831	2838	2844	2851	2858	2864	2871	2877	7	6 7
46	2884	2891	2897	2904	2911	2917	2924	2931	2938	2944	7	7 8
47	2951	2958	2965	2972	2979	2985	2992	2999	3006	3013	7	8 9
48	3020	3027	3034	3041	3048	3055	3062	3069	3076	3083	7	10 10
49	3090	3097	3105	3112	3119	3126	3133	3141	3148	3155	7	11 12

n	0	1	2	3	4	5	6	7	8	9	d	pp.
50	3162	3170	3177	3184	3192	3199	3206	3214	3221	3228	8	1415
51	3236	3243	3251	3258	3266	3273	3281	3289	3296	3304	7	1 2
52	3311	3319	3327	3334	3342	3350	3357	3365	3373	3381	7	3 3
53	3388	3396	3404	3412	3420	3428	3436	3443	3451	3459	8	4 5
54	3467	3475	3483	3491	3499	3508	3516	3524	3532	3540	8	6 6
55	3548	3556	3565	3573	3581	3589	3597	3606	3614	3622	9	7 8
56	3631	3639	3648	3656	3664	3673	3681	3690	3698	3707	8	8 9
57	3715	3724	3733	3741	3750	3758	3767	3776	3784	3793	9	10 11
58	3802	3811	3819	3828	3837	3846	3855	3864	3873	3882	8	11 12
59	3890	3899	3908	3917	3926	3936	3945	3954	3963	3972	9	13 14
60	3981	3990	3999	4009	4018	4027	4036	4046	4055	4064	10	1617
61	4074	4083	4093	4102	4111	4121	4130	4140	4150	4159	10	2 2
62	4169	4178	4188	4198	4207	4217	4227	4236	4246	4256	10	3 3
63	4266	4276	4285	4295	4305	4315	4325	4335	4345	4355	10	5 5
64	4365	4375	4385	4395	4406	4416	4426	4436	4446	4457	10	6 7
65	4467	4477	4487	4498	4508	4519	4529	4539	4550	4560	11	8 9
66	4571	4581	4592	4603	4613	4624	4634	4645	4656	4667	10	10 10
67	4677	4688	4699	4710	4721	4732	4742	4753	4764	4775	11	11 12
68	4786	4797	4808	4819	4831	4842	4853	4864	4875	4887	11	13 14
69	4898	4909	4920	4932	4943	4955	4966	4977	4989	5000	12	14 15
70	5012	5023	5035	5047	5058	5070	5082	5093	5105	5117	12	1819
71	5129	5140	5152	5164	5176	5188	5200	5212	5224	5236	12	2 2
72	5248	5260	5272	5284	5297	5309	5321	5333	5346	5358	12	4 4
73	5370	5383	5395	5408	5420	5433	5445	5458	5470	5483	12	5 6
74	5495	5508	5521	5534	5546	5559	5572	5585	5598	5610	13	7 8
75	5623	5636	5649	5662	5675	5689	5702	5715	5728	5741	13	9 10
76	5754	5768	5781	5794	5808	5821	5834	5848	5861	5875	13	11 11
77	5888	5902	5916	5929	5943	5957	5970	5984	5998	6012	14	13 13
78	6026	6039	6053	6067	6081	6095	6109	6124	6138	6152	14	14 15
79	6166	6180	6194	6209	6223	6237	6252	6266	6281	6295	15	16 17
80	6310	6324	6339	6353	6368	6383	6397	6412	6427	6442	15	2021
81	6457	6471	6486	6501	6516	6531	6546	6561	6577	6592	15	2 2
82	6607	6622	6637	6653	6668	6683	6699	6714	6730	6745	16	4 4
83	6761	6776	6792	6808	6823	6839	6855	6871	6887	6902	16	6 6
84	6918	6934	6950	6966	6982	6998	7015	7031	7047	7063	16	8 8
85	7079	7096	7112	7129	7145	7161	7178	7194	7211	7228	16	10 11
86	7244	7261	7278	7295	7311	7328	7345	7362	7379	7396	17	12 13
87	7413	7430	7447	7464	7482	7499	7516	7534	7551	7568	18	14 15
88	7586	7603	7621	7638	7656	7674	7691	7709	7727	7745	18	16 17
89	7762	7780	7798	7816	7834	7852	7870	7889	7907	7925	18	18 19
90	7943	7962	7980	7998	8017	8035	8054	8072	8091	8110	18	2223
91	8128	8147	8166	8185	8204	8222	8241	8260	8279	8299	19	2 2
92	8318	8337	8356	8375	8395	8414	8433	8453	8472	8492	19	4 5
93	8511	8531	8551	8570	8590	8610	8630	8650	8670	8690	20	7 7
94	8710	8730	8750	8770	8790	8810	8831	8851	8872	8892	21	9 9
95	8913	8933	8954	8974	8995	9016	9036	9057	9078	9099	21	11 12
96	9120	9141	9162	9183	9204	9226	9247	9268	9290	9311	22	13 14
97	9333	9354	9376	9397	9419	9441	9462	9484	9506	9528	22	15 16
98	9550	9572	9594	9616	9638	9661	9683	9705	9727	9750	22	18 18
99	9772	9795	9817	9840	9863	9886	9908	9931	9954	9977	23	20 21

log n	0	1	2	3	4	5	6	7	8	9	d	pp.
6.	0.0000	0001	0001	0001	0001	0001	0002	0002	0003	0003	1	
7.0	0.0004	0004	0005	0005	0005	0005	0005	0005	0005	0005	0	1 2
1	0005	0006	0006	0006	0006	0006	0006	0006	0007	0007	0	0 0
2	0007	0007	0007	0007	0008	0008	0008	0008	0008	0008	1	0 0
3	0009	0009	0009	0009	0009	0010	0010	0010	0010	0011	0	0 1
4	0011	0011	0011	0012	0012	0012	0013	0013	0013	0013	1	0 1
5	0014	0014	0014	0015	0015	0015	0016	0016	0016	0017	0	1 1
6	0017	0018	0018	0018	0019	0019	0020	0020	0021	0021	1	1 1
7	0022	0022	0023	0023	0024	0024	0025	0025	0026	0027	0	1 1
8	0027	0028	0029	0029	0030	0031	0031	0032	0033	0034	0	1 2
9	0034	0035	0036	0037	0038	0039	0039	0040	0041	0042	1	1 2
8.0	0.0043	0044	0045	0046	0047	0048	0050	0051	0052	0053	1	3 4
1	0054	0056	0057	0058	0060	0061	0062	0064	0065	0067	1	0 0
2	0068	0070	0071	0073	0075	0077	0078	0080	0082	0084	2	1 1
3	0086	0088	0090	0092	0094	0096	0098	0101	0103	0105	3	1 1
4	0108	0110	0113	0115	0118	0121	0123	0126	0129	0132	3	1 2
5	0135	0138	0141	0145	0148	0151	0155	0158	0162	0166	4	2 2
6	0170	0173	0177	0181	0186	0190	0194	0199	0203	0208	4	2 2
7	0212	0217	0222	0227	0232	0238	0243	0248	0254	0260	6	2 3
8	0266	0272	0278	0284	0291	0297	0304	0311	0318	0325	7	2 3
9	0332	0339	0347	0355	0363	0371	0379	0387	0396	0405	9	3 4
9.0	0414	0423	0432	0442	0452	0462	0472	0482	0493	0504	11	
1	0515	0526	0538	0550	0562	0574	0586	0599	0612	0625	14	
9.20	0.0639	0640	0642	0643	0644	0646	0647	0649	0650	0651	2	5 6
21	0653	0654	0656	0657	0658	0660	0661	0663	0664	0665	2	1 1
22	0667	0668	0670	0671	0673	0674	0675	0677	0678	0680	1	1 1
23	0681	0683	0684	0686	0687	0689	0690	0691	0693	0694	2	2 2
24	0696	0697	0699	0700	0702	0703	0705	0706	0708	0709	2	2 2
25	0711	0712	0714	0715	0717	0718	0720	0721	0723	0725	1	3 3
26	0726	0728	0729	0731	0732	0734	0735	0737	0738	0740	2	3 4
27	0742	0743	0745	0746	0748	0749	0751	0753	0754	0756	1	4 4
28	0757	0759	0761	0762	0764	0766	0767	0769	0770	0772	2	4 5
29	0774	0775	0777	0779	0780	0782	0783	0785	0787	0788	2	5 5
9.30	0.0790	0792	0793	0795	0797	0798	0800	0802	0804	0805	2	7 8
31	0807	0809	0810	0812	0814	0815	0817	0819	0821	0822	2	1 1
32	0824	0826	0827	0829	0831	0833	0834	0836	0838	0840	1	1 2
33	0841	0843	0845	0847	0849	0850	0852	0854	0856	0857	2	2 2
34	0859	0861	0863	0865	0866	0868	0870	0872	0874	0876	1	3 3
35	0877	0879	0881	0883	0885	0887	0888	0890	0892	0894	2	4 4
36	0896	0898	0900	0901	0903	0905	0907	0909	0911	0913	2	4 5
37	0915	0917	0918	0920	0922	0924	0926	0928	0930	0932	2	5 6
38	0934	0936	0938	0940	0942	0944	0945	0947	0949	0951	2	6 6
39	0953	0955	0957	0959	0961	0963	0965	0967	0969	0971	2	6 7
9.40	0.0973	0975	0977	0979	0981	0983	0985	0987	0989	0991	2	9
41	0993	0996	0998	1000	1002	1004	1006	1008	1010	1012	2	1
42	1014	1016	1018	1020	1022	1025	1027	1029	1031	1033	2	2
43	1035	1037	1039	1042	1044	1046	1048	1050	1052	1054	3	3
44	1057	1059	1061	1063	1065	1067	1070	1072	1074	1076	2	4
45	1078	1081	1083	1085	1087	1089	1092	1094	1096	1098	3	5
46	1101	1103	1105	1107	1110	1112	1114	1116	1119	1121	2	5
47	1123	1125	1128	1130	1132	1135	1137	1139	1141	1144	2	6
48	1146	1148	1151	1153	1155	1158	1160	1162	1165	1167	2	7
49	1169	1172	1174	1177	1179	1181	1184	1186	1189	1191	2	8

log n	0	1	2	3	4	5	6	7	8	9	d	pp.
9.50	0.1193	1196	1198	1201	1203	1205	1208	1210	1213	1215	3	**10**
51	1218	1220	1222	1225	1227	1230	1232	1235	1237	1240	2	1
52	1242	1245	1247	1250	1252	1255	1257	1260	1262	1265	2	2
53	1267	1270	1272	1275	1277	1280	1283	1285	1288	1290	3	3
54	1293	1295	1298	1301	1303	1306	1308	1311	1314	1316	3	4
55	1319	1321	1324	1327	1329	1332	1335	1337	1340	1343	2	5
56	1345	1348	1351	1353	1356	1359	1361	1364	1367	1369	3	6
57	1372	1375	1377	1380	1383	1386	1388	1391	1394	1397	2	7
58	1399	1402	1405	1408	1410	1413	1416	1419	1422	1424	3	8
59	1427	1430	1433	1436	1438	1441	1444	1447	1450	1453	2	9
9.60	0.1455	1458	1461	1464	1467	1470	1473	1475	1478	1481	3	**11**
61	1484	1487	1490	1493	1496	1499	1502	1504	1507	1510	3	1
62	1513	1516	1519	1522	1525	1528	1531	1534	1537	1540	3	2
63	1543	1546	1549	1552	1555	1558	1561	1564	1567	1570	3	3
64	1573	1576	1579	1582	1585	1588	1591	1594	1598	1601	3	4
65	1604	1607	1610	1613	1616	1619	1622	1625	1629	1632	3	6
66	1635	1638*	1641	1644	1647	1651	1654	1657	1660	1663	3	7
67	1666	1670	1673	1676	1679	1682	1686	1689	1692	1695	4	8
68	1699	1702	1705	1708	1712	1715	1718	1721	1725	1728	3	9
69	1731	1735	1738	1741	1744	1748	1751	1754	1758	1761	3	10
9.70	0.1764	1768	1771	1774	1778	1781	1784	1788	1791	1795	3	**12**
71	1798	1801	1805	1808	1812	1815	1818	1822	1825	1829	3	1
72	1832	1836	1839	1842	1846	1849	1853	1856	1860	1863	4	2
73	1867	1870	1874	1877	1881	1884	1888	1891	1895	1898	4	4
74	1902	1906	1909	1913	1916	1920	1923	1927	1931	1934	4	5
75	1938	1941	1945	1949	1952	1956	1959	1963	1967	1970	4	6
76	1974	1978	1981	1985	1989	1992	1996	2000	2003	2007	4	7
77	2011	2015	2018	2022	2026	2029	2033	2037	2041	2044	4	8
78	2048	2052	2056	2059	2063	2067	2071	2075	2078	2082	4	10
79	2086	2090	2094	2097	2101	2105	2109	2113	2117	2121	3	11
9.80	0.2124	2128	2132	2136	2140	2144	2148	2152	2156	2159	4	**13**
81	2163	2167	2171	2175	2179	2183	2187	2191	2195	2199	4	1
82	2203	2207	2211	2215	2219	2223	2227	2231	2235	2239	4	3
83	2243	2247	2251	2255	2259	2263	2267	2271	2275	2279	5	4
84	2284	2288	2292	2296	2300	2304	2308	2312	2316	2321	4	5
85	2325	2329	2333	2337	2341	2346	2350	2354	2358	2362	4	7
86	2366	2371	2375	2379	2383	2388	2392	2396	2400	2405	4	8
87	2409	2413	2417	2422	2426	2430	2434	2439	2443	2447	5	9
88	2452	2456	2460	2465	2469	2473	2478	2482	2486	2491	4	10
89	2495	2499	2504	2508	2513	2517	2521	2526	2530	2535	4	12
9.90	0.2539	2543	2548	2552	2557	2561	2566	2570	2575	2579	5	**14**
91	2584	2588	2593	2597	2602	2606	2611	2615	2620	2624	5	1
92	2629	2633	2638	2642	2647	2651	2656	2661	2665	2670	4	3
93	2674	2679	2684	2688	2693	2697	2702	2707	2711	2716	5	4
94	2721	2725	2730	2735	2739	2744	2749	2753	2758	2763	4	6
95	2767	2772	2777	2782	2786	2791	2796	2801	2805	2810	5	7
96	2815	2820	2824	2829	2834	2839	2844	2848	2853	2858	5	8
97	2863	2868	2873	2877	2882	2887	2892	2897	2902	2907	4	10
98	2911	2916	2921	2926	2931	2936	2941	2946	2951	2956	5	11
99	2961	2966	2970	2975	2980	2985	2990	2995	3000	3005	5	13

IV. SUBTRACTION LOGARITHMS. $\log\left(\dfrac{1}{1-n}\right)$

log n	0	1	2	3	4	5	6	7	8	9	d	pp.
6.	0.0000	0001	0001	0001	0001	0001	0002	0002	0003	0003	1	
7.0	0.0004	0004	0005	0005	0005	0005	0005	0005	0005	0005	0	1 2
1	0005	0006	0006	0006	0006	0006	0006	0006	0007	0007	0	0 0
2	0007	0007	0007	0007	0008	0008	0008	0008	0008	0008	1	0 0
3	0009	0009	0009	0009	0010	0010	0010	0010	0010	0011	0	0 1
4	0011	0011	0011	0012	0012	0012	0013	0013	0013	0013	1	0 1
5	0014	0014	0014	0015	0015	0015	0016	0016	0017	0017	0	1 1
6	0017	0018	0018	0019	0019	0019	0020	0020	0021	0021	1	1 1
7	0022	0022	0023	0023	0024	0024	0025	0026	0026	0027	0	1 1
8	0027	0028	0029	0029	0030	0031	0032	0032	0033	0034	1	1 2
9	0035	0035	0036	0037	0038	0039	0040	0041	0042	0043	1	1 2
8.0	0.0044	0045	0046	0047	0048	0049	0050	0051	0053	0054	1	3 4
1	0055	0056	0058	0059	0060	0062	0063	0065	0066	0068	1	0 0
2	0069	0071	0073	0074	0076	0078	0080	0082	0084	0086	2	1 1
3	0088	0090	0092	0094	0096	0098	0101	0103	0105	0108	2	1 1
4	0110	0113	0116	0118	0121	0124	0127	0130	0133	0136	4	1 2
5	0140	0143	0146	0150	0153	0157	0161	0164	0168	0172	4	2 2
6	0176	0181	0185	0189	0194	0198	0203	0208	0213	0218	5	2 2
7	0223	0229	0234	0240	0245	0251	0257	0264	0270	0276	7	2 3
8	0283	0290	0297	0304	0311	0319	0327	0335	0343	0351	8	2 3
9	0359	0368	0377	0386	0396	0405	0415	0425	0436	0447	11	3 4
9.0	0458	0469	0480	0492	0504	0517	0530	0543	0556	0570	14	
.1	0584	0599	0614	0629	0645	0661	0678	0695	0713	0731	18	
9.20	0.0749	0751	0753	0755	0757	0759	0761	0763	0765	0767	1	5 6
21	0768	0770	0772	0774	0776	0778	0780	0782	0784	0786	2	1 1
22	0788	0790	0792	0794	0796	0798	0800	0802	0804	0806	2	1 1
23	0808	0810	0812	0814	0817	0819	0821	0823	0825	0827	2	2 2
24	0829	0831	0833	0835	0838	0840	0842	0844	0846	0848	2	2 2
25	0850	0853	0855	0857	0859	0861	0863	0866	0868	0870	2	3 3
26	0872	0875	0877	0879	0881	0884	0886	0888	0890	0893	2	3 4
27	0895	0897	0899	0902	0904	0906	0909	0911	0913	0916	2	4 4
28	0918	0920	0923	0925	0928	0930	0932	0935	0937	0940	2	4 5
29	0942	0944	0947	0949	0952	0954	0957	0959	0962	0964	3	5 5
9.30	0.0967	0969	0972	0974	0977	0979	0982	0984	0987	0989	3	7 8
31	0992	0994	0997	1000	1002	1005	1007	1010	1013	1015	3	1 1
32	1018	1020	1023	1026	1028	1031	1034	1037	1039	1042	3	1 2
33	1045	1047	1050	1053	1056	1058	1061	1064	1067	1069	3	2 2
34	1072	1075	1078	1081	1084	1086	1089	1092	1095	1098	3	3 3
35	1101	1104	1106	1109	1112	1115	1118	1121	1124	1127	3	4 4
36	1130	1133	1136	1139	1142	1145	1148	1151	1154	1157	3	4 5
37	1160	1163	1166	1169	1172	1176	1179	1182	1185	1188	3	5 6
38	1191	1194	1198	1201	1204	1207	1210	1214	1217	1220	3	6 6
39	1223	1226	1230	1233	1236	1240	1243	1246	1250	1253	3	6 7
9.40	0.1256	1260	1263	1266	1270	1273	1277	1280	1283	1287	3	9 11
41	1290	1294	1297	1301	1304	1308	1311	1315	1318	1322	3	1 1
42	1325	1329	1333	1336	1340	1343	1347	1351	1354	1358	4	2 2
43	1362	1365	1369	1373	1377	1380	1384	1388	1392	1395	4	3 3
44	1399	1403	1407	1411	1414	1418	1422	1426	1430	1434	4	4 4
45	1438	1442	1446	1450	1454	1458	1462	1466	1470	1474	4	5 6
46	1478	1482	1486	1490	1494	1498	1502	1506	1511	1515	4	5 7
47	1519	1523	1527	1531	1536	1540	1544	1549	1553	1557	4	6 8
48	1561	1566	1570	1574	1579	1583	1588	1592	1596	1601	4	7 9
49	1605	1610	1614	1619	1623	1628	1633	1637	1642	1646	5	8 10

log n	0	1	2	3	4	5	6	7	8	9	d	pp.
9.50	0.1651	1656	1660	1665	1670	1674	1679	1684	1688	1693	5	12 13
51	1698	1703	1708	1712	1717	1722	1727	1732	1737	1742	5	1 1
52	1747	1752	1757	1762	1767	1772	1777	1782	1787	1792	5	2 3
53	1797	1802	1807	1812	1818	1823	1828	1833	1839	1844	5	4 4
54	1849	1854	1860	1865	1871	1876	1881	1887	1892	1898	5	5 5
55	1903	1909	1914	1920	1925	1931	1936	1942	1948	1953	6	6 7
56	1959	1965	1971	1976	1982	1988	1994	2000	2005	2011	6	7 8
57	2017	2023	2029	2035	2041	2047	2053	2059	2065	2071	6	8 9
58	2077	2084	2090	2096	2102	2108	2115	2121	2127	2134	6	10 10
59	2140	2146	2153	2159	2166	2172	2179	2185	2192	2198	7	11 12
9.60	0.2205	2211	2218	2225	2231	2238	2245	2252	2259	2265	7	14 15
61	2272	2279	2286	2293	2300	2307	2314	2321	2328	2335	7	1 2
62	2342	2350	2357	2364	2371	2378	2386	2393	2400	2408	7	3 3
63	2415	2423	2430	2438	2445	2453	2460	2468	2476	2483	8	4 5
64	2491	2499	2507	2515	2522	2530	2538	2546	2554	2562	8	6 6
65	2570	2578	2586	2595	2603	2611	2619	2628	2636	2644	9	7 8
66	2653	2661	2670	2678	2687	2695	2704	2713	2721	2730	9	8 9
67	2739	2748	2756	2765	2774	2783	2792	2801	2810	2819	10	10 11
68	2829	2838	2847	2856	2866	2875	2884	2894	2903	2913	9	11 12
69	2922	2932	2942	2951	2961	2971	2981	2991	3001	3011	10	13 14
9.70	0.3021	3031	3041	3051	3061	3071	3082	3092	3103	3113	10	16 17
71	3123	3134	3145	3155	3166	3177	3188	3198	3209	3220	11	2 2
72	3231	3242	3253	3265	3276	3287	3299	3310	3321	3333	11	3 3
73	3344	3356	3368	3380	3391	3403	3415	3427	3439	3451	12	5 5
74	3463	3476	3488	3500	3513	3525	3538	3550	3563	3576	13	6 7
75	3589	3602	3614	3627	3641	3654	3667	3680	3694	3707	14	8 9
76	3721	3734	3748	3762	3775	3789	3803	3817	3831	3846	14	10 10
77	3860	3874	3889	3903	3918	3933	3947	3962	3977	3992	15	11 12
78	4007	4022	4038	4053	4069	4084	4100	4116	4131	4147	16	13 14
79	4163	4180	4196	4212	4229	4245	4262	4278	4295	4312	17	14 15
9.80	0.4329	4346	4364	4381	4398	4416	4434	4452	4470	4488	18	18 19
81	4506	4524	4542	4561	4580	4598	4617	4636	4655	4675	19	2 2
82	4694	4714	4733	4753	4773	4793	4813	4834	4854	4875	21	4 4
83	4896	4917	4938	4959	4980	5002	5024	5046	5068	5090	22	5 6
84	5112	5135	5157	5180	5203	5227	5250	5273	5297	5321	24	7 8
85	5345	5370	5394	5419	5444	5469	5494	5520	5546	5572	26	9 10
86	5598	5624	5651	5678	5705	5732	5760	5787	5815	5844	28	11 11
87	5872	5901	5930	5959	5989	6019	6049	6079	6110	6141	31	13 13
88	6172	6204	6236	6268	6300	6333	6366	6400	6434	6468	34	14 15
89	6502	6537	6572	6608	6644	6680	6717	6754	6792	6830	38	16 17

pp.	20	21	22	23	24	25	26	27	28	29	30	31	32	33	34	35	36	37	88
1	2	2	2	2	2	3	3	3	3	3	3	3	3	3	3	4	4	4	4
2	4	4	4	5	5	5	5	5	6	6	6	6	6	7	7	7	7	7	8
3	6	6	7	7	7	8	8	8	8	9	9	9	10	10	10	11	11	11	11
4	8	8	9	9	10	10	10	11	11	12	12	12	13	13	14	14	14	15	15
5	10	10	11	12	12	13	13	14	14	15	15	16	16	17	17	18	18	19	19
6	12	12	13	13	14	14	15	16	16	17	17	18	19	19	20	20	21	22	22
7	14	15	15	16	17	18	18	19	20	20	21	22	22	23	24	25	25	26	27
8	16	17	18	18	19	20	21	22	22	23	24	25	26	26	27	28	29	30	30
9	18	19	20	21	22	23	23	24	25	26	27	28	29	30	31	32	32	33	34

IV. SUBTRACTION LOGARITHMS $\log\left(\frac{1}{1-n}\right)$

log n	0	1	2	3	4	5	6	7	8	9	d	pp.
9.900	0.6868	6872	6876	6880	6884	6888	6892	6895	6899	6903	4	**4 5**
901	6907	6911	6915	6919	6923	6927	6931	6935	6938	6942	4	0 1
902	6946	6950	6954	6958	6962	6966	6970	6974	6978	6982	4	1 1
903	6986	6990	6994	6998	7002	7006	7010	7014	7018	7022	4	1 2
904	7026	7030	7034	7038	7042	7047	7051	7055	7059	7063	4	2 2
905	7067	7071	7075	7079	7083	7087	7092	7096	7100	7104	4	2 3
906	7108	7112	7116	7121	7125	7129	7133	7137	7141	7146	4	2 3
907	7150	7154	7158	7162	7167	7171	7175	7179	7183	7188	4	3 4
908	7192	7196	7200	7205	7209	7213	7217	7222	7226	7230	4	3 4
909	7234	7239	7243	7247	7252	7256	7260	7265	7269	7273	5	4 5
9.910	0.7278	7282	7286	7291	7295	7299	7304	7308	7313	7317	4	**6 7**
911	7321	7326	7330	7335	7339	7343	7348	7352	7357	7361	5	1 1
912	7366	7370	7375	7379	7383	7388	7392	7397	7401	7406	4	1 1
913	7410	7415	7419	7424	7428	7433	7438	7442	7447	7451	5	2 2
914	7456	7460	7465	7469	7474	7479	7483	7488	7492	7497	5	2 3
915	7502	7506	7511	7516	7520	7525	7530	7534	7539	7544	4	3 4
916	7548	7553	7558	7562	7567	7572	7577	7581	7586	7591	4	4 4
917	7595	7600	7605	7610	7614	7619	7624	7629	7634	7638	5	4 5
918	7643	7648	7653	7658	7663	7667	7672	7677	7682	7687	5	5 6
919	7692	7697	7701	7706	7711	7716	7721	7726	7731	7736	5	5 6
9.920	0.7741	7746	7751	7756	7761	7766	7771	7776	7781	7786	5	**8 9**
921	7791	7796	7801	7806	7811	7816	7821	7826	7831	7836	5	1 1
922	7841	7846	7851	7856	7861	7867	7872	7877	7882	7887	5	2 2
923	7892	7897	7903	7908	7913	7918	7923	7929	7934	7939	5	2 3
924	7944	7949	7955	7960	7965	7970	7976	7981	7986	7992	5	3 4
925	7997	8002	8007	8013	8018	8023	8029	8034	8040	8045	5	4 5
926	8050	8056	8061	8066	8072	8077	8083	8088	8094	8099	6	5 5
927	8105	8110	8115	8121	8126	8132	8137	8143	8148	8154	6	6 6
928	8160	8165	8171	8176	8182	8187	8193	8199	8204	8210	5	6 7
929	8215	8221	8227	8232	8238	8244	8249	8255	8261	8266	6	7 8
9.930	0.8272	8278	8284	8289	8295	8301	8307	8312	8318	8324	6	**1011**
931	8330	8336	8341	8347	8353	8359	8365	8371	8377	8382	6	1 1
932	8388	8394	8400	8406	8412	8418	8424	8430	8436	8442	6	2 2
933	8448	8454	8460	8466	8472	8478	8484	8490	8496	8502	6	3 3
934	8508	8514	8520	8527	8533	8539	8545	8551	8557	8563	7	4 4
935	8570	8576	8582	8588	8595	8601	8607	8613	8620	8626	6	5 6
936	8632	8638	8645	8651	8657	8664	8670	8676	8683	8689	7	6 7
937	8696	8702	8708	8715	8721	8728	8734	8741	8747	8754	6	7 8
938	8760	8767	8773	8780	8786	8793	8800	8806	8813	8819	7	8 9
939	8826	8833	8839	8846	8853	8859	8866	8873	8879	8886	7	9 10
9.940	0.8893	8900	8906	8913	8920	8927	8934	8940	8947	8954	7	**1213**
941	8961	8968	8975	8982	8989	8996	9002	9009	9016	9023	7	1 1
942	9030	9037	9044	9051	9058	9065	9073	9080	9087	9094	7	2 3
943	9101	9108	9115	9122	9130	9137	9144	9151	9158	9166	7	4 4
944	9173	9180	9188	9195	9202	9209	9217	9224	9232	9239	7	5 5
945	9246	9254	9261	9269	9276	9284	9291	9299	9306	9314	7	6 7
946	9321	9329	9336	9344	9351	9359	9367	9374	9382	9390	7	7 8
947	9397	9405	9413	9421	9428	9436	9444	9452	9460	9467	8	8 9
948	9475	9483	9491	9499	9507	9515	9523	9531	9539	9547	8	10 10
949	9555	9563	9571	9579	9587	9595	9603	9611	9619	9628	8	11 12

log n	0	1	2	3	4	5	6	7	8	9	d	pp.
9.950	0.9636	9644	9652	9660	9669	9677	9685	9694	9702	9710	9	14 15
951	9719	9727	9735	9744	9752	9761	9769	9778	9786	9795	8	1 2
952	9803	9812	9820	9829	9838	9846	9855	9864	9872	9881	9	3 3
953	9890	9899	9907	9916	9925	9934	9943	9951	9960	9969	9	4 5
954	9978	9987	9996	*0005	*0014	*0023	*0032	*0041	*0050	*0060	9	6 6
955	1.0069	0078	0087	0096	0106	0115	0124	0133	0143	0152	9	7 8
956	0161	0171	0180	0190	0199	0209	0218	0228	0237	0247	9	8 9
957	0256	0266	0276	0285	0295	0305	0314	0324	0334	0344	10	10 11
958	0354	0364	0373	0383	0393	0403	0413	0423	0433	0443	10	11 12
959	0453	0464	0474	0484	0494	0504	0514	0525	0535	0545	11	13 14
9.960	1.0556	0566	0576	0587	0597	0608	0618	0629	0640	0650	11	16 17
961	0661	0671	0682	0693	0704	0714	0725	0736	0747	0758	11	2 2
962	0769	0780	0791	0802	0813	0824	0835	0846	0857	0868	12	3 3
963	0880	0891	0902	0913	0925	0936	0948	0959	0971	0982	12	5 5
964	0994	1005	1017	1028	1040	1052	1064	1075	1087	1099	12	6 7
965	1111	1123	1135	1147	1159	1171	1183	1195	1207	1220	12	8 9
966	1232	1244	1257	1269	1281	1294	1306	1319	1331	1344	13	10 10
967	1357	1369	1382	1395	1408	1420	1433	1446	1459	1472	13	11 12
968	1485	1498	1512	1525	1538	1551	1565	1578	1591	1605	13	13 14
969	1618	1632	1645	1659	1673	1686	1700	1714	1728	1742	14	14 15
9.970	1.1756	1770	1784	1798	1812	1826	1841	1855	1869	1884	14	18 19
971	1898	1913	1927	1942	1956	1971	1986	2001	2016	2031	15	2 2
972	2046	2061	2076	2091	2106	2121	2137	2152	2167	2183	16	4 4
973	2199	2214	2230	2246	2261	2277	2293	2309	2325	2341	16	5 6
974	2357	2374	2390	2406	2423	2439	2456	2473	2489	2506	17	7 8
975	2523	2540	2557	2574	2591	2608	2625	2643	2660	2678	17	9 10
976	2695	2713	2731	2748	2766	2784	2802	2820	2838	2857	18	11 11
977	2875	2893	2912	2931	2949	2968	2987	3006	3025	3044	19	13 13
978	3063	3082	3102	3121	3141	3161	3180	3200	3220	3240	20	14 15
979	3260	3280	3301	3321	3342	3362	3383	3404	3425	3446	21	16 17
9.980	1.3467	3488	3510	3531	3553	3575	3596	3618	3640	3663	22	20 21
981	3685	3707	3730	3753	3775	3798	3821	3845	3868	3891	24	2 2
982	3915	3939	3962	3986	4010	4035	4059	4084	4108	4133	25	4 4
983	4158	4183	4208	4234	4259	4285	4311	4337	4363	4390	26	6 6
984	4416	4443	4470	4497	4524	4552	4579	4607	4635	4663	29	8 8
985	4692	4720	4749	4778	4807	4836	4866	4896	4926	4956	30	10 11
986	4986	5017	5048	5079	5110	5142	5174	5206	5238	5270	33	12 13
987	5303	5336	5370	5403	5437	5471	5505	5540	5575	5610	36	14 15
988	5646	5682	5718	5754	5791	5828	5866	5903	5942	5980	39	16 17
989	6019	6058	6097	6137	6178	6218	6259	6301	6343	6385	43	18 19
9.990	1.6428	6471	6514	6559	6603	6648	6693	6739	6786	6833	47	22 23
991	6880	6928	6977	7026	7076	7126	7177	7228	7281	7333	54	2 2
992	7387	7441	7496	7551	7608	7665	7722	7781	7840	7901	61	4 5
993	7962	8024	8087	8151	8215	8281	8348	8416	8485	8555	71	7 7
994	8626	8699	8773	8848	8924	9002	9081	9162	9244	9328	85	9 9
995	9413	9500	9589	9680	9773	9868	9965	*0065	*0166	*0270		11 12
996	2.0377	0487	0599	0714	0833	0955	1080	1209	1342	1480		13 14
997	1622	1768	1920	2078	2241	2411	2588	2772	2965	3166		15 16
998	3378	3600	3834	4082	4345	4624	4924	5245	5592	5969		18 18
999	6383	6840	7351	7930	8599	9391	*0359	*1608	*3369	*6378		20 21

log sin n°   log cos n°

n°	.0	.1	.2	.3	.4	.5	.6	.7	.8	.9	1.0		d
0	7.	2419	5429	7190	8439	9408	*0200	*0870	*1450	*1961	*2419	89	
1	8.2419	2832	3210	3558	3880	4179	4459	4723	4971	5206	5428	88	
2	5428	5640	5842	6035	6220	6397	6567	6731	6889	7041	7188	87	
3	7188	7330	7468	7602	7731	7857	7979	8098	8213	8326	8436	86	
4	8436	8543	8647	8749	8849	8946	9042	9135	9226	9315	9403	85	88
5	9403	9489	9573	9655	9736	9816	9894	9970	*0046	*0120	*0192	84	72
6	9.0192	0264	0334	0403	0472	0539	0605	0670	0734	0797	0859	83	62
7	0859	0920	0981	1040	1099	1157	1214	1271	1326·	1381	1436	82	55
8	1436	1489	1542	1594	1646	1697	1747	1797	1847	1895	1943	81	48
9	1943	1991	2038	2085	2131	2176	2221	2266	2310	2353	2397	80	44
10	9.2397	2439	2482	2524	2565	2606	2647	2687	2727	2767	2806	79	39
11	2806	2845	2883	2921	2959	2997	3034	3070	3107	3143	3179	78	36
12	3179	3214	3250	3284	3319	3353	3387	3421	3455	3488	3521	77	33
13	3521	3554	3586	3618	3650	3682	3713	3745	3775	3806	3837	76	31
14	3837	3867	3897	3927	3957	3986	4015	4044	4073	4102	4130	75	28
15	4130	4158	4186	4214	4242	4269	4296	4323	4350	4377	4403	74	26
16	4403	4430	4456	4482	4508	4533	4559	4584	4609	4634	4659	73	25
17	4659	4684	4709	4733	4757	4781	4805	4829	4853	4876	4900	72	24
18	4900	4923	4946	4969	4992	5015	5037	5060	5082	5104	5126	71	22
19	5126	5148	5170	5192	5213	5235	5256	5278	5299	5320	5341	70	21
20	9.5341	5361	5382	5402	5423	5443	5463	5484	5504	5523	5543	69	20
21	5543	5563	5583	5602	5621	5641	5660	5679	5698	5717	5736	68	19
22	5736	5754	5773	5792	5810	5828	5847	5865	5883	5901	5919	67	18
23	5919	5937	5954	5972	5990	6007	6024	6042	6059	6076	6093	66	17
24	6093	6110	6127	6144	6161	6177	6194	6210	6227	6243	6259	65	16
25	6259	6276	6292	6308	6324	6340	6356	6371	6387	6403	6418	64	15
26	6418	6434	6449	6465	6480	6495	6510	6526	6541	6556	6570	63	14
27	6570	6585	6600	6615	6629	6644	6659	6673	6687	6702	6716	62	14
28	6716	6730	6744	6759	6773	6787	6801	6814	6828	6842	6856	61	14
29	6856	6869	6883	6896	6910	6923	6937	6950	6963	6977	6990	60	13
30	9.6990	7003	7016	7029	7042	7055	7068	7080	7093	7106	7118	59	12
31	7118	7131	7144	7156	7168	7181	7193	7205	7218	7230	7242	58	12
32	7242	7254	7266	7278	7290	7302	7314	7326	7338	7349	7361	57	12
33	7361	7373	7384	7396	7407	7419	7430	7442	7453	7464	7476	56	12
34	7476	7487	7498	7509	7520	7531	7542	7553	7564	7575	7586	55	11
35	7586	7597	7607	7618	7629	7640	7650	7661	7671	7682	7692	54	10
36	7692	7703	7713	7723	7734	7744	7754	7764	7774	7785	7795	53	10
37	7795	7805	7815	7825	7835	7844	7854	7864	7874	7884	7893	52	9
38	7893	7903	7913	7922	7932	7941	7951	7960	7970	7979	7989	51	10
39	7989	7998	8007	8017	8026	8035	8044	8053	8063	8072	8081	50	9
40	9.8081	8090	8099	8108	8117	8125	8134	8143	8152	8161	8169	49	8
41	8169	8178	8187	8195	8204	8213	8221	8230	8238	8247	8255	48	8
42	.8255	8264	8272	8280	8289	8297	8305	8313	8322	8330	8338	47	8
43	8338	8346	8354	8362	8370	8378	8386	8394	8402	8410	8418	46	8
44	8418	8426	8433	8441	8449	8457	8464	8472	8480	8487	8495	45	8
45	8495	8502	8510	8517	8525	8532	8540	8547	8555	8562	8569	44	7
46	8569	8577	8584	8591	8598	8606	8613	8620	8627	8634	8641	43	7
47	8641	8648	8655	8662	8669	8676	8683	8690	8697	8704	8711	42	7
48	8711	8718	8724	8731	8738	8745	8751	8758	8765	8771	8778	41	7
49	8778	8784	8791	8797	8804	8810	8817	8823	8830	8836	8843	40	7
	1.0	.9	.8	.7	.6	.5	.4	.3	.2	.1	.0	n°	d

log sin $n°$ log cos $n°$

n°	.0	.1	.2	.3	.4	.5	.6	.7	.8	.9	1.0		d
50	9.8843	8849	8855	8862	8868	8874	8880	8887	8893	8899	8905	39	6
51	8905	8911	8917	8923	8929	8935	8941	8947	8953	8959	8965	38	6
52	8965	8971	8977	8983	8989	8995	9000	9006	9012	9018	9023	37	5
53	9023	9029	9035	9041	9046	9052	9057	9063	9069	9074	9080	36	6
54	9080	9085	9091	9096	9101	9107	9112	9118	9123	9128	9134	35	6
55	9134	9139	9144	9149	9155	9160	9165	9170	9175	9181	9186	34	5
56	9186	9191	9196	9201	9206	9211	9216	9221	9226	9231	9236	33	5
57	9236	9241	9246	9251	9255	9260	9265	9270	9275	9279	9284	32	5
58	9284	9289	9294	9298	9303	9308	9312	9317	9322	9326	9331	31	5
59	9331	9335	9340	9344	9349	9353	9358	9362	9367	9371	9375	30	4
60	9.9375	9380	9384	9388	9393	9397	9401	9406	9410	9414	9418	29	4
61	9418	9422	9427	9431	9435	9439	9443	9447	9451	9455	9459	28	4
62	9459	9463	9467	9471	9475	9479	9483	9487	9491	9495	9499	27	4
63	9499	9503	9507	9510	9514	9518	9522	9525	9529	9533	9537	26	4
64	9537	9540	9544	9548	9551	9555	9558	9562	9566	9569	9573	25	4
65	9573	9576	9580	9583	9587	9590	9594	9597	9601	9604	9607	24	3
66	9607	9611	9614	9617	9621	9624	9627	9631	9634	9637	9640	23	3
67	9640	9643	9647	9650	9653	9656	9659	9662	9666	9669	9672	22	3
68	9672	9675	9678	9681	9684	9687	9690	9693	9696	9699	9702	21	3
69	9702	9704	9707	9710	9713	9716	9719	9722	9724	9727	9730	20	3
70	9.9730	9733	9735	9738	9741	9743	9746	9749	9751	9754	9757	19	3
71	9757	9759	9762	9764	9767	9770	9772	9775	9777	9780	9782	18	2
72	9782	9785	9787	9789	9792	9794	9797	9799	9801	9804	9806	17	2
73	9806	9808	9811	9813	9815	9817	9820	9822	9824	9826	9828	16	2
74	9828	9831	9833	9835	9837	9839	9841	9843	9845	9847	9849	15	2
75	9849	9851	9853	9855	9857	9859	9861	9863	9865	9867	9869	14	2
76	9869	9871	9873	9875	9876	9878	9880	9882	9884	9885	9887	13	2
77	9887	9889	9891	9892	9894	9896	9897	9899	9901	9902	9904	12	2
78	9904	9906	9907	9909	9910	9912	9913	9915	9916	9918	9919	11	1
79	9919	9921	9922	9924	9925	9927	9928	9929	9931	9932	9934	10	2
80	9.9934	9935	9936	9937	9939	9940	9941	9943	9944	9945	9946	9	1
81	9946	9947	9949	9950	9951	9952	9953	9954	9955	9956	9958	8	2
82	9958	9959	9960	9961	9962	9963	9964	9965	9966	9967	9968	7	1
83	9968	9968	9969	9970	9971	9972	9973	9974	9975	9975	9976	6	1
84	9976	9977	9978	9978	9979	9980	9981	9981	9982	9983	9983	5	0
85	9983	9984	9985	9985	9986	9987	9987	9988	9988	9989	9989	4	0
86	9989	9990	9990	9991	9991	9992	9992	9993	9993	9994	9994	3	0
87	9994	9994	9995	9995	9996	9996	9996	9996	9997	9997	9997	2	0
88	9997	9998	9998	9998	9998	9999	9999	9999	9999	9999	9999	1	0
89	9999	9999	0000	0000	0000	0000	0000	0000	0000	0000	0000	0	0
	1.0	.9	.8	.7	.6	.5	.4	.3	.2	.1	.0	n°	d

pp.	11	12	13	14	15	16	17	18	19	20	21	22	23	24	25	26	27	28	29	30
1	1	1	1	1	2	2	2	2	2	2	2	2	2	2	3	3	3	3	3	3
2	2	2	3	3	3	3	3	4	4	4	4	4	5	5	5	5	5	6	6	6
3	3	4	4	4	5	5	5	5	6	6	6	7	7	7	8	8	8	8	9	9
4	4	5	5	6	6	6	7	7	8	8	8	9	9	10	10	10	11	11	12	12
5	6	6	7	7	8	8	9	9	10	10	11	11	12	12	13	13	14	14	15	15
6	7	7	8	8	9	10	10	11	11	12	13	13	14	14	15	16	16	17	17	18
7	8	8	9	10	11	11	12	13	13	14	15	15	16	17	18	18	19	20	20	21
8	9	10	10	11	12	13	14	14	15	16	17	18	18	19	20	21	22	22	23	24
9	10	11	12	13	14	14	15	16	17	18	19	20	21	22	23	23	24	25	26	27

log sin *n*°   log cos *n*°

n°	0	1	2	3	4	5	6	7	8	9	10		d
0.0	6.	2419	5429	7190	8439	9408	*0200	*0870	*1450	*1961	*2419	89.9	
0.1	7.2419	2833	3211	3558	3880	4180	4460	4723	4971	5206	5429	89.8	
0.2	5429	5641	5843	6036	6221	6398	6568	6732	6890	7043	7190	89.7	
0.3	7190	7332	7470	7604	7734	7859	7982	8101	8217	8329	8439	89.6	
0.4	8439	8547	8651	8753	8853	8951	9046	9140	9231	9321	9408	89.5	87
0.5	9408	9494	9579	9661	9743	9822	9901	9977	*0053	*0127	*0200	89.4	73
0.6	8.0200	0272	0343	0412	0480	0548	0614	0679	0744	0807	0870	89.3	63
0.7	0870	0931	0992	1052	1111	1169	1227	1284	1340	1395	1450	89.2	55
0.8	1450	1503	1557	1609	1661	1713	1764	1814	1863	1912	1961	89.1	49
0.9	1961	2009	2056	2103	2150	2196	2241	2286	2331	2375	2419	89.0	44
1.0	8.2419	2462	2505	2547	2589	2630	2672	2712	2753	2793	2832	88.9	39
1.1	2832	2872	2911	2949	2988	3025	3063	3100	3137	3174	3210	88.8	36
1.2	3210	3246	3282	3317	3353	3388	3422	3456	3491	3524	3558	88.7	34
1.3	3558	3591	3624	3657	3689	3722	3754	3786	3817	3848	3880	88.6	32
1.4	3880	3911	3941	3972	4002	4032	4062	4091	4121	4150	4179	88.5	29
1.5	4179	4208	4237	4265	4293	4322	4349	4377	4405	4432	4459	88.4	27
1.6	4459	4486	4513	4540	4567	4593	4619	4645	4671	4697	4723	88.3	26
1.7	4723	4748	4773	4799	4824	4848	4873	4898	4922	4947	4971	88.2	24
1.8	4971	4995	5019	5043	5066	5090	5113	5136	5160	5183	5206	88.1	23
1.9	5206	5228	5251	5274	5296	5318	5340	5363	5385	5406	5428	88.0	22
2.0	8.5428	5450	5471	5493	5514	5535	5557	5578	5598	5619	5640	87.9	21
2.1	5640	5661	5681	5702	5722	5742	5762	5782	5802	5822	5842	87.8	20
2.2	5842	5862	5881	5901	5920	5939	5959	5978	5997	6016	6035	87.7	19
2.3	6035	6054	6072	6091	6110	6128	6147	6165	6183	6201	6220	87.6	19
2.4	6220	6238	6256	6274	6291	6309	6327	6344	6362	6379	6397	87.5	18
2.5	6397	6414	6431	6449	6466	6483	6500	6517	6534	6550	6567	87.4	17
2.6	6567	6584	6600	6617	6633	6650	6666	6682	6699	6715	6731	87.3	16
2.7	6731	6747	6763	6779	6795	6810	6826	6842	6858	6873	6889	87.2	16
2.8	6889	6904	6920	6935	6950	6965	6981	6996	7011	7026	7041	87.1	15
2.9	7041	7056	7071	7086	7100	7115	7130	7144	7159	7174	7188	87.0	14
3.0	8.7188	7202	7217	7231	7245	7260	7274	7288	7302	7316	7330	86.9	14
3.1	7330	7344	7358	7372	7386	7400	7413	7427	7441	7454	7468	86.8	14
3.2	7468	7482	7495	7508	7522	7535	7549	7562	7575	7588	7602	86.7	14
3.3	7602	7615	7628	7641	7654	7667	7680	7693	7705	7718	7731	86.6	13
3.4	7731	7744	7756	7769	7782	7794	7807	7819	7832	7844	7857	86.5	13
3.5	7857	7869	7881	7894	7906	7918	7930	7943	7955	7967	7979	86.4	12
3.6	7979	7991	8003	8015	8027	8039	8051	8062	8074	8086	8098	86.3	12
3.7	8098	8109	8121	8133	8144	8156	8168	8179	8191	8202	8213	86.2	11
3.8	8213	8225	8236	8248	8259	8270	8281	8293	8304	8315	8326	86.1	11
3.9	8326	8337	8348	8359	8370	8381	8392	8403	8414	8425	8436	86.0	11
4.0	8.8436	8447	8457	8468	8479	8490	8500	8511	8522	8532	8543	85.9	11
4.1	8543	8553	8564	8575	8585	8595	8606	8616	8627	8637	8647	85.8	10
4.2	8647	8658	8668	8678	8688	8699	8709	8719	8729	8739	8749	85.7	10
4.3	8749	8759	8769	8780	8790	8799	8809	8819	8829	8839	8849	85.6	10
4.4	8849	8859	8869	8878	8888	8898	8908	8917	8927	8937	8946	85.5	9
4.5	8946	8956	8966	8975	8985	8994	9004	9013	9023	9032	9042	85.4	10
4.6	9042	9051	9060	9070	9079	9089	9098	9107	9116	9126	9135	85.3	9
4.7	9135	9144	9153	9162	9172	9181	9190	9199	9208	9217	9226	85.2	9
4.8	9226	9235	9244	9253	9262	9271	9280	9289	9298	9307	9315	85.1	8
4.9	9315	9324	9333	9342	9351	9359	9368	9377	9386	9394	9403	85.0	9
	10	9	8	7	6	5	4	3	2	1	0	n°	d

log sin n°   log cos n°

n°	0	1	2	3	4	5	6	7	8	9	10		d
5.0	8.9403	9412	9420	9429	9437	9446	9455	9463	9472	9480	9489	84.9	9
5.1	9489	9497	9506	9514	9523	9531	9539	9548	9556	9565	9573	84.8	8
5.2	9573	9581	9589	9598	9606	9614	9623	9631	9639	9647	9655	84.7	8
5.3	9655	9664	9672	9680	9688	9696	9704	9712	9720	9728	9736	84.6	8
5.4	9736	9744	9752	9760	9768	9776	9784	9792	9800	9808	9816	84.5	8
5.5	9816	9824	9831	9839	9847	9855	9863	9870	9878	9886	9894	84.4	8
5.6	9894	9901	9909	9917	9925	9932	9940	9948	9955	9963	9970	84.3	7
5.7	9970	9978	9986	9993	*0001	*0008	*0016	*0023	*0031	*0038	*0046	84.2	8
5.8	9.0046	0053	0061	0068	0075	0083	0090	0098	0105	0112	0120	84.1	8
5.9	0120	0127	0134	0142	0149	0156	0163	0171	0178	0185	0192	84.0	7
6.0	9.0192	0200	0207	0214	0221	0228	0235	0243	0250	0257	0264	83.9	7
6.1	0264	0271	0278	0285	0292	0299	0306	0313	0320	0327	0334	83.8	7
6.2	0334	0341	0348	0355	0362	0369	0376	0383	0390	0397	0403	83.7	6
6.3	0403	0410	0417	0424	0431	0438	0444	0451	0458	0465	0472	83.6	7
6.4	0472	0478	0485	0492	0498	0505	0512	0519	0525	0532	0539	83.5	7
6.5	0539	0545	0552	0558	0565	0572	0578	0585	0591	0598	0605	83.4	7
6.6	0605	0611	0618	0624	0631	0637	0644	0650	0657	0663	0670	83.3	7
6.7	0670	0676	0683	0689	0695	0702	0708	0715	0721	0727	0734	83.2	7
6.8	0734	0740	0746	0753	0759	0765	0772	0778	0784	0790	0797	83.1	7
6.9	0797	0803	0809	0816	0822	0828	0834	0840	0847	0853	0859	83.0	6
7.0	9.0859	0865	0871	0877	0884	0890	0896	0902	0908	0914	0920	82.9	6
7.1	0920	0926	0932	0938	0945	0951	0957	0963	0969	0975	0981	82.8	6
7.2	0981	0987	0993	0999	1005	1011	1017	1022	1028	1034	1040	82.7	6
7.3	1040	1046	1052	1058	1064	1070	1076	1081	1087	1093	1099	82.6	6
7.4	1099	1105	1111	1116	1122	1128	1134	1140	1145	1151	1157	82.5	6
7.5	1157	1163	1168	1174	1180	1186	1191	1197	1203	1208	1214	82.4	6
7.6	1214	1220	1226	1231	1237	1242	1248	1254	1259	1265	1271	82.3	6
7.7	1271	1276	1282	1287	1293	1299	1304	1310	1315	1321	1326	82.2	5
7.8	1326	1332	1337	1343	1348	1354	1359	1365	1370	1376	1381	82.1	5
7.9	1381	1387	1392	1398	1403	1409	1414	1419	1425	1430	1436	82.0	6
8.0	9.1436	1441	1446	1452	1457	1462	1468	1473	1478	1484	1489	81.9	5
8.1	1489	1494	1500	1505	1510	1516	1521	1526	1532	1537	1542	81.8	5
8.2	1542	1547	1553	1558	1563	1568	1574	1579	1584	1589	1594	81.7	5
8.3	1594	1600	1605	1610	1615	1620	1625	1631	1636	1641	1646	81.6	5
8.4	1646	1651	1656	1661	1666	1672	1677	1682	1687	1692	1697	81.5	5
8.5	1697	1702	1707	1712	1717	1722	1727	1732	1737	1742	1747	81.4	5
8.6	1747	1752	1757	1762	1767	1772	1777	1782	1787	1792	1797	81.3	5
8.7	1797	1802	1807	1812	1817	1822	1827	1832	1837	1842	1847	81.2	5
8.8	1847	1851	1856	1861	1866	1871	1876	1881	1886	1890	1895	81.1	5
8.9	1895	1900	1905	1910	1915	1919	1924	1929	1934	1939	1943	81.0	4
	10	9	8	7	6	5	4	3	2	1	0	n°	

°	0	1	2	3	4	5	6	7	8	9	°	S	log sin
.1	6	6.6	7.2	7.8	8.4	9	9.6	10.2	10.8	11.4	0.00	1.7581	
.2	12	12.6	13.2	13.8	14.4	15	15.6	16.2	16.8	17.4	1.11	1.7582	8.2872
.3	18	18.6	19.2	19.8	20.4	21	21.6	22.2	22.8	23.4	2.40	1.7583	8.6220
.4	24	24.6	25.2	25.8	26.4	27	27.6	28.2	28.8	29.4	3.21	1.7584	8.7482
.5	30	30.6	31.2	31.8	32.4	33	33.6	34.2	34.8	35.4	3.85	1.7585	8.8270
.6	36	36.6	37.2	37.8	38.4	39	39.6	40.2	40.8	41.4	4.40		8.8849
.7	42	42.6	43.2	43.8	44.4	45	45.6	46.2	46.8	47.4			
.8	48	48.6	49.2	49.8	50.4	51	51.6	52.2	52.8	53.4			
.9	54	54.6	55.2	55.8	56.4	57	57.6	58.2	58.8	59.4			

log tan n°   log cotan n°

n°	.0	.1	.2	.3	.4	.5	.6	.7	.8	.9	1.0		d
0	7.	2419	5429	7190	8439	9409	*0200	*0870	*1450	*1962	*2419	89	
1	8.2419	2833	3211	3559	3881	4181	4461	4725	4973	5208	5431	88	
2	5431	5643	5845	6038	6223	6401	6571	6736	6894	7046	7194	87	
3	7194	7337	7475	7609	7739	7865	7988	8107	8223	8336	8446	86	
4	8446	8554	8659	8762	8862	8960	9056	9150	9241	9331	9420	85	89
5	9420	9506	9591	9674	9756	9836	9915	9992	*0068	*0143	*0216	84	73
6	9.0216	0289	0360	0430	0499	0567	0633	0699	0764	0828	0891	83	63
7	0891	0954	1015	1076	1135	1194	1252	1310	1367	1423	1478	82	55
8	1478	1533	1587	1640	1693	1745	1797	1848	1898	1948	1997	81	49
9	1997	2046	2094	2142	2189	2236	2282	2328	2374	2419	2463	80	44
10	9.2463	2507	2551	2594	2637	2680	2722	2764	2805	2846	2887	79	41
11	2887	2927	2967	3006	3046	3085	3123	3162	3200	3237	3275	78	38
12	3275	3312	3349	3385	3422	3458	3493	3529	3564	3599	3634	77	35
13	3634	3668	3702	3736	3770	3804	3837	3870	3903	3935	3968	76	33
14	3968	4000	4032	4064	4095	4127	4158	4189	4220	4250	4281	75	31
15	4281	4311	4341	4371	4400	4430	4459	4488	4517	4546	4575	74	29
16	4575	4603	4632	4660	4688	4716	4744	4771	4799	4826	4853	73	27
17	4853	4880	4907	4934	4961	4987	5014	5040	5066	5092	5118	72	26
18	5118	5143	5169	5195	5220	5245	5270	5295	5320	5345	5370	71	25
19	5370	5394	5419	5443	5467	5491	5516	5539	5563	5587	5611	70	24
20	9.5611	5634	5658	5681	5704	5727	5750	5773	5796	5819	5842	69	23
21	5842	5864	5887	5909	5932	5954	5976	5998	6020	6042	6064	68	22
22	6064	6086	6108	6129	6151	6172	6194	6215	6236	6257	6279	67	22
23	6279	6300	6321	6341	6362	6383	6404	6424	6445	6465	6486	66	21
24	6486	6506	6527	6547	6567	6587	6607	6627	6647	6667	6687	65	20
25	6687	6706	6726	6746	6765	6785	6804	6824	6843	6863	6882	64	19
26	6882	6901	6920	6939	6958	6977	6996	7015	7034	7053	7072	63	19
27	7072	7090	7109	7128	7146	7165	7183	7202	7220	7238	7257	62	19
28	7257	7275	7293	7311	7330	7348	7366	7384	7402	7420	7438	61	18
29	7438	7455	7473	7491	7509	7526	7544	7562	7579	7597	7614	60	17
30	9.7614	7632	7649	7667	7684	7701	7719	7736	7753	7771	7788	59	17
31	7788	7805	7822	7839	7856	7873	7890	7907	7924	7941	7958	58	17
32	7958	7975	7992	8008	8025	8042	8059	8075	8092	8109	8125	57	16
33	8125	8142	8158	8175	8191	8208	8224	8241	8257	8274	8290	56	16
34	8290	8306	8323	8339	8355	8371	8388	8404	8420	8436	8452	55	16
35	8452	8468	8484	8501	8517	8533	8549	8565	8581	8597	8613	54	16
36	8613	8629	8644	8660	8676	8692	8708	8724	8740	8755	8771	53	16
37	8771	8787	8803	8818	8834	8850	8865	8881	8897	8912	8928	52	16
38	8928	8944	8959	8975	8990	9006	9022	9037	9053	9068	9084	51	16
39	9084	9099	9115	9130	9146	9161	9176	9192	9207	9223	9238	50	15
40	9.9238	9254	9269	9284	9300	9315	9330	9346	9361	9376	9392	49	16
41	9392	9407	9422	9438	9453	9468	9483	9499	9514	9529	9544	48	15
42	9544	9560	9575	9590	9605	9621	9636	9651	9666	9681	9697	47	16
43	9697	9712	9727	9742	9757	9772	9788	9803	9818	9833	9848	46	15
44	9848	9864	9879	9894	9909	9924	9939	9955	9970	9985	*0000	45	15
45	0.0000	0015	0030	0045	0061	0076	0091	0106	0121	0136	0152	44	16
46	0152	0167	0182	0197	0212	0228	0243	0258	0273	0288	0303	43	15
47	0303	0319	0334	0349	0364	0379	0395	0410	0425	0440	0456	42	16
48	0456	0471	0486	0501	0517	0532	0547	0562	0578	0593	0608	41	15
49	0608	0624	0639	0654	0670	0685	0700	0716	0731	0746	0762	40	16
	1.0	.9	.8	.7	.6	.5	.4	.3	.2	.1	.0	n°	d

log tan n°   log cotan n°

n°	.0	.1	.2	.3	.4	.5	.6	.7	.8	.9	1.0		d
50	0.0762	0777	0793	0808	0824	0839	0854	0870	0885	0901	0916	39	15
51	0916	0932	0947	0963	0978	0994	1010	1025	1041	1056	1072	38	16
52	1072	1088	1103	1119	1135	1150	1166	1182	1197	1213	1229	37	16
53	1229	1245	1260	1276	1292	1308	1324	1340	1356	1371	1387	36	16
54	1387	1403	1419	1435	1451	1467	1483	1499	1516	1532	1548	35	16
55	1548	1564	1580	1596	1612	1629	1645	1661	1677	1694	1710	34	16
56	1710	1726	1743	1759	1776	1792	1809	1825	1842	1858	1875	33	17
57	1875	1891	1908	1925	1941	1958	1975	1992	2008	2025	2042	32	17
58	2042	2059	2076	2093	2110	2127	2144	2161	2178	2195	2212	31	17
59	2212	2229	2247	2264	2281	2299	2316	2333	2351	2368	2386	30	18
60	0.2386	2403	2421	2438	2456	2474	2491	2509	2527	2545	2562	29	17
61	2562	2580	2598	2616	2634	2652	2670	2689	2707	2725	2743	28	18
62	2743	2762	2780	2798	2817	2835	2854	2872	2891	2910	2928	27	18
63	2928	2947	2966	2985	3004	3023	3042	3061	3080	3099	3118	26	19
64	3118	3137	3157	3176	3196	3215	3235	3254	3274	3294	3313	25	19
65	3313	3333	3353	3373	3393	3413	3433	3453	3473	3494	3514	24	20
66	3514	3535	3555	3576	3596	3617	3638	3659	3679	3700	3721	23	21
67	3721	3743	3764	3785	3806	3828	3849	3871	3892	3914	3936	22	22
68	3936	3958	3980	4002	4024	4046	4068	4091	4113	4136	4158	21	22
69	4158	4181	4204	4227	4250	4273	4296	4319	4342	4366	4389	20	23
70	0.4389	4413	4437	4461	4484	4509	4533	4557	4581	4606	4630	19	24
71	4630	4655	4680	4705	4730	4755	4780	4805	4831	4857	4882	18	25
72	4882	4908	4934	4960	4986	5013	5039	5066	5093	5120	5147	17	27
73	5147	5174	5201	5229	5256	5284	5312	5340	5368	5397	5425	16	28
74	5425	5454	5483	5512	5541	5570	5600	5629	5659	5689	5719	15	30
75	5719	5750	5780	5811	5842	5873	5905	5936	5968	6000	6032	14	32
76	6032	6065	6097	6130	6163	6196	6230	6264	6298	6332	6366	13	34
77	6366	6401	6436	6471	6507	6542	6578	6615	6651	6688	6725	12	37
78	6725	6763	6800	6838	6877	6915	6954	6994	7033	7073	7113	11	40
79	7113	7154	7195	7236	7278	7320	7363	7406	7449	7493	7537	10	44
80	0.7537	7581	7626	7672	7718	7764	7811	7858	7906	7954	8003	9	49
81	8003	8052	8102	8152	8203	8255	8307	8360	8413	8467	8522	8	55
82	8522	8577	8633	8690	8748	8806	8865	8924	8985	9046	9109	7	63
83	9109	9172	9236	9301	9367	9433	9501	9570	9640	9711	9784	6	73
84	9784	9857	9932	*0008	*0085	*0164	*0244	*0326	*0409	*0494	*0580	5	86
85	1.0580	0669	0759	0850	0944	1040	1138	1238	1341	1446	1554	4	
86	1554	1664	1777	1893	2012	2135	2261	2391	2525	2663	2806	3	
87	2806	2954	3106	3264	3429	3599	3777	3962	4155	4357	4569	2	
88	4569	4792	5027	5275	5539	5819	6119	6441	6789	7167	7581	1	
89	7581	8038	8550	9130	9800	*0591	*1561	*2810	*4571	*7581		0	
	1.0	.9	.8	.7	.6	.5	.4	.3	.2	.1	.0	n°	d

pp.	31	32	33	34	35	36	37	38	39	40	41	42	43	44	45	46	47	48	49	50
1	3	3	3	3	4	4	4	4	4	4	4	4	4	4	5	5	5	5	5	5
2	6	6	7	7	7	7	7	8	8	8	8	8	9	9	9	9	9	10	10	10
3	9	10	10	10	11	11	11	11	12	12	12	13	13	13	14	14	14	14	15	15
4	12	13	13	14	14	14	15	15	16	16	16	17	17	18	18	18	19	19	20	20
5	16	16	17	17	18	18	19	19	20	20	21	21	22	22	23	23	24	24	25	25
6	19	19	20	20	21	22	22	23	23	24	25	25	26	26	27	28	28	29	29	30
7	22	22	23	24	25	25	26	27	27	28	29	29	30	31	32	32	33	34	34	35
8	25	26	26	27	28	29	30	30	31	32	33	34	34	35	36	37	38	38	39	40
9	28	29	30	31	32	32	33	34	35	36	37	38	39	40	41	41	42	43	44	45

log tan n°   log cotan n°

n°	0	1	2	3	4	5	6	7	8	9	10		d
0.0	6.	2419	5429	7190	8439	9408	*0200	*0870	*1450	*1961	*2419	89.9	
0.1	7.2419	2833	3211	3558	3880	4180	4460	4723	4972	5206	5429	89.8	
0.2	5429	5641	5843	6036	6221	6398	6569	6732	6890	7043	7190	89.7	
0.3	7190	7332	7470	7604	7734	7860	7982	8101	8217	8329	8439	89.6	
0.4	8439	8547	8651	8754	8853	8951	9046	9140	9231	9321	9409	89.5	88
0.5	9409	9495	9579	9662	9743	9823	9901	9978	*0053	*0127	*0200	89.4	73
0.6	8.0200	0272	0343	0412	0481	0548	0614	0680	0744	0807	0870	89.3	63
0.7	0870	0932	0992	1052	1111	1170	1227	1284	1340	1395	1450	89.2	55
0.8	1450	1504	1557	1610	1662	1713	1764	1814	1864	1913	1962	89.1	49
0.9	1962	2010	2057	2104	2150	2196	2242	2287	2331	2376	2419	89.0	43
1.0	8.2419	2462	2505	2548	2590	2631	2672	2713	2754	2794	2833	88.9	39
1.1	2833	2873	2912	2950	2988	3026	3064	3101	3138	3175	3211	88.8	36
1.2	3211	3247	3283	3318	3354	3389	3423	3458	3492	3525	3559	88.7	34
1.3	3559	3592	3625	3658	3691	3723	3755	3787	3818	3850	3881	88.6	31
1.4	3881	3912	3943	3973	4003	4033	4063	4093	4122	4152	4181	88.5	29
1.5	4181	4210	4238	4267	4295	4323	4351	4379	4406	4434	4461	88.4	27
1.6	4461	4488	4515	4542	4568	4595	4621	4647	4673	4699	4725	88.3	26
1.7	4725	4750	4775	4801	4826	4851	4875	4900	4924	4949	4973	88.2	24
1.8	4973	4997	5021	5045	5068	5092	5115	5139	5162	5185	5208	88.1	23
1.9	5208	5231	5253	5276	5298	5321	5343	5365	5387	5409	5431	88.0	22
2.0	8.5431	5453	5474	5496	5517	5538	5559	5580	5601	5622	5643	87.9	21
2.1	5643	5664	5684	5705	5725	5745	5765	5785	5805	5825	5845	87.7	20
2.2	5845	5865	5884	5904	5923	5943	5962	5981	6000	6019	6038	87.6	19
2.3	6038	6057	6076	6095	6113	6132	6150	6169	6187	6205	6223	87.8	18
2.4	6223	6242	6260	6277	6295	6313	6331	6348	6366	6384	6401	87.5	17
2.5	6401	6418	6436	6453	6470	6487	6504	6521	6538	6555	6571	87.4	16
2.6	6571	6588	6605	6621	6638	6654	6671	6687	6703	6719	6736	87.3	17
2.7	6736	6752	6768	6784	6800	6815	6831	6847	6863	6878	6894	87.2	16
2.8	6894	6909	6925	6940	6956	6971	6986	7001	7016	7031	7046	87.1	15
2.9	7046	7061	7076	7091	7106	7121	7136	7150	7165	7179	7194	87.0	15
3.0	8.7194	7208	7223	7237	7252	7266	7280	7294	7308	7323	7337	86.9	14
3.1	7337	7351	7365	7379	7392	7406	7420	7434	7448	7461	7475	86.8	14
3.2	7475	7488	7502	7515	7529	7542	7556	7569	7582	7596	7609	86.7	13
3.3	7609	7622	7635	7648	7661	7674	7687	7700	7713	7726	7739	86.6	13
3.4	7739	7751	7764	7777	7790	7802	7815	7827	7840	7852	7865	86.5	13
3.5	7865	7877	7890	7902	7914	7927	7939	7951	7963	7975	7988	86.4	13
3.6	7988	8000	8012	8024	8036	8048	8059	8071	8083	8095	8107	86.3	12
3.7	8107	8119	8130	8142	8154	8165	8177	8188	8200	8212	8223	86.2	11
3.8	8223	8234	8246	8257	8269	8280	8291	8302	8314	8325	8336	86.1	11
3.9	8336	8347	8358	8370	8381	8392	8403	8414	8425	8436	8446	86.0	10
4.0	8.8446	8457	8468	8479	8490	8501	8511	8522	8533	8543	8554	85.9	11
4.1	8554	8565	8575	8586	8596	8607	8617	8628	8638	8649	8659	85.8	10
4.2	8659	8669	8680	8690	8700	8711	8721	8731	8741	8751	8762	85.7	11
4.3	8762	8772	8782	8792	8802	8812	8822	8832	8842	8852	8862	85.6	10
4.4	8862	8872	8882	8891	8901	8911	8921	8931	8940	8950	8960	85.5	10
4.5	8960	8970	8979	8989	8998	9008	9018	9027	9037	9046	9056	85.4	10
4.6	9056	9065	9075	9084	9093	9103	9112	9122	9131	9140	9150	85.3	10
4.7	9150	9159	9168	9177	9186	9196	9205	9214	9223	9232	9241	85.2	9
4.8	9241	9250	9260	9269	9278	9287	9296	9305	9313	9322	9331	85.1	9
4.9	9331	9340	9349	9358	9367	9376	9384	9393	9402	9411	9420	85.0	9
	10	9	8	7	6	5	4	3	2	1	0	n°	d

log tan $n°$ log cotan $n°$

n°	0	1	2	3	4	5	6	7	8	9	10		d
5.0	8.9420	9428	9437	9446	9454	9463	9472	9480	9489	9497	9506	84.9	9
5.1	9506	9515	9523	9532	9540	9549	9557	9565	9574	9582	9591	84.8	9
5.2	9591	9599	9608	9616	9624	9633	9641	9649	9657	9666	9674	84.7	8
5.3	9674	9682	9690	9699	9707	9715	9723	9731	9739	9747	9756	84.6	9
5.4	9756	9764	9772	9780	9788	9796	9804	9812	9820	9828	9836	84.5	8
5.5	9836	9844	9852	9860	9867	9875	9883	9891	9899	9907	9915	84.4	8
5.6	9915	9922	9930	9938	9946	9953	9961	9969	9977	9984	9992	84.3	8
5.7	9992	*0000	*0007	*0015	*0022	*0030	*0038	*0045	*0053	+0060	0068	84.2	8
5.8	9.0068	0075	0083	0090	0098	0105	0113	0120	0128	0135	0143	84.1	8
5.9	0143	0150	0157	0165	0172	0180	0187	0194	0202	0209	0216	84.0	7
6.0	9.0216	0223	0231	0238	0245	0253	0260	0267	0274	0281	0289	83.9	8
6.1	0289	0296	0303	0310	0317	0324	0331	0338	0346	0353	0360	83.8	7
6.2	0360	0367	0374	0381	0388	0395	0402	0409	0416	0423	0430	83.7	7
6.3	0430	0437	0444	0451	0457	0464	0471	0478	0485	0492	0499	83.6	7
6.4	0499	0506	0512	0519	0526	0533	0540	0546	0553	0560	0567	83.5	7
6.5	0567	0573	0580	0587	0593	0600	0607	0614	0620	0627	0633	83.4	6
6.6	0633	0640	0647	0653	0660	0667	0673	0680	0686	0693	0699	83.3	6
6.7	0699	0706	0712	0719	0725	0732	0738	0745	0751	0758	0764	83.2	6
6.8	0764	0771	0777	0784	0790	0796	0803	0809	0816	0822	0828	83.1	6
6.9	0828	0835	0841	0847	0854	0860	0866	0873	0879	0885	0891	83.0	6
7.0	9.0891	0898	0904	0910	0916	0923	0929	0935	0941	0947	0954	82.9	7
7.1	0954	0960	0966	0972	0978	0984	0991	0997	1003	1009	1015	82.8	6
7.2	1015	1021	1027	1033	1039	1045	1051	1058	1064	1070	1076	82.7	6
7.3	1076	1082	1088	1094	1100	1106	1112	1117	1123	1129	1135	82.6	6
7.4	1135	1141	1147	1153	1159	1165	1171	1177	1183	1188	1194	82.5	6
7.5	1194	1200	1206	1212	1218	1223	1229	1235	1241	1247	1252	82.4	5
7.6	1252	1258	1264	1270	1276	1281	1287	1293	1299	1304	1310	82.3	6
7.7	1310	1316	1321	1327	1333	1338	1344	1350	1355	1361	1367	82.2	6
7.8	1367	1372	1378	1384	1389	1395	1400	1406	1412	1417	1423	82.1	6
7.9	1423	1428	1434	1439	1445	1450	1456	1461	1467	1473	1478	82.0	5
8.0	9.1478	1484	1489	1494	1500	1505	1511	1516	1522	1527	1533	81.9	6
8.1	1533	1538	1544	1549	1554	1560	1565	1571	1576	1581	1587	81.8	6
8.2	1587	1592	1597	1603	1608	1613	1619	1624	1629	1635	1640	81.7	5
8.3	1640	1645	1651	1656	1661	1667	1672	1677	1682	1688	1693	81.6	5
8.4	1693	1698	1703	1709	1714	1719	1724	1729	1735	1740	1745	81.5	5
8.5	1745	1750	1755	1761	1766	1771	1776	1781	1786	1791	1797	81.4	5
8.6	1797	1802	1807	1812	1817	1822	1827	1832	1837	1842	1848	81.3	6
8.7	1848	1853	1858	1863	1868	1873	1878	1883	1888	1893	1898	81.2	5
8.8	1898	1903	1908	1913	1918	1923	1928	1933	1938	1943	1948	81.1	5
8.9	1948	1953	1958	1963	1968	1973	1977	1982	1987	1992	1997	81.0	5
	10	9	8	7	6	5	4	3	2	1	0	n°	

′	0	1	2	3	4	5	6	7	8	9	°	T	log tan
0	0	.016	.03	.05	.06	.083	.1	.116	.13	.15	0.00	1.7581	
											1.28	1.7580	8.3492
1	.16	.183	.2	.216	.23	.25	.26	.283	.3	.316	1.98	1.7579	8.5387
2	.3	.35	.36	.383	.4	.416	.43	.45	.46	.483	2.49	1.7578	8.6384
											2.91	1.7577	8.7061
3	.5	.516	.53	.55	.56	.583	.6	.616	.63	.65	3.27	1.7576	8.7569
4	.6	.683	.7	.716	.73	.75	.76	.783	.8	.816	3.60	1.7575	8.7988
5	.83	.85	.86	.883	.9	.916	.93	.95	.96	.983	3.90	1.7574	8.8336
											4.18		8.8638

log sin   log cos

n°	0'	10'	20'	30'	40'	50'	60'		d	pp
0	7.4637	7648	9408	*0658	*1627	*2419	89			45 46 47 48 49
1	8.2419	3088	3668	4179	4637	5050	5428	88		5 5 5 5 5
2	5428	5776	6097	6397	6677	6940	7188	87		9 9 9 10 10
3	7188	7423	7645	7857	8059	8251	8436	86		14 14 14 14 15
4	8436	8613	8783	8946	9104	9256	9403	85		18 18 19 19 20
5	9403	9545	9682	9816	9945	*0070	*0192	84		23 23 24 24 25
6	9.0192	0311	0426	0539	0648	0755	0859	83		27 28 28 29 29
7	0859	0961	1060	1157	1252	1345	1436	82	91	32 32 33 34 34
8	1436	1525	1612	1697	1781	1863	1943	81	80	36 37 38 38 39
9	1943	2022	2100	2176	2251	2324	2397	80	73	41 41 42 43 44
10	9.2397	2468	2538	2606	2674	2740	2806	79	66	40 41 42 43 44
11	2806	2870	2934	2997	3058	3119	3179	78	60	4 4 4 4 4
12	3179	3238	3296	3353	3410	3466	3521	77	55	8 8 8 9 9
13	3521	3575	3629	3682	3734	3786	3837	76	51	12 12 13 13 13
14	3837	3887	3937	3986	4035	4083	4130	75	47	16 16 17 17 18
15	4130	4177	4223	4269	4314	4359	4403	74	44	20 21 21 22 22
16	4403	4447	4491	4533	4576	4618	4659	73	41	24 25 25 26 26
17	4659	4700	4741	4781	4821	4861	4900	72	39	28 29 29 30 31
18	4900	4939	4977	5015	5052	5090	5126	71	36	32 33 34 34 35
19	5126	5163	5199	5235	5270	5306	5341	70	35	36 37 38 39 40
20	9.5341	5375	5409	5443	5477	5510	5543	69	33	35 36 37 38 39
21	5543	5576	5609	5641	5673	5704	5736	68	32	4 4 4 4 4
22	5736	5767	5798	5828	5859	5889	5919	67	30	7 7 7 8 8
23	5919	5948	5978	6007	6036	6065	6093	66	28	11 11 11 11 12
24	6093	6121	6149	6177	6205	6232	6259	65	27	14 14 15' 15 16
25	6259	6286	6313	6340	6366	6392	6418	64	26	18 18 19 19 20
26	6418	6444	6470	6495	6521	6546	6570	63	24	21 22 22 23 23
27	6570	6595	6620	6644	6668	6692	6716	62	24	25 25 26 27 27
28	6716	6740	6763	6787	6810	6833	6856	61	23	28 29 30 30 31
29	6856	6878	6901	6923	6946	6968	6990	60	22	32 32 33 34 35
30	9.6990	7012	7033	7055	7076	7097	7118	59	21	30 31 32 33 34
31	7118	7139	7160	7181	7201	7222	7242	58	20	3 3 3 3 3
32	7242	7262	7282	7302	7322	7342	7361	57	19	6 6 6 7 7
33	7361	7380	7400	7419	7438	7457	7476	56	19	9 9 10 10 10
34	7476	7494	7513	7531	7550	7568	7586	55	18	12 12 13 13 14
35	7586	7604	7622	7640	7657	7675	7692	54	17	15 16 16 17 17
36	7692	7710	7727	7744	7761	7778	7795	53	17	18 19 19 20 20
37	7795	7811	7828	7844	7861	7877	7893	52	16	21 22 22 23 24
38	7893	7910	7926	7941	7957	7973	7989	51	16	24 25 26 26 27
39	7989	8004	8020	8035	8050	8066	8081	50	15	27 28 29 30 31
40	9.8081	8096	8111	8125	8140	8155	8169	49	14	25 26 27 28 29
41	8169	8184	8198	8213	8227	8241	8255	48	14	3 3 3 3 3
42	8255	8269	8283	8297	8311	8324	8338	47	14	5 5 5 6 6
43	8338	8351	8365	8378	8391	8405	8418	46	13	8 8 8 8 9
44	8418	8431	8444	8457	8469	8482	8495	45	13	10 10 11 11 12
45	8495	8507	8520	8532	8545	8557	8569	44	12	13 13 14 14 15
46	8569	8582	8594	8606	8618	8629	8641	43	12	15 16 16 17 17
47	8641	8653	8665	8676	8688	8699	8711	42	12	18 18 19 20 20
48	8711	8722	8733	8745	8756	8767	8778	41	11	20 21 22 22 23
49	8778	8789	8800	8810	8821	8832	8843	40	11	23 23 24 25 26
	60'	50'	40'	30'	20'	10'	0'	n°	d	

log sin   **log cos**

n°	0'	10'	20'	30'	40'	50'	60'	d	pp				
50	9.8843	8853	8864	8874	8884	8895	8905	39	10	20	21	22	23	24
51	8905	8915	8925	8935	8945	8955	8965	38	10	2	2	2	2	2
52	8965	8975	8985	8995	9004	9014	9023	37	9	4	4	4	5	5
53	9023	9033	9042	9052	9061	9070	9080	36	10	6	6	7	7	7
54	9080	9089	9098	9107	9116	9125	9134	35	9	8	8	9	9	10
55	9134	9142	9151	9160	9169	9177	9186	34	9	10	11	11	12	12
56	9186	9194	9203	9211	9219	9228	9236	33	8	12	13	13	14	14
57	9236	9244	9252	9260	9268	9276	9284	32	8	14	15	15	16	17
58	9284	9292	9300	9308	9315	9323	9331	31	8	16	17	18	18	19
59	9331	9338	9346	9353	9361	9368	9375	30	7	18	19	20	21	22
60	9.9375	9383	9390	9397	9404	9411	9418	29	7	15	16	17	18	19
61	9418	9425	9432	9439	9446	9453	9459	28	6	2	2	2	2	2
62	9459	9466	9473	9479	9486	9492	9499	27	7	3	3	3	4	4
63	9499	9505	9512	9518	9524	9530	9537	26	7	5	5	5	5	6
64	9537	9543	9549	9555	9561	9567	9573	25	6	6	6	7	7	8
65	9573	9579	9584	9590	9596	9602	9607	24	5	8	8	9	9	10
66	9607	9613	9618	9624	9629	9635	9640	23	5	9	10	10	11	11
67	9640	9646	9651	9656	9661	9667	9672	22	5	11	11	12	13	13
68	9672	9677	9682	9687	9692	9697	9702	21	5	12	13	14	14	15
69	9702	9706	9711	9716	9721	9725	9730	20	5	14	14	15	16	17
70	9.9730	9734	9739	9743	9748	9752	9757	19	5	10	11	12	13	14
71	9757	9761	9765	9770	9774	9778	9782	18	4	1	1	1	1	1
72	9782	9786	9790	9794	9798	9802	9806	17	4	2	2	2	3	3
73	9806	9810	9814	9817	9821	9825	9828	16	3	3	3	4	4	4
74	9828	9832	9836	9839	9843	9846	9849	15	3	4	4	5	5	6
75	9849	9853	9856	9859	9863	9866	9869	14	3	5	6	6	7	7
76	9869	9872	9875	9878	9881	9884	9887	13	3	6	7	7	8	8
77	9887	9890	9893	9896	9899	9901	9904	12	3	7	8	8	9	10
78	9904	9907	9909	9912	9914	9917	9919	11	2	8	9	10	10	11
79	9919	9922	9924	9927	9929	9931	9934	10	3	9	10	11	12	13
80	9.9934	9936	9938	9940	9942	9944	9946	9	2	5	6	7	8	9
81	9946	9948	9950	9952	9954	9956	9958	8	2	1	1	1	1	1
82	9958	9959	9961	9963	9964	9966	9968	7	2	1	1	1	2	2
83	9968	9969	9971	9972	9973	9975	9976	6	1	2	2	2	2	3
84	9976	9977	9979	9980	9981	9982	9983	5	1	2	2	3	3	4
85	9983	9985	9986	9987	9988	9989	9989	4	0	3	3	4	4	5
86	9989	9990	9991	9992	9993	9993	9994	3	1	3	4	4	5	5
87	9994	9995	9995	9996	9996	9997	9997	2	0	4	4	5	6	6
88	9997	9998	9998	9999	9999	9999	9999	1	0	4	5	6	6	7
89	9999	*0000	*0000	*0000	*0000	*0000	*0000	0	0	5	5	6	7	8

	60'	50'	40'	30'	20'	10'	0'	n°	d	1	2	3	4

° '	'	S	log sin	° '	'	S	log sin		1	2	3	4
									0	0	0	0
									0	0	1	1
									0	1	1	1
0 00	0	3.5363		5 07	307	3.5369	8.9503		0	1	1	2
1 51	111	3.5364	8.5090	5 32	332	3.5370	8.9842		1	1	2	2
2 50	170	3.5365	8.6940	5 56	356	3.5371	9.0144		1	1	2	3
3 32	212	3.5366	8.7898	6 18	378	3.5372	9.0403		1	2	2	3
4 08	248	3.5367	8.8578	6 39	399	3.5373	9.0637		1	2	3	3
4 39	279	3.5368	8.9089	6 59	419		9.0849		1	2	3	4

log tan   log cotan

n°	0'	10'	20'	30'	40'	50'	60'		d	pp
0		7.4637	7648	9409	*0658	*1627	*2419	89		95 96 97 98 99
1	8.2419	3089	3669	4181	4638	5053	5431	88		10 10 10 10 10
2	5431	5779	6101	6401	6682	6945	7194	87		19 19 19 20 20
3	7194	7429	7652	7865	8067	8261	8446	86		29 29 29 29 30
4	8446	8624	8795	8960	9118	9272	9420	85		38 38 39 39 40
5	9420	9563	9701	9836	9966	*0093	*0216	84		48 48 49 49 50
6	9.0216	0336	0453	0567	0678	0786	0891	83	105	57 58 58 59 59
7	0891	0995	1096	1194	1291	1385	1478	82	93	67 67 68 69 69
8	1478	1569	1658	1745	1831	1915	1997	81	82	76 77 78 78 79
9	1997	2078	2158	2236	2313	2389	2463	80	74	86 86 87 88 89
10	9.2463	2536	2609	2680	2750	2819	2887	79	68	90 91 92 93 94
11	2887	2953	3020	3085	3149	3212	3275	78	63	9 9 9 9 9
12	3275	3336	3397	3458	3517	3576	3634	77	58	18 18 18 19 19
13	3634	3691	3748	3804	3859	3914	3968	76	54	27 27 28 28 28
14	3968	4021	4074	4127	4178	4230	4281	75	51	36 36 37 37 38
15	4281	4331	4381	4430	4479	4527	4575	74	48	45 46 46 47 47
16	4575	4622	4669	4716	4762	4808	4853	73	45	54 55 55 56 56
17	4853	4898	4943	4987	5031	5075	5118	72	43	63 64 64 65 66
18	5118	5161	5203	5245	5287	5329	5370	71	41	72 73 74 74 75
19	5370	5411	5451	5491	5531	5571	5611	70	40	81 82 83 84 85
20	9.5611	5650	5689	5727	5766	5804	5842	69	38	85 86 87 88 89
21	5842	5879	5917	5954	5991	6028	6064	68	36	9 9 9 9 9
22	6064	6100	6136	6172	6208	6243	6279	67	36	17 17 17 18 18
23	6279	6314	6348	6383	6417	6452	6486	66	34	26 26 26 26 27
24	6486	6520	6553	6587	6620	6654	6687	65	33	34 34 35 35 36
25	6687	6720	6752	6785	6817	6850	6882	64	32	43 43 44 44 45
26	6882	6914	6946	6977	7009	7040	7072	63	32	51 52 52 53 53
27	7072	7103	7134	7165	7196	7226	7257	62	31	60 60 61 62 62
28	7257	7287	7317	7348	7378	7408	7438	61	30	68 69 70 70 71
29	7438	7467	7497	7526	7556	7585	7614	60	29	77 77 78 79 80
30	9.7614	7644	7673	7701	7730	7759	7788	59	29	80 81 82 83 84
31	7788	7816	7845	7873	7902	7930	7958	58	28	8 8 8 8 8
32	7958	7986	8014	8042	8070	8097	8125	57	28	16 16 16 17 17
33	8125	8153	8180	8208	8235	8263	8290	56	27	24 24 25 25 25
34	8290	8317	8344	8371	8398	8425	8452	55	27	32 32 33 33 34
35	8452	8479	8506	8533	8559	8586	8613	54	27	40 41 41 42 42
36	8613	8639	8666	8692	8718	8745	8771	53	26	48 49 49 50 50
37	8771	8797	8824	8850	8876	8902	8928	52	26	56 57 57 58 59
38	8928	8954	8980	9006	9032	9058	9084	51	26	64 65 66 66 67
39	9084	9110	9135	9161	9187	9212	9238	50	26	72 73 74 75 76
40	9.9238	9264	9289	9315	9341	9366	9392	49	26	75 76 77 78 79
41	9392	9417	9443	9468	9494	9519	9544	48	25	8 8 8 8 8
42	9544	9570	9595	9621	9646	9671	9697	47	26	15 15 15 16 16
43	9697	9722	9747	9772	9798	9823	9848	46	25	23 23 23 23 24
44	9848	9874	9899	9924	9949	9975	*0000	45	25	30 30 31 31 32
45	0.0000	0025	0051	0076	0101	0126	0152	44	26	38 38 39 39 40
46	0152	0177	0202	0228	0253	0278	0303	43	25	45 46 46 47 47
47	0303	0329	0354	0379	0405	0430	0456	42	26	53 53 54 55 55
48	0456	0481	0506	0532	0557	0583	0608	41	25	60 61 62 62 63
49	0608	0634	0659	0685	0711	0736	0762	40	26	68 68 69 70 71
	60'	50'	40'	30'	20'	10'	0'	n°	d	

log tan　　　　　　　　**log cotan**

n°	0'	10'	20'	30'	40'	50'	60'	d	pp
50	0.0762	0788	0813	0839	0865	0890	0916	39	26	70 71 72 73 74
51	0916	0942	0968	0994	1020	1046	1072	38	26	7 7 7 7 7
52	1072	1098	1124	1150	1176	1203	1229	37	26	14 14 14 15 15
53	1229	1255	1282	1308	1334	1361	1387	36	26	21 21 22 22 22
54	1387	1414	1441	1467	1494	1521	1548	35	27	28 28 29 29 30
55	1548	1575	1602	1629	1656	1683	1710	34	27	35 36 36 37 37
56	1710	1737	1765	1792	1820	1847	1875	33	28	42 43 43 44 44
57	1875	1903	1930	1958	1986	2014	2042	32	28	49 50 50 51 52
58	2042	2070	2098	2127	2155	2184	2212	31	28	56 57 58 58 59
59	2212	2241	2270	2299	2327	2356	2386	30	30	63 64 65 66 67
60	0.2386	2415	2444	2474	2503	2533	2562	29	29	65 66 67 68 69
61	2562	2592	2622	2652	2683	2713	2743	28	30	7 7 7 7 7
62	2743	2774	2804	2835	2866	2897	2928	27	31	13 13 13 14 14
63	2928	2960	2991	3023	3054	3086	3118	26	32	20 20 20 20 21
64	3118	3150	3183	3215	3248	3280	3313	25	33	26 26 27 27 28
65	3313	3346	3380	3413	3447	3480	3514	24	34	33 33 34 34 35
66	3514	3548	3583	3617	3652	3686	3721	23	35	39 40 40 41 41
67	3721	3757	3792	3828	3864	3900	3936	22	36	46 46 47 48 48
68	3936	3972	4009	4046	4083	4121	4158	21	37	52 53 54 54 55
69	4158	4196	4234	4273	4311	4350	4389	20	39	59 59 60 61 62
70	0.4389	4429	4469	4509	4549	4589	4630	19	41	60 61 62 63 64
71	4630	4671	4713	4755	4797	4839	4882	18	43	6 6 6 6 6
72	4882	4925	4969	5013	5057	5102	5147	17	45	12 12 12 13 13
73	5147	5192	5238	5284	5331	5378	5425	16	47	18 18 19 19 19
74	5425	5473	5521	5570	5619	5669	5719	15	50	24 24 25 25 26
75	5719	5770	5822	5873	5926	5979	6032	14	53	30 31 31 32 32
76	6032	6086	6141	6196	6252	6309	6366	13	57	36 37 37 38 38
77	6366	6424	6483	6542	6603	6664	6725	12	61	42 43 43 44 45
78	6725	6788	6851	6915	6980	7047	7113	11	66	48 49 50 50 51
79	7113	7181	7250	7320	7391	7464	7537	10	73	54 55 56 57 58
80	0.7537	7611	7687	7764	7842	7922	8003	9	81	55 56 57 58 59
81	8003	8085	8169	8255	8342	8431	8522	8	91	6 6 6 6 6
82	8522	8615	8709	8806	8904	9005	9109	7	104	11 11 11 12 12
83	9109	9214	9322	9433	9547	9664	9784	6	120	17 17 17 17 18
84	9784	9907	*0034	*0164	*0299	*0437	*0580	5		22 22 23 23 24
85	1.0580	0728	0882	1040	1205	1376	1554	4		28 28 29 29 30
86	1554	1739	1933	2135	2348	2571	2806	3		33 34 34 35 35
87	2806	3055	3318	3599	3899	4221	4569	2		39 39 40 41 41
88	4569	4947	5362	5819	6331	6911	7581	1		44 45 46 46 47
89	7581	8373	9342	*0591	*2352	*5363		0		50 50 51 52 53
	60'	50'	40'	30'	20'	10'	0'	n°	d	

° '	'	T	log tan	° '	'	T	log tan	50 51 52 53 54
0 00	0	3.5363		4 19	259	3.5354	8.8778	5 5 5 5 5
0 44	44	3.5362	8.1072	4 34	274	3.5353	8.9024	10 10 10 11 11
1 41	101	3.5361	8.4682	4 49	289	3.5352	8.9256	15 15 16 16 16
2 15	135	3.5360	8.5943	5 03	303	3.5351	8.9463	20 20 21 21 22
2 43	163	3.5359	8.6762	5 16	316	3.5350	8.9646	25 26 26 27 27
3 06	186	3.5358	8.7337	5 28	328	3.5349	8.9809	30 31 31 32 32
3 27	207	3.5357	8.7802	5 41	341	3.5348	8.9979	35 36 36 37 38
3 46	226	3.5356	8.8185	5 52	352	3.5347	9.0118	40 41 42 42 43
4 03	243	3.5355	8.8501	6 04	364		9.0265	45 46 47 48 49

sin n°　　　　　　　　　　　　　　　　　　　　　　cos n°

n°	.0 0'	.1 6'	.2 12'	.3 18'	.4 24'	.5 30'	.6 36'	.7 42'	.8 48'	.9 54'	1.0 60'		d
0	0.0000	0017	0035	0052	0070	0087	0105	0122	0140	0157	0175	89	18
1	0175	0192	0209	0227	0244	0262	0279	0297	0314	0332	0349	88	17
2	0349	0366	0384	0401	0419	0436	0454	0471	0488	0506	0523	87	17
3	0523	0541	0558	0576	0593	0610	0628	0645	0663	0680	0698	86	18
4	0698	0715	0732	0750	0767	0785	0802	0819	0837	0854	0872	85	18
5	0872	0889	0906	0924	0941	0958	0976	0993	1011	1028	1045	84	17
6	1045	1063	1080	1097	1115	1132	1149	1167	1184	1201	1219	83	18
7	1219	1236	1253	1271	1288	1305	1323	1340	1357	1374	1392	82	18
8	1392	1409	1426	1444	1461	1478	1495	1513	1530	1547	1564	81	17
9	1564	1582	1599	1616	1633	1650	1668	1685	1702	1719	1736	80	17
10	0.1736	1754	1771	1788	1805	1822	1840	1857	1874	1891	1908	79	17
11	1908	1925	1942	1959	1977	1994	2011	2028	2045	2062	2079	78	17
12	2079	2096	2113	2130	2147	2164	2181	2198	2215	2233	2250	77	17
13	2250	2267	2284	2300	2317	2334	2351	2368	2385	2402	2419	76	17
14	2419	2436	2453	2470	2487	2504	2521	2538	2554	2571	2588	75	17
15	2588	2605	2622	2639	2656	2672	2689	2706	2723	2740	2756	74	16
16	2756	2773	2790	2807	2823	2840	2857	2874	2890	2907	2924	73	17
17	2924	2940	2957	2974	2990	3007	3024	3040	3057	3074	3090	72	16
18	3090	3107	3123	3140	3156	3173	3190	3206	3223	3239	3256	71	17
19	3256	3272	3289	3305	3322	3338	3355	3371	3387	3404	3420	70	16
20	0.3420	3437	3453	3469	3486	3502	3518	3535	3551	3567	3584	69	17
21	3584	3600	3616	3633	3649	3665	3681	3697	3714	3730	3746	68	16
22	3746	3762	3778	3795	3811	3827	3843	3859	3875	3891	3907	67	16
23	3907	3923	3939	3955	3971	3987	4003	4019	4035	4051	4067	66	16
24	4067	4083	4099	4115	4131	4147	4163	4179	4195	4210	4226	65	16
25	4226	4242	4258	4274	4289	4305	4321	4337	4352	4368	4384	64	16
26	4384	4399	4415	4431	4446	4462	4478	4493	4509	4524	4540	63	16
27	4540	4555	4571	4586	4602	4617	4633	4648	4664	4679	4695	62	16
28	4695	4710	4726	4741	4756	4772	4787	4802	4818	4833	4848	61	15
29	4848	4863	4879	4894	4909	4924	4939	4955	4970	4985	5000	60	15
30	0.5000	5015	5030	5045	5060	5075	5090	5105	5120	5135	5150	59	15
31	5150	5165	5180	5195	5210	5225	5240	5255	5270	5284	5299	58	15
32	5299	5314	5329	5344	5358	5373	5388	5402	5417	5432	5446	57	14
33	5446	5461	5476	5490	5505	5519	5534	5548	5563	5577	5592	56	15
34	5592	5606	5621	5635	5650	5664	5678	5693	5707	5721	5736	55	15
35	5736	5750	5764	5779	5793	5807	5821	5835	5850	5864	5878	54	14
36	5878	5892	5906	5920	5934	5948	5962	5976	5990	6004	6018	53	14
37	6018	6032	6046	6060	6074	6088	6101	6115	6129	6143	6157	52	14
38	6157	6170	6184	6198	6211	6225	6239	6252	6266	6280	6293	51	13
39	6293	6307	6320	6334	6347	6361	6374	6388	6401	6414	6428	50	14
40	0.6428	6441	6455	6468	6481	6494	6508	6521	6534	6547	6561	49	14
41	6561	6574	6587	6600	6613	6626	6639	6652	6665	6678	6691	48	13
42	6691	6704	6717	6730	6743	6756	6769	6782	6794	6807	6820	47	13
43	6820	6833	6845	6858	6871	6884	6896	6909	6921	6934	6947	46	13
44	6947	6959	6972	6984	6997	7009	7022	7034	7046	7059	7071	45	12
45	7071	7083	7096	7108	7120	7133	7145	7157	7169	7181	7193	44	12
46	7193	7206	7218	7230	7242	7254	7266	7278	7290	7302	7314	43	12
47	7314	7325	7337	7349	7361	7373	7385	7396	7408	7420	7431	42	11
48	7431	7443	7455	7466	7478	7490	7501	7513	7524	7536	7547	41	11
49	7547	7559	7570	7581	7593	7604	7615	7627	7638	7649	7660	40	11
	60'	54'	48'	42'	36'	30'	24'	18'	12'	6'	0'		
	1.0	.9	.8	.7	.6	.5	.4	.3	.2	.1	.0	n°	d

sin n°　　　　　　　　　　　　　　　　　　　cos n°

n°	.0 0′	.1 6′	.2 12′	.3 18′	.4 24′	.5 30′	.6 36′	.7 42′	.8 48′	.9 54′	1.0 60′		d
50	0.7660	7672	7683	7694	7705	7716	7727	7738	7749	7760	7771	39	11
51	7771	7782	7793	7804	7815	7826	7837	7848	7859	7869	7880	38	11
52	7880	7891	7902	7912	7923	7934	7944	7955	7965	7976	7986	37	10
53	7986	7997	8007	8018	8028	8039	8049	8059	8070	8080	8090	36	10
54	8090	8100	8111	8121	8131	8141	8151	8161	8171	8181	8192	35	11
55	8192	8202	8211	8221	8231	8241	8251	8261	8271	8281	8290	34	9
56	8290	8300	8310	8320	8329	8339	8348	8358	8368	8377	8387	33	10
57	8387	8396	8406	8415	8425	8434	8443	8453	8462	8471	8480	32	9
58	8480	8490	8499	8508	8517	8526	8536	8545	8554	8563	8572	31	9
59	8572	8581	8590	8599	8607	8616	8625	8634	8643	8652	8660	30	8
60	0.8660	8669	8678	8686	8695	8704	8712	8721	8729	8738	8746	29	8
61	8746	8755	8763	8771	8780	8788	8796	8805	8813	8821	8829	28	8
62	8829	8838	8846	8854	8862	8870	8878	8886	8894	8902	8910	27	8
63	8910	8918	8926	8934	8942	8949	8957	8965	8973	8980	8988	26	8
64	8988	8996	9003	9011	9018	9026	9033	9041	9048	9056	9063	25	7
65	9063	9070	9078	9085	9092	9100	9107	9114	9121	9128	9135	24	7
66	9135	9143	9150	9157	9164	9171	9178	9184	9191	9198	9205	23	7
67	9205	9212	9219	9225	9232	9239	9245	9252	9259	9265	9272	22	7
68	9272	9278	9285	9291	9298	9304	9311	9317	9323	9330	9336	21	6
69	9336	9342	9348	9354	9361	9367	9373	9379	9385	9391	9397	20	6
70	0.9397	9403	9409	9415	9421	9426	9432	9438	9444	9449	9455	19	6
71	9455	9461	9466	9472	9478	9483	9489	9494	9500	9505	9511	18	6
72	9511	9516	9521	9527	9532	9537	9542	9548	9553	9558	9563	17	5
73	9563	9568	9573	9578	9583	9588	9593	9598	9603	9608	9613	16	5
74	9613	9617	9622	9627	9632	9636	9641	9646	9650	9655	9659	15	4
75	9659	9664	9668	9673	9677	9681	9686	9690	9694	9699	9703	14	4
76	9703	9707	9711	9715	9720	9724	9728	9732	9736	9740	9744	13	4
77	9744	9748	9751	9755	9759	9763	9767	9770	9774	9778	9781	12	3
78	9781	9785	9789	9792	9796	9799	9803	9806	9810	9813	9816	11	3
79	9816	9820	9823	9826	9829	9833	9836	9839	9842	9845	9848	10	3
80	0.9848	9851	9854	9857	9860	9863	9866	9869	9871	9874	9877	9	3
81	9877	9880	9882	9885	9888	9890	9893	9895	9898	9900	9903	8	3
82	9903	9905	9907	9910	9912	9914	9917	9919	9921	9923	9925	7	2
83	9925	9928	9930	9932	9934	9936	9938	9940	9942	9943	9945	6	2
84	9945	9947	9949	9951	9952	9954	9956	9957	9959	9960	9962	5	2
85	9962	9963	9965	9966	9968	9969	9971	9972	9973	9974	9976	4	2
86	9976	9977	9978	9979	9980	9981	9982	9983	9984	9985	9986	3	1
87	9986	9987	9988	9989	9990	9990	9991	9992	9993	9993	9994	2	1
88	9994	9995	9995	9996	9996	9997	9997	9997	9998	9998	9998	1	0
89	9998	9999	9999	9999	9999	1.000	1.000	1.000	1.000	1.000	1.000	0	0
	60′ 1.0	54′ .9	48′ .8	42′ .7	36′ .6	30′ .5	24′ .4	18′ .3	12′ .2	6′ .1	0′ .0	n°	d

	1	2	3	4	5	6	7	8	9	10	11	12	13	14	15	16	17	18	19
1	0	0	1	1	1	1	1	1	2	2	2	2	2	2	3	3	3	3	3
2	0	1	1	1	2	2	2	3	3	3	4	4	4	5	5	5	6	6	6
3	1	1	2	2	3	3	4	4	5	5	6	6	7	7	8	8	9	9	10
4	1	1	2	3	3	4	5	5	6	7	7	8	9	9	10	11	11	12	13
5	1	2	3	3	4	5	6	7	8	8	9	10	11	12	13	13	14	15	16

tan n°   cot n°

n°	.0 0'	.1 6'	.2 12'	.3 18'	.4 24'	.5 30'	.6 36'	.7 42'	.8 48'	.9 54'	1.0 60'		d
0	0.0000	0017	0035	0052	0070	0087	0105	0122	0140	0157	0175	89	18
1	.0175	0192	0209	0227	0244	0262	0279	0297	0314	0332	0349	88	17
2	0349	0367	0384	0402	0419	0437	0454	0472	0489	0507	0524	87	17
3	0524	0542	0559	0577	0594	0612	0629	0647	0664	0682	0699	86	17
4	0699	0717	0734	0752	0769	0787	0805	0822	0840	0857	0875	85	18
5	0875	0892	0910	0928	0945	0963	0981	0998	1016	1033	1051	84	18
6	1051	1069	1086	1104	1122	1139	1157	1175	1192	1210	1228	83	18
7	1228	1246	1263	1281	1299	1317	1334	1352	1370	1388	1405	82	17
8	1405	1423	1441	1459	1477	1495	1512	1530	1548	1566	1584	81	18
9	1584	1602	1620	1638	1655	1673	1691	1709	1727	1745	1763	80	18
10	0.1763	1781	1799	1817	1835	1853	1871	1890	1908	1926	1944	79	18
11	1944	1962	1980	1998	2016	2035	2053	2071	2089	2107	2126	78	19
12	2126	2144	2162	2180	2199	2217	2235	2254	2272	2290	2309	77	19
13	2309	2327	2345	2364	2382	2401	2419	2438	2456	2475	2493	76	19
14	2493	2512	2530	2549	2568	2586	2605	2623	2642	2661	2679	75	18
15	2679	2698	2717	2736	2754	2773	2792	2811	2830	2849	2867	74	18
16	2867	2886	2905	2924	2943	2962	2981	3000	3019	3038	3057	73	19
17	3057	3076	3096	3115	3134	3153	3172	3191	3211	3230	3249	72	19
18	3249	3269	3288	3307	3327	3346	3365	3385	3404	3424	3443	71	19
19	3443	3463	3482	3502	3522	3541	3561	3581	3600	3620	3640	70	20
20	0.3640	3659	3679	3699	3719	3739	3759	3779	3799	3819	3839	69	20
21	3839	3859	3879	3899	3919	3939	3959	3979	4000	4020	4040	68	20
22	4040	4061	4081	4101	4122	4142	4163	4183	4204	4224	4245	67	21
23	4245	4265	4286	4307	4327	4348	4369	4390	4411	4431	4452	66	21
24	4452	4473	4494	4515	4536	4557	4578	4599	4621	4642	4663	65	21
25	4663	4684	4706	4727	4748	4770	4791	4813	4834	4856	4877	64	21
26	4877	4899	4921	4942	4964	4986	5008	5029	5051	5073	5095	63	22
27	5095	5117	5139	5161	5184	5206	5228	5250	5272	5295	5317	62	22
28	5317	5340	5362	5384	5407	5430	5452	5475	5498	5520	5543	61	23
29	5543	5566	5589	5612	5635	5658	5681	5704	5727	5750	5774	60	24
30	0.5774	5797	5820	5844	5867	5890	5914	5938	5961	5985	6009	59	24
31	6009	6032	6056	6080	6104	6128	6152	6176	6200	6224	6249	58	25
32	6249	6273	6297	6322	6346	6371	6395	6420	6445	6469	6494	57	25
33	6494	6519	6544	6569	6594	6619	6644	6669	6694	6720	6745	56	25
34	6745	6771	6796	6822	6847	6873	6899	6924	6950	6976	7002	55	26
35	7002	7028	7054	7080	7107	7133	7159	7186	7212	7239	7265	54	26
36	7265	7292	7319	7346	7373	7400	7427	7454	7481	7508	7536	53	28
37	7536	7563	7590	7618	7646	7673	7701	7729	7757	7785	7813	52	28
38	7813	7841	7869	7898	7926	7954	7983	8012	8040	8069	8098	51	29
39	8098	8127	8156	8185	8214	8243	8273	8302	8332	8361	8391	50	30
40	0.8391	8421	8451	8481	8511	8541	8571	8601	8632	8662	8693	49	31
41	8693	8724	8754	8785	8816	8847	8878	8910	8941	8972	9004	48	32
42	9004	9036	9067	9099	9131	9163	9195	9228	9260	9293	9325	47	32
43	9325	9358	9391	9424	9457	9490	9523	9556	9590	9623	9657	46	34
44	9657	9691	9725	9759	9793	9827	9861	9896	9930	9965	*0000	45	35
45	1.0000	0035	0070	0105	0141	0176	0212	0247	0283	0319	0355	44	36
46	0355	0392	0428	0464	0501	0538	0575	0612	0649	0686	0724	43	38
47	0724	0761	0799	0837	0875	0913	0951	0990	1028	1067	1106	42	39
48	1106	1145	1184	1224	1263	1303	1343	1383	1423	1463	1504	41	41
49	1504	1544	1585	1626	1667	1708	1750	1792	1833	1875	1918	40	43
	60' 1.0	54' .9	48' .8	42' .7	36' .6	30' .5	24' .4	18' .3	12' .2	6' .1	0' .0	n°	d

tan n°   cot n°

n°	.0 / 0'	.1 / 6'	.2 / 12'	.3 / 18'	.4 / 24'	.5 / 30'	.6 / 36'	.7 / 42'	.8 / 48'	.9 / 54'	1.0 / 60'		d
50	1.1918	1960	2002	2045	2088	2131	2174	2218	2261	2305	2349	39	44
51	2349	2393	2437	2482	2527	2572	2617	2662	2708	2753	2799	38	46
52	2799	2846	2892	2938	2985	3032	3079	3127	3175	3222	3270	37	48
53	3270	3319	3367	3416	3465	3514	3564	3613	3663	3713	3764	36	51
54	3764	3814	3865	3916	3968	4019	4071	4124	4176	4229	4281	35	52
55	4281	4335	4388	4442	4496	4550	4605	4659	4715	4770	4826	34	56
56	4826	4882	4938	4994	5051	5108	5166	5224	5282	5340	5399	33	59
57	5399	5458	5517	5577	5637	5697	5757	5818	5880	5941	6003	32	62
58	6003	6066	6128	6191	6255	6319	6383	6447	6512	6577	6643	31	66
59	6643	6709	6775	6842	6909	6977	7045	7113	7182	7251	7321	30	70
60	1.7321	7391	7461	7532	7603	7675	7747	7820	7893	7966	8040	29	74
61	8040	8115	8190	8265	8341	8418	8495	8572	8650	8728	8807	28	79
62	8807	8887	8967	9047	9128	9210	9292	9375	9458	9542	9626	27	84
63	9626	9711	9797	9883	9970	*0057	*0145	*0233	*0323	*0413	*0503	26	90
64	2.0503	0594	0686	0778	0872	0965	1060	1155	1251	1348	1445	25	97
65	1445	1543	1642	1742	1842	1943	2045	2148	2251	2355	2460	24	105
66	2460	2566	2673	2781	2889	2998	3109	3220	3332	3445	3559	23	114
67	3559	3673	3789	3906	4023	4142	4262	4383	4504	4627	4751	22	124
68	4751	4876	5002	5129	5257	5386	5517	5649	5782	5916	6051	21	135
69	6051	6187	6325	6464	6605	6746	6889	7034	7179	7326	7475	20	149
70	2.7475	7625	7776	7929	8083	8239	8397	8556	8716	8878	9042	19	164
71	9042	9208	9375	9544	9714	9887	*0061	*0237	*0415	*0595	*0777	18	182
72	3.0777	0961	1146	1334	1524	1716	1910	2106	2305	2506	2709	17	203
73	2709	2914	3122	3332	3544	3759	3977	4197	4420	4646	4874	16	228
74	4874	5105	5339	5576	5816	6059	6305	6554	6806	7062	7321	15	
75	7321	7583	7848	8118	8391	8667	8947	9232	9520	9812	*0108	14	
76	4.0108	0408	0713	1022	1335	1653	1976	2303	2635	2972	3315	13	
77	3315	3662	4015	4373	4737	5107	5483	5864	6252	6646	7046	12	
78	7046	7453	7867	8288	8716	9152	9594	*0045	*0504	*0970	*1446	11	
79	5.1446	1929	2422	2924	3435	3955	4486	5026	5578	6140	6713	10	
80	5.6713	7297	7894	8502	9124	9758	*0405	*1066	*1742	*2432	*3138	9	
81	6.3138	3859	4596	5350	6122	6912	7720	8548	9395	*0264	*1154	8	
82	7.1154	2066	3002	3962	4947	5958	6996	8062	9158	*0285	*1443	7	
83	8.1443	2636	3863	5126	6427	7769	9152	*0579	*2052	*3572	*5144	6	
84	9.514	9.677	9.845	10.02	10.20	10.39	10.58	10.78	10.99	11.20	11.43	5	
85	11.43	11.66	11.91	12.16	12.43	12.71	13.00	13.30	13.62	13.95	14.30	4	
86	14.30	14.67	15.06	15.46	15.89	16.35	16.83	17.34	17.89	18.46	19.08	3	
87	19.08	19.74	20.45	21.20	22.02	22.90	23.86	24.90	26.03	27.27	28.64	2	
88	28.64	30.14	31.82	33.69	35.80	38.19	40.92	44.07	47.74	52.08	57.29	1	
89	57.29	63.66	71.62	81.85	95.49	114.6	143.2	191 0	286.5	573.0		0	
	1.0	.9	.8	.7	.6	.5	.4	.3	.2	.1	.0	n°	d

20	21	22	23	24	25	26	27	28	29	30	31	32	33	34	35	36	37	38	39
3	4	4	4	4	4	4	5	5	5	5	5	6	6	6	6	6	6	7	
7	7	7	8	8	8	9	9	9	10	10	10	11	11	11	12	12	12	13	13
10	11	11	12	12	13	13	14	14	15	15	16	16	17	17	18	18	19	19	20
13	14	15	15	16	17	17	18	19	19	20	21	21	22	23	23	24	25	25	26
17	18	18	19	20	21	22	23	23	24	25	26	27	28	28	29	30	31	32	33

40	41	42	43	44	45	46	47	48	49	50	51	52	53	54	55	56	57	58	59
7	7	7	7	8	8	8	8	8	8	8	9	9	9	9	9	9	10	10	10
13	14	14	14	15	15	15	16	16	16	17	17	18	18	18	19	19	19	20	
20	21	21	22	22	23	23	24	24	25	25	26	26	27	27	28	28	29	29	30
27	27	28	29	29	30	31	31	32	33	33	34	35	35	36	37	37	38	39	39
33	34	35	36	37	38	38	39	40	41	42	43	43	44	45	46	47	48	48	49

sec *n*°   cosec *n*°

n°	.0 0'	.1 6'	.2 12'	.3 18'	.4 24'	.5 30'	.6 36'	.7 42'	.8 48'	.9 54'	1.0 60'		d
0	1.0000	0000	0000	0000	0000	0000	0001	0001	0001	0001	0002	89	1
1	0002	0002	0002	0003	0003	0003	0004	0004	0005	0006	0006	88	0
2	0006	0007	0007	0008	0009	0010	0010	0011	0012	0013	0014	87	1
3	0014	0015	0016	0017	0018	0019	0020	0021	0022	0023	0024	86	1
4	0024	0026	0027	0028	0030	0031	0032	0034	0035	0037	0038	85	1
5	0038	0040	0041	0043	0045	0046	0048	0050	0051	0053	0055	84	2
6	0055	0057	0059	0061	0063	0065	0067	0069	0071	0073	0075	83	2
7	0075	0077	0079	0082	0084	0086	0089	0091	0093	0096	0098	82	2
8	0098	0101	0103	0106	0108	0111	0114	0116	0119	0122	0125	81	3
9	0125	0127	0130	0133	0136	0139	0142	0145	0148	0151	0154	80	3
10	1.0154	0157	0161	0164	0167	0170	0174	0177	0180	0184	0187	79	3
11	0187	0191	0194	0198	0201	0205	0209	0212	0216	0220	0223	78	3
12	0223	0227	0231	0235	0239	0243	0247	0251	0255	0259	0263	77	4
13	0263	0267	0271	0276	0280	0284	0288	0293	0297	0302	0306	76	4
14	0306	0311	0315	0320	0324	0329	0334	0338	0343	0348	0353	75	5
15	0353	0358	0363	0367	0372	0377	0382	0388	0393	0398	0403	74	5
16	0403	0408	0413	0419	0424	0429	0435	0440	0446	0451	0457	73	6
17	0457	0463	0468	0474	0480	0485	0491	0497	0503	0509	0515	72	6
18	0515	0521	0527	0533	0539	0545	0551	0557	0564	0570	0576	71	6
19	0576	0583	0589	0595	0602	0608	0615	0622	0628	0635	0642	70	7
20	1.0642	0649	0655	0662	0669	0676	0683	0690	0697	0704	0711	69	7
21	0711	0719	0726	0733	0740	0748	0755	0763	0770	0778	0785	68	7
22	0785	0793	0801	0808	0816	0824	0832	0840	0848	0856	0864	67	8
23	0864	0872	0880	0888	0896	0904	0913	0921	0929	0938	0946	66	8
24	0946	0955	0963	0972	0981	0989	0998	1007	1016	1025	1034'	65	9
25	1034	1043	1052	1061	1070	1079	1089	1098	1107	1117	1126	64	9
26	1126	1136	1145	1155	1164	1174	1184	1194	1203	1213	1223	63	10
27	1223	1233	1243	1253	1264	1274	1284	1294	1305	1315	1326	62	11
28	1326	1336	1347	1357	1368	1379	1390	1401	1412	1423	1434	61	11
29	1434	1445	1456	1467	1478	1490	1501	1512	1524	1535	1547	60	12
30	1.1547	1559	1570	1582	1594	1606	1618	1630	1642	1654	1666	59	12
31	1666	1679	1691	1703	1716	1728	1741	1753	1766	1779	1792	58	13
32	1792	1805	1818	1831	1844	1857	1870	1883	1897	1910	1924	57	14
33	1924	1937	1951	1964	1978	1992	2006	2020	2034	2048	2062	56	14
34	2062	2076	2091	2105	2120	2134	2149	2163	2178	2193	2208	55	15
35	2208	2223	2238	2253	2268	2283	2299	2314	2329	2345	2361	54	16
36	2361	2376	2392	2408	2424	2440	2456	2472	2489	2505	2521	53	16
37	2521	2538	2554	2571	2588	2605	2622	2639	2656	2673	2690	52	17
38	2690	2708	2725	2742	2760	2778	2796	2813	2831	2849	2868	51	19
39	2868	2886	2904	2923	2941	2960	2978	2997	3016	3035	3054	50	19
40	1.3054	3073	3093	3112	3131	3151	3171	3190	3210	3230	3250	49	20
41	3250	3270	3291	3311	3331	3352	3373	3393	3414	3435	3456	48	21
42	3456	3478	3499	3520	3542	3563	3585	3607	3629	3651	3673	47	22
43	3673	3696	3718	3741	3763	3786	3809	3832	3855	3878	3902	46	24
44	3902	3925	3949	3972	3996	4020	4044	4069	4093	4118	4142	45	24
45	4142	4167	4192	4217	4242	4267	4293	4318	4344	4370	4396	44	26
46	4396	4422	4448	4474	4501	4527	4554	4581	4608	4635	4663	43	28
47	4663	4690	4718	4746	4774	4802	4830	4859	4887	4916	4945	42	29
48	4945	4974	5003	5032	5062	5092	5121	5151	5182	5212	5243	41	31
49	5243	5273	5304	5335	5366	5398	5429	5461	5493	5525	5557	40	32
	60'	54'	48'	42'	36'	30'	24'	18'	12'	6'	0'		
	1.0	.9	.8	.7	.6	.5	.4	.3	.2	.1	.0	n°	d

sec $n°$ cosec $n°$

$n°$	.0 0'	.1 6'	.2 12'	.3 18'	.4 24'	.5 30'	.6 36'	.7 42'	.8 48'	.9 54'	1.0 60'		d
50	1.5557	5590	5622	5655	5688	5721	5755	5788	5822	5856	5890	39	34
51	5890	5925	5959	5994	6029	6064	6099	6135	6171	6207	6243	38	36
52	6243	6279	6316	6353	6390	6427	6464	6502	6540	6578	6616	37	38
53	6616	6655	6694	6733	6772	6812	6852	6892	6932	6972	7013	36	41
54	7013	7054	7095	7137	7179	7221	7263	7305	7348	7391	7434	35	43
55	7434	7478	7522	7566	7610	7655	7700	7745	7791	7837	7883	34	46
56	7883	7929	7976	8023	8070	8118	8166	8214	8263	8312	8361	33	49
57	8361	8410	8460	8510	8561	8612	8663	8714	8766	8818	8871	32	53
58	8871	8924	8977	9031	9084	9139	9194	9249	9304	9360	9416	31	56
59	9416	9473	9530	9587	9645	9703	9762	9821	9880	9940	*0000	30	60
60	2.0000	0061	0122	0183	0245	0308	0371	0434	0498	0562	0627	29	65
61	0627	0692	0757	0824	0890	0957	1025	1093	1162	1231	1301	28	70
62	1301	1371	1441	1513	1584	1657	1730	1803	1877	1952	2027	27	75
63	2027	2103	2179	2256	2333	2412	2490	2570	2650	2730	2812	26	82
64	2812	2894	2976	3060	3144	3228	3314	3400	3486	3574	3662	25	88
65	3662	3751	3841	3931	4022	4114	4207	4300	4395	4490	4586	24	96
66	4586	4683	4780	4879	4978	5078	5180	5282	5384	5488	5593	23	105
67	5593	5699	5805	5913	6022	6131	6242	6354	6466	6580	6695	22	115
68	6695	6811	6927	7046	7165	7285	7407	7529	7653	7778	7904	21	126
69	7904	8032	8161	8291	8422	8555	8688	8824	8960	9099	9238	20	139
70	2.9238	9379	9521	9665	9811	9957	*0106	*0256	*0407	*0561	*0716	19	155
71	3.0716	0872	1030	1190	1352	1515	1681	1848	2017	2188	2361	18	173
72	2361	2535	2712	2891	3072	3255	3440	3628	3817	4009	4203	17	194
73	4203	4399	4598	4799	5003	5209	5418	5629	5843	6060	6280	16	220
74	6280	6502	6727	6955	7186	7420	7657	7897	8140	8387	8637	15	
75	8637	8890	9147	9408	9672	9939	*0211	*0486	*0765	*1048	*1336	14	
76	4.1336	1627	1923	2223	2527	2837	3150	3469	3792	4121	4454	13	
77	4454	4793	5137	5486	5841	6202	6569	6942	7321	7706	8097	12	
78	8097	8496	8901	9313	9732	*0159	*0593	*1034	*1484	*1942	*2408	11	
79	5.2408	2883	3367	3860	4362	4874	5396	5928	6470	7023	7588	10	
80	5.7588	8164	8751	9351	9963	*0589	1227	1880	2546	3228	3925	9	
81	6.3925	4637	5366	6111	6874	7655	8454	9273	*0112	*0972	*1853	8	
82	7.1853	2757	3684	4635	5611	6613	7642	8700	9787	*0905	*2055	7	
83	8.2055	3238	4457	5711	7004	8337	9711	*1129	*2593	*4105	*5668	6	
84	9.567	9.728	9.895	10.07	10.25	10.43	10.63	10.83	11.03	11.25	11.47	5	
85	11.47	11.71	11.95	12.20	12.47	12.75	13.03	13.34	13.65	13.99	14.34	4	
86	14.34	14.70	15.09	15.50	15.93	16.38	16.86	17.37	17.91	18.49	19.11	3	
87	19.11	19.77	20.47	21.23	22.04	22.93	23.88	24.92	26.05	27.29	28.65	2	
88	28.65	30.16	31.84	33.71	35.81	38.20	40.93	44.08	47.75	52.09	57.30	1	
89	57.30	63.66	71.62	81 85	95 49	114.6	143.2	191.0	286.5	573.0		0	
	1.0	.9	.8	.7	.6	.5	.4	.3	.2	.1	.0	$n°$	d

	60	61	62	63	64	65	66	67	68	69	70	71	72	73	74	75	76	77	78	79
1	10	10	10	11	11	11	11	11	11	12	12	12	12	12	12	13	13	13	13	13
2	20	20	21	21	21	22	22	22	23	23	23	24	24	24	25	25	25	26	26	26
3	30	31	31	32	32	33	33	34	34	35	35	36	36	37	37	38	38	39	39	40
4	40	41	41	42	43	43	44	45	45	46	47	47	48	49	49	50	51	51	52	53
5	50	51	52	53	53	54	55	56	57	58	58	59	60	61	62	63	63	64	65	66

	80	81	82	83	84	85	86	87	88	89	90	91	92	93	94	95	96	97	98	99
1	13	14	14	14	14	14	14	15	15	15	15	15	15	16	16	16	16	16	16	17
2	27	27	27	28	28	28	29	29	29	30	30	30	31	31	31	32	32	32	33	33
3	40	41	41	42	42	43	43	44	44	45	45	46	46	47	47	48	48	49	49	50
4	53	54	55	55	56	57	57	58	59	59	60	61	61	62	63	63	64	65	65	66
5	67	68	68	69	70	71	72	73	73	74	75	76	77	78	78	79	80	81	82	83

n°	.0	.1	.2	.3	.4	.5	.6	.7	.8	.9	p	h m
10	0.1745	1763	1780	1798	1815	1833	1850	1868	1885	1902	.0278	0 40
11	1920	1937	1955	1972	1990	2007	2025	2042	2059	2077	.0306	0 44
12	2094	2112	2129	2147	2164	2182	2199	2217	2234	2251	.0333	0 48
13	2269	2286	2304	2321	2339	2356	2374	2391	2409	2426	.0361	0 52
14	2443	2461	2478	2496	2513	2531	2548	2566	2583	2601	.0389	0 56
15	2618	2635	2653	2670	2688	2705	2723	2740	2758	2775	.0417	1 0
16	2793	2810	2827	2845	2862	2880	2897	2915	2932	2950	.0444	1 4
17	2967	2985	3002	3019	3037	3054	3072	3089	3107	3124	.0472	1 8
18	3142	3159	3176	3194	3211	3229	3246	3264	3281	3299	.0500	1 12
19	3316	3334	3351	3368	3386	3403	3421	3438	3456	3473	.0528	1 16
20	0.3491	3508	3526	3543	3560	3578	3595	3613	3630	3648	.0556	1 20
21	3665	3683	3700	3718	3735	3752	3770	3787	3805	3822	.0583	1 24
22	3840	3857	3875	3892	3910	3927	3944	3962	3979	3997	.0611	1 28
23	4014	4032	4049	4067	4084	4102	4119	4136	4154	4171	.0639	1 32
24	4189	4206	4224	4241	4259	4276	4294	4311	4328	4346	.0667	1 36
25	4363	4381	4398	4416	4433	4451	4468	4485	4503	4520	.0694	1 40
26	4538	4555	4573	4590	4608	4625	4643	4660	4677	4695	.0722	1 44
27	4712	4730	4747	4765	4782	4800	4817	4835	4852	4869	.0750	1 48
28	4887	4904	4922	4939	4957	4974	4992	5009	5027	5044	.0778	1 52
29	5061	5079	5096	5114	5131	5149	5166	5184	5201	5219	.0806	1 56
30	0.5236	5253	5271	5288	5306	5323	5341	5358	5376	5393	.0833	2 0
31	5411	5428	5445	5463	5480	5498	5515	5533	5550	5568	.0861	2 4
32	5585	5603	5620	5637	5655	5672	5690	5707	5725	5742	.0889	2 8
33	5760	5777	5794	5812	5829	5847	5864	5882	5899	5917	.0917	2 12
34	5934	5952	5969	5986	6004	6021	6039	6056	6074	6091	.0944	2 16
35	6109	6126	6144	6161	6178	6196	6213	6231	6248	6266	.0972	2 20
36	6283	6301	6318	6336	6353	6370	6388	6405	6423	6440	.1000	2 24
37	6458	6475	6493	6510	6528	6545	6562	6580	6597	6615	.1028	2 28
38	6632	6650	6667	6685	6702	6720	6737	6754	6772	6789	.1056	2 32
39	6807	6824	6842	6859	6877	6894	6912	6929	6946	6964	.1083	2 36
40	0.6981	6999	7016	7034	7051	7069	7086	7103	7121	7138	.1111	2 40
41	7156	7173	7191	7208	7226	7243	7261	7278	7295	7313	.1139	2 44
42	7330	7348	7365	7383	7400	7418	7435	7453	7470	7487	.1167	2 48
43	7505	7522	7540	7557	7575	7592	7610	7627	7645	7662	.1194	2 52
44	7679	7697	7714	7732	7749	7767	7784	7802	7819	7837	.1222	2 56
45	7854	7871	7889	7906	7924	7941	7959	7976	7994	8011	.1250	3 0
46	8029	8046	8063	8081	8098	8116	8133	8151	8168	8186	.1278	3 4
47	8203	8221	8238	8255	8273	8290	8308	8325	8343	8360	.1306	3 8
48	8378	8395	8412	8430	8447	8465	8482	8500	8517	8535	.1333	3 12
49	8552	8570	8587	8604	8622	8639	8657	8674	8692	8709	.1361	3 16
50	0.8727	8744	8762	8779	8796	8814	8831	8849	8866	8884	.1389	3 20
51	8901	8919	8936	8954	8971	8988	9006	9023	9041	9058	.1417	3 24
52	9076	9093	9111	9128	9146	9163	9180	9198	9215	9233	.1444	3 28
53	9250	9268	9285	9303	9320	9338	9355	9372	9390	9407	.1472	3 32
54	9425	9442	9460	9477	9495	9512	9529	9547	9564	9582	.1500	3 36
55	9599	9617	9634	9652	9669	9687	9704	9721	9739	9756	.1528	3 40
56	9774	9791	9809	9826	9844	9861	9879	9896	9913	9931	.1556	3 44
57	9948	9966	9983	*0001	*0018	*0036	*0053	*0071	*0088	*0105	.1583	3 48
58	1.0123	0140	0158	0175	0193	0210	0228	0245	0263	0280	.1611	3 52
59	0297	0315	0332	0350	0367	0385	0402	0420	0437	0455	.1639	3 56

n°	.0	.1	.2	.3	.4	.5	.6	.7	.8	.9	p	h m
60	1.0472	0489	0507	0524	0542	0559	0577	0594	0612	0629	.1667	4 0
61	0647	0664	0681	0699	0716	0734	0751	0769	0786	0804	.1694	4 4
62	0821	0838	0856	0873	0891	0908	0926	0943	0961	0978	.1722	4 8
63	0996	1013	1030	1048	1065	1083	1100	1118	1135	1153	.1750	4 12
64	1170	1188	1205	1222	1240	1257	1275	1292	1310	1327	.1778	4 16
65	1345	1362	1380	1397	1414	1432	1449	1467	1484	1502	.1806	4 20
66	1519	1537	1554	1572	1589	1606	1624	1641	1659	1676	.1833	4 24
67	1694	1711	1729	1746	1764	1781	1798	1816	1833	1851	.1861	4 28
68	1868	1886	1903	1921	1938	1956	1973	1990	2008	2025	.1889	4 32
69	2043	2060	2078	2095	2113	2130	2147	2165	2182	2200	.1917	4 36
70	1.2217	2235	2252	2270	2287	2305	2322	2339	2357	2374	.1944	4 40
71	2392	2409	2427	2444	2462	2479	2497	2514	2531	2549	.1972	4 44
72	2566	2584	2601	2619	2636	2654	2671	2689	2706	2723	.2000	4 48
73	2741	2758	2776	2793	2811	2828	2846	2863	2881	2898	.2028	4 52
74	2915	2933	2950	2968	2985	3003	3020	3038	3055	3073	.2056	4 56
75	3090	3107	3125	3142	3160	3177	3195	3212	3230	3247	.2083	5 0
76	3265	3282	3299	3317	3334	3352	3369	3387	3404	3422	.2111	5 4
77	3439	3456	3474	3491	3509	3526	3544	3561	3579	3596	.2139	5 8
78	3614	3631	3648	3666	3683	3701	3718	3736	3753	3771	.2167	5 12
79	3788	3806	3823	3840	3858	3875	3893	3910	3928	3945	.2194	5 16
80	1.3963	3980	3998	4015	4032	4050	4067	4085	4102	4120	.2222	5 20
81	4137	4155	4172	4190	4207	4224	4242	4259	4277	4294	.2250	5 24
82	4312	4329	4347	4364	4382	4399	4416	4434	4451	4469	.2278	5 28
83	4486	4504	4521	4539	4556	4573	4591	4608	4626	4643	.2306	5 32
84	4661	4678	4696	4713	4731	4748	4765	4783	4800	4818	.2333	5 36
85	4835	4853	4870	4888	4905	4923	4940	4957	4975	4992	.2361	5 40
86	5010	5027	5045	5062	5080	5097	5115	5132	5149	5167	.2389	5 44
87	.5184	5202	5219	5237	5254	5272	5289	5307	5324	5341	.2417	5 48
88	5359	5376	5394	5411	5429	5446	5464	5481	5499	5516	.2444	5 52
89	5533	5551	5568	5586	5603	5621	5638	5656	5673	5691	.2472	5 56
90	1.5708	5725	5743	5760	5778	5795	5813	5830	5848	5865	.2500	6 0
91	5882	5900	5917	5935	5952	5970	5987	6005	6022	6040	.2528	6 4
92	6057	6074	6092	6109	6127	6144	6162	6179	6197	6214	.2556	6 8
93	6232	6249	6266	6284	6301	6319	6336	6354	6371	6389	.2583	6 12
94	6406	6424	6441	6458	6476	6493	6511	6528	6546	6563	.2611	6 16
95	6581	6598	6616	6633	6650	6668	6685	6703	6720	6738	.2639	6 20
96	6755	6773	6790	6808	6825	6842	6860	6877	6895	6912	.2667	6 24
97	6930	6947	6965	6982	7000	7017	7034	7052	7069	7087	.2694	6 28
98	7104	7122	7139	7157	7174	7191	7209	7226	7244	7261	.2722	6 32
99	7279	7296	7314	7331	7349	7366	7383	7401	7418	7436	.2750	6 36

n'	0	1	2	3	4	5	6	7	8	9	p	s
1	.00 2909	3200	3491	3782	4072	4363	4654	4945	5236	5527	.000 0463	4
2	.00 5818	6109	6400	6690	6981	7272	7563	7854	8145	8436	0926	8
3	.00 8727	9018	9308	9599	9890	*0181	*0472	*0763	*1054	*1345	1389	12
4	.01 1636	1926	2217	2508	2799	3090	3381	3672	3963	4254	1852	16
5	.01 4544	4835	5126	5417	5708	5999	6290	6581	6872	7162	2315	20
6	.01 7453	7744	8035	8326	8617	8908	9199	9490	9780	*0071	2778	24
7	.02 0362	0653	0944	1235	1526	1817	2108	2398	2689	2980	3241	28
8	.02 3271	3562	3853	4144	4435	4725	5016	5307	5598	5889	3704	32
9	.02 6180	6471	6762	7053	7343	7634	7925	8216	8507	8798	4167	36

n	0	1	2	3	4	5	6	7	8	9	d
1.0	1.0000	9901	9804	9709	9615	9524	9434	9346	9259	9174	83
1.1	0.9091	9009	8929	8850	8772	8696	8621	8547	8475	8403	70
1.2	8333	8264	8197	8130	8065	8000	7937	7874	7813	7752	60
1.3	7692	7634	7576	7519	7463	7407	7353	7299	7246	7194	51
1.4	7143	7092	7042	6993	6944	6897	6849	6803	6757	6711	44
1.5	6667	6623	6579	6536	6494	6452	6410	6369	6329	6289	39
1.6	6250	6211	6173	6135	6098	6061	6024	5988	5952	5917	35
1.7	5882	5848	5814	5780	5747	5714	5682	5650	5618	5587	31
1.8	5556	5525	5495	5464	5435	5405	5376	5348	5319	5291	28
1.9	5263	5236	5208	5181	5155	5128	5102	5076	5051	5025	25
2.0	0.5000	4975	4950	4926	4902	4878	4854	4831	4808	4785	23
2.1	4762	4739	4717	4695	4673	4651	4630	4608	4587	4566	21
2.2	4545	4525	4505	4484	4464	4444	4425	4405	4386	4367	19
2.3	4348	4329	4310	4292	4274	4255	4237	4219	4202	4184	17
2.4	4167	4149	4132	4115	4098	4082	4065	4049	4032	4016	16
2.5	4000	3984	3968	3953	3937	3922	3906	3891	3876	3861	15
2.6	3846	3831	3817	3802	3788	3774	3759	3745	3731	3717	13
2.7	3704	3690	3676	3663	3650	3636	3623	3610	3597	3584	13
2.8	3571	3559	3546	3534	3521	3509	3497	3484	3472	3460	12
2.9	3448	3436	3425	3413	3401	3390	3378	3367	3356	3344	11
3.0	0.3333	3322	3311	3300	3289	3279	3268	3257	3247	3236	10
3.1	3226	3215	3205	3195	3185	3175	3165	3155	3145	3135	10
3.2	3125	3115	3106	3096	3086	3077	3067	3058	3049	3040	10
3.3	3030	3021	3012	3003	2994	2985	2976	2967	2959	2950	9
3.4	2941	2933	2924	2915	2907	2899	2890	2882	2874	2865	8
3.5	2857	2849	2841	2833	2825	2817	2809	2801	2793	2786	8
3.6	2778	2770	2762	2755	2747	2740	2732	2725	2717	2710	7
3.7	2703	2695	2688	2681	2674	2667	2660	2653	2646	2639	7
3.8	2632	2625	2618	2611	2604	2597	2591	2584	2577	2571	7
3.9	2564	2558	2551	2545	2538	2532	2525	2519	2513	2506	6
4.0	0.2500	2494	2488	2481	2475	2469	2463	2457	2451	2445	6
4.1	2439	2433	2427	2421	2415	2410	2404	2398	2392	2387	6
4.2	2381	2375	2370	2364	2358	2353	2347	2342	2336	2331	5
4.3	2326	2320	2315	2309	2304	2299	2294	2288	2283	2278	5
4.4	2273	2268	2262	2257	2252	2247	2242	2237	2232	2227	5
4.5	2222	2217	2212	2208	2203	2198	2193	2188	2183	2179	5
4.6	2174	2169	2165	2160	2155	2151	2146	2141	2137	2132	4
4.7	2128	2123	2119	2114	2110	2105	2101	2096	2092	2088	5
4.8	2083	2079	2075	2070	2066	2062	2058	2053	2049	2045	4
4.9	2041	2037	2033	2028	2024	2020	2016	2012	2008	2004	4
5.0	0.2000	1996	1992	1988	1984	1980	1976	1972	1969	1965	4
5.1	1961	1957	1953	1949	1946	1942	1938	1934	1931	1927	4
5.2	1923	1919	1916	1912	1908	1905	1901	1898	1894	1890	3
5.3	1887	1883	1880	1876	1873	1869	1866	1862	1859	1855	3
5.4	1852	1848	1845	1842	1838	1835	1832	1828	1825	1821	3
5.5	1818	1815	1812	1808	1805	1802	1799	1795	1792	1789	3
5.6	1786	1783	1779	1776	1773	1770	1767	1764	1761	1757	3
*5.7	1754	1751	1748	1745	1742	1739	1736	1733	1730	1727	3
5.8	1724	1721	1718	1715	1712	1709	1706	1704	1701	1698	3
5.9	1695	1692	1689	1686	1684	1681	1678	1675	1672	1669	2

n	0	1	2	3	4	5	6	7	8	9	d
6.0	0.1667	1664	1661	1658	1656	1653	1650	1647	1645	1642	3
6.1	1639	1637	1634	1631	1629	1626	1623	1621	1618	1616	3
6.2	1613	1610	1608	1605	1603	1600	1597	1595	1592	1590	3
6.3	1587	1585	1582	1580	1577	1575	1572	1570	1567	1565	2
6.4	1563	1560	1558	1555	1553	1550	1548	1546	1543	1541	3
6.5	1538	1536	1534	1531	1529	1527	1524	1522	1520	1517	2
6.6	1515	1513	1511	1508	1506	1504	1502	1499	1497	1495	2
6.7	1493	1490	1488	1486	1484	1481	1479	1477	1475	1473	2
6.8	1471	1468	1466	1464	1462	1460	1458	1456	1453	1451	2
6.9	1449	1447	1445	1443	1441	1439	1437	1435	1433	1431	2
7.0	0.1429	1427	1425	1422	1420	1418	1416	1414	1412	1410	2
7.1	1408	1406	1404	1403	1401	1399	1397	1395	1393	1391	2
7.2	1389	1387	1385	1383	1381	1379	1377	1376	1374	1372	2
7.3	1370	1368	1366	1364	1362	1361	1359	1357	1355	1353	2
7.4	1351	1350	1348	1346	1344	1342	1340	1339	1337	1335	2
7.5	1333	1332	1330	1328	1326	1325	1323	1321	1319	1318	2
7.6	1316	1314	1312	1311	1309	1307	1305	1304	1302	1300	1
7.7	1299	1297	1295	1294	1292	1290	1289	1287	1285	1284	2
7.8	1282	1280	1279	1277	1276	1274	1272	1271	1269	1267	1
7.9	1266	1264	1263	1261	1259	1258	1256	1255	1253	1252	2
8.0	0.1250	1248	1247	1245	1244	1242	1241	1239	1238	1236	1
8.1	1235	1233	1232	1230	1229	1227	1225	1224	1222	1221	1
8.2	1220	1218	1217	1215	1214	1212	1211	1209	1208	1206	1
8.3	1205	1203	1202	1200	1199	1198	1196	1195	1193	1192	2
8.4	1190	1189	1188	1186	1185	1183	1182	1181	1179	1178	2
8.5	1176	1175	1174	1172	1171	1170	1168	1167	1166	1164	1
8.6	1163	1161	1160	1159	1157	1156	1155	1153	1152	1151	2
8.7	1149	1148	1147	1145	1144	1143	1142	1140	1139	1138	2
8.8	1136	1135	1134	1133	1131	1130	1129	1127	1126	1125	1
8.9	1124	1122	1121	1120	1119	1117	1116	1115	1114	1112	1
9.0	0.1111	1110	1109	1107	1106	1105	1104	1103	1101	1100	1
9.1	1099	1098	1096	1095	1094	1093	1092	1091	1089	1088	1
9.2	1087	1086	1085	1083	1082	1081	1080	1079	1078	1076	1
9.3	1075	1074	1073	1072	1071	1070	1068	1067	1066	1065	1
9.4	1064	1063	1062	1060	1059	1058	1057	1056	1055	1054	1
9.5	1053	1052	1050	1049	1048	1047	1046	1045	1044	1043	1
9.6	1042	1041	1040	1038	1037	1036	1035	1034	1033	1032	1
9.7	1031	1030	1029	1028	1027	1026	1025	1024	1022	1021	1
9.8	1020	1019	1018	1017	1016	1015	1014	1013	1012	1011	1
9.9	1010	1009	1008	1007	1006	1005	1004	1003	1002	1001	1

	2	3	4	5	6	7	8	9	11	12	13	14	15	16
1	.5	.(3)	.25	.2	.1(6)	.1429	.125	.(1)	.(09)	.08(3)	.0769	.0714	.0(6)	.0625
2		.(6)	.5	.4	.(3)	.2857	.25	.(2)	.(18)	.1(6)	.1538	.1429	.1(3)	.125
3			.75	.6	.5	.4286	.375	.(3)	.(27)	.25	.2308	.2143	.2	.1875
4				.8	.(6)	.5714	.5	.(4)	.(36)	.(3)	.3077	.2857	.2(6)	.25
5					.8(3)	.7143	.625	.(5)	.(45)	.41(6)	.3846	.3571	.(3)	.3125
6						.8571	.75	.(6)	.(54)	.5	.4615	.4286	.4	.375
7							.875	.(7)	.(63)	.58(3)	.5385	.5	.4(6)	.4375
8								.(8)	.(72)	.(6)	.6154	.5714	.5(3)	.5
9									.(81)	.75	.6923	.6429	.6	.5625

n	0	1	2	3	4	5	6	7	8	9	d
1.0	1.000	1.020	1.040	1.061	1.082	1.103	1.124	1.145	1.166	1.188	22
1.1	1.210	1.232	1.254	1.277	1.300	1.323	1.346	1.369	1.392	1.416	24
1.2	1.440	1.464	1.488	1.513	1.538	1.563	1.588	1.613	1.638	1.664	26
1.3	1.690	1.716	1.742	1.769	1.796	1.823	1.850	1.877	1.904	1.932	28
1.4	1.960	1.988	2.016	2.045	2.074	2.103	2.132	2.161	2.190	2.220	30
1.5	2.250	2.280	2.310	2.341	2.372	2.403	2.434	2.465	2.496	2.528	32
1.6	2.560	2.592	2.624	2.657	2.690	2.723	2.756	2.789	2.822	2.856	34
1.7	2.890	2.924	2.958	2.993	3.028	3.063	3.098	3.133	3.168	3.204	36
1.8	3.240	3.276	3.312	3.349	3.386	3.423	3.460	3.497	3.534	3.572	38
1.9	3.610	3.648	3.686	3.725	3.764	3.803	3.842	3.881	3.920	3.960	40
2.0	4.000	4.040	4.080	4.121	4.162	4.203	4.244	4.285	4.326	4.368	42
2.1	4.410	4.452	4.494	4.537	4.580	4.623	4.666	4.709	4.752	4.796	44
2.2	4.840	4.884	4.928	4.973	5.018	5.063	5.108	5.153	5.198	5.244	46
2.3	5.290	5.336	5.382	5.429	5.476	5.523	5.570	5.617	5.664	5.712	48
2.4	5.760	5.808	5.856	5.905	5.954	6.003	6.052	6.101	6.150	6.200	50
2.5	6.250	6.300	6.350	6.401	6.452	6.503	6.554	6.605	6.656	6.708	52
2.6	6.760	6.812	6.864	6.917	6.970	7.023	7.076	7.129	7.182	7.236	54
2.7	7.290	7.344	7.398	7.453	7.508	7.563	7.618	7.673	7.728	7.784	56
2.8	7.840	7.896	7.952	8.009	8.066	8.123	8.180	8.237	8.294	8.352	58
2.9	8.410	8.468	8.526	8.585	8.644	8.703	8.762	8.821	8.880	8.940	60
3.0	9.000	9.060	9.120	9.181	9.242	9.303	9.364	9.425	9.486	9.548	62
3.1	9.610	9.672	9.734	9.797	9.860	9.923	9.986	10.05	10.11	10.18	6
3.2	10.24	10.30	10.37	10.43	10.50	10.56	10.63	10.69	10.76	10.82	7
3.3	10.89	10.96	11.02	11.09	11.16	11.22	11.29	11.36	11.42	11.49	7
3.4	11.56	11.63	11.70	11.76	11.83	11.90	11.97	12.04	12.11	12.18	7
3.5	12.25	12.32	12.39	12.46	12.53	12.60	12.67	12.74	12.82	12.89	7
3.6	12.96	13.03	13.10	13.18	13.25	13.32	13.40	13.47	13.54	13.62	7
3.7	13.69	13.76	13.84	13.91	13.99	14.06	14.14	14.21	14.29	14.36	8
3.8	14.44	14.52	14.59	14.67	14.75	14.82	14.90	14.98	15.05	15.13	8
3.9	15.21	15.29	15.37	15.44	15.52	15.60	15.68	15.76	15.84	15.92	8
4.0	16.00	16.08	16.16	16.24	16.32	16.40	16.48	16.56	16.65	16.73	8
4.1	16.81	16.89	16.97	17.06	17.14	17.22	17.31	17.39	17.47	17.56	8
4.2	17.64	17.72	17.81	17.89	17.98	18.06	18.15	18.23	18.32	18.40	9
4.3	18.49	18.58	18.66	18.75	18.84	18.92	19.01	19.10	19.18	19.27	9
4.4	19.36	19.45	19.54	19.62	19.71	19.80	19.89	19.98	20.07	20.16	9
4.5	20.25	20.34	20.43	20.52	20.61	20.70	20.79	20.88	20.98	21.07	9
4.6	21.16	21.25	21.34	21.44	21.53	21.62	21.72	21.81	21.90	22.00	9
4.7	22.09	22.18	22.28	22.37	22.47	22.56	22.66	22.75	22.85	22.94	10
4.8	23.04	23.14	23.23	23.33	23.43	23.52	23.62	23.72	23.81	23.91	10
4.9	24.01	24.11	24.21	24.30	24.40	24.50	24.60	24.70	24.80	24.90	10
5.0	25.00	25.10	25.20	25.30	25.40	25.50	25.60	25.70	25.81	25.91	10
5.1	26.01	26.11	26.21	26.32	26.42	26.52	26.63	26.73	26.83	26.94	10
5.2	27.04	27.14	27.25	27.35	27.46	27.56	27.67	27.77	27.88	27.98	11
5.3	28.09	28.20	28.30	28.41	28.52	28.62	28.73	28.84	28.94	29.05	11
5.4	29.16	29.27	29.38	29.48	29.59	29.70	29.81	29.92	30.03	30.14	11
5.5	30.25	30.36	30.47	30.58	30.69	30.80	30.91	31.02	31.14	31.25	11
5.6	31.36	31.47	31.58	31.70	31.81	31.92	32.04	32.15	32.26	32.38	11
5.7	32.49	32.60	32.72	32.83	32.95	33.06	33.18	33.29	33.41	33.52	12
5.8	33.64	33.76	33.87	33.99	34.11	34.22	34.34	34.46	34.57	34.69	12
5.9	34.81	34.93	35.05	35.16	35.28	35.40	35.52	35.64	35.76	35.88	12

n	0	1	2	3	4	5	6	7	8	9	d
6.0	36.00	36.12	36.24	36.36	36.48	36.60	36.72	36.84	36.97	37.09	12
6.1	37.21	37.33	37.45	37.58	37.70	37.82	37.95	38.07	38.19	38.32	12
6.2	38.44	38.56	38.69	38.81	38.94	39.06	39.19	39.31	39.44	39.56	13
6.3	39.69	39.82	39.94	40.07	40.20	40.32	40.45	40.58	40.70	40.83	13
6.4	40.96	41.09	41.22	41.34	41.47	41.60	41.73	41.86	41.99	42.12	13
6.5	42.25	42.38	42.51	42.64	42.77	42.90	43.03	43.16	43.30	43.43	13
6.6	43.56	43.69	43.82	43.96	44.09	44.22	44.36	44.49	44.62	44.76	13
6.7	44.89	45.02	45.16	45.29	45.43	45.56	45.70	45.83	45.97	46.10	14
6.8	46.24	46.38	46.51	46.65	46.79	46.92	47.06	47.20	47.33	47.47	14
6.9	47.61	47.75	47.89	48.02	48.16	48.30	48.44	48.58	48.72	48.86	14
7.0	49.00	49.14	49.28	49.42	49.56	49.70	49.84	49.98	50.13	50.27	14
7.1	50.41	50.55	50.69	50.84	50.98	51.12	51.27	51.41	51.55	51.70	14
7.2	51.84	51.98	52.13	52.27	52.42	52.56	52.71	52.85	53.00	53.14	15
7.3	53.29	53.44	53.58	53.73	53.88	54.02	54.17	54.32	54.46	54.61	15
7.4	54.76	54.91	55.06	55.20	55.35	55.50	55.65	55.80	55.95	56.10	15
7.5	56.25	56.40	56.55	56.70	56.85	57.00	57.15	57.30	57.46	57.61	15
7.6	57.76	57.91	58.06	58.22	58.37	58.52	58.68	58.83	58.98	59.14	15
7.7	59.29	59.44	59.60	59.75	59.91	60.06	60.22	60.37	60.53	60.68	16
7.8	60.84	61.00	61.15	61.31	61.47	61.62	61.78	61.94	62.09	62.25	16
7.9	62.41	62.57	62.73	62.88	63.04	63.20	63.36	63.52	63.68	63.84	16
8.0	64.00	64.16	64.32	64.48	64.64	64.80	64.96	65.12	65.29	65.45	16
8.1	65.61	65.77	65.93	66.10	66.26	66.42	66.59	66.75	66.91	67.08	16
8.2	67.24	67.40	67.57	67.73	67.90	68.06	68.23	68.39	68.56	68.72	17
8.3	68.89	69.06	69.22	69.39	69.56	69.72	69.89	70.06	70.22	70.39	17
8.4	70.56	70.73	70.90	71.06	71.23	71.40	71.57	71.74	71.91	72.08	17
8.5	72.25	72.42	72.59	72.76	72.93	73.10	73.27	73.44	73.62	73.79	17
8.6	73.96	74.13	74.30	74.48	74.65	74.82	75.00	75.17	75.34	75.52	17
8.7	75.69	75.86	76.04	76.21	76.39	76.56	76.74	76.91	77.09	77.26	18
8.8	77.44	77.62	77.79	77.97	78.15	78.32	78.50	78.68	78.85	79.03	18
8.9	79.21	79.39	79.57	79.74	79.92	80.10	80.28	80.46	80.64	80.82	18
9.0	81.00	81.18	81.36	81.54	81.72	81.90	82.08	82.26	82.45	82.63	18
9.1	82.81	82.99	83.17	83.36	83.54	83.72	83.91	84.09	84.27	84.46	18
9.2	84.64	84.82	85.01	85.19	85.38	85.56	85.75	85.93	86.12	86.30	19
9.3	86.49	86.68	86.86	87.05	87.24	87.42	87.61	87.80	87.98	88.17	19
9.4	88.36	88.55	88.74	88.92	89.11	89.30	89.49	89.68	89.87	90.06	19
9.5	90.25	90.44	90.63	90.82	91.01	91.20	91.39	91.58	91.78	91.97	19
9.6	92.16	92.35	92.54	92.74	92.93	93.12	93.32	93.51	93.70	93.90	19
9.7	94.09	94.28	94.48	94.67	94.87	95.06	95.26	95.45	95.65	95.84	20
9.8	96.04	96.24	96.43	96.63	96.83	97.02	97.22	97.42	97.61	97.81	20
9.9	98.01	98.21	98.41	98.60	98.80	99.00	99.20	99.40	99.60	99.80	20

n	.0	.1	.2	.3	.4	.5	.6	.7	.8	.9	d
1	1.000	*826	*694	*592	*510	*444	*391	*346	*309	*277	27
2	0.250	227	207	189	174	160	148	137	128	119	8
3	0.111	104	*977	*918	*865	*816	*772	*730	*693	*657	32
4	0.0 625	595	567	541	517	494	473	453	434	416	16
5	0.0 400	384	370	356	343	331	319	308	297	287	9
6	0.0 278	269	260	252	244	237	230	223	216	210	6
7	0.0 204	198	193	188	183	178	173	169	164	160	4
8	0.0 156	152	149	145	142	138	135	132	129	126	3
9	0.0 123	121	118	116	113	111	109	106	104	102	2

n	0	1	2	3	4	5	6	7	8	9	d
1.0	1.000	1.030	1.061	1.093	1.125	1.158	1.191	1.225	1.260	1.295	36
1.1	1.331	1.368	1.405	1.443	1.482	1.521	1.561	1.602	1.643	1.685	43
1.2	1.728	1.772	1.816	1.861	1.907	1.953	2.000	2.048	2.097	2.147	50
1.3	2.197	2.248	2.300	2.353	2.406	2.460	2.515	2.571	2.628	2.686	58
1.4	2.744	2.803	2.863	2.924	2.986	3.049	3.112	3.177	3.242	3.308	67
1.5	3.375	3.443	3.512	3.582	3.652	3.724	3.796	3.870	3.944	4.020	76
1.6	4.096	4.173	4.252	4.331	4.411	4.492	4.574	4.657	4.742	4.827	86
1.7	4.913	5.000	5.088	5.178	5.268	5.359	5.452	5.545	5.640	5.735	97
1.8	5.832	5.930	6.029	6.128	6.230	6.332	6.435	6.539	6.645	6.751	108
1.9	6.859	6.968	7.078	7.189	7.301	7.415	7.530	7.645	7.762	7.881	119
2.0	8.000	8.121	8.242	8.365	8.490	8.615	8.742	8.870	8.999	9.129	132
2.1	9.261	9.394	9.528	9.664	9.800	9.938	10.08	10.22	10.36	10.50	15
2.2	10.648	10.79	10.94	11.09	11.24	11.39	11.54	11.70	11.85	12.01	16
2.3	12.167	12.33	12.49	12.65	12.81	12.98	13.14	13.31	13.48	13.65	17
2.4	13.824	14.00	14.17	14.35	14.53	14.71	14.89	15.07	15.25	15.44	19
2.5	15.625	15.81	16.00	16.19	16.39	16.58	16.78	16.97	17.17	17.37	21
2.6	17.576	17.78	17.98	18.19	18.40	18.61	18.82	19.03	19.25	19.47	21
2.7	19.683	19.90	20.12	20.35	20.57	20.80	21.02	21.25	21.48	21.72	23
2.8	21.952	22.19	22.43	22.67	22.91	23.15	23.39	23.64	23.89	24.14	25
2.9	24.389	24.64	24.90	25.15	25.41	25.67	25.93	26.20	26.46	26.73	27
3.0	27.000	27.27	27.54	27.82	28.09	28.37	28.65	28.93	29.22	29.50	29
3.1	29.791	30.08	30.37	30.66	30.96	31.26	31.55	31.86	32.16	32.46	31
3.2	32.768	33.08	33.39	33.70	34.01	34.33	34.65	34.97	35.29	35.61	33
3.3	35.937	36.26	36.59	36.93	37.26	37.60	37.93	38.27	38.61	38.96	34
3.4	39.304	39.65	40.00	40.35	40.71	41.06	41.42	41.78	42.14	42.51	37
3.5	42.875	43.24	43.61	43.99	44.36	44.74	45.12	45.50	45.88	46.27	39
3.6	46.656	47.05	47.44	47.83	48.23	48.63	49.03	49.43	49.84	50.24	41
3.7	50.653	51.06	51.48	51.90	52.31	52.73	53.16	53.58	54.01	54.44	43
3.8	54.872	55.31	55.74	56.18	56.62	57.07	57.51	57.96	58.41	58.86	46
3.9	59.319	59.78	60.24	60.70	61.16	61.63	62.10	62.57	63.04	63.52	48
4.0	64.000	64.48	64.96	65.45	65.94	66.43	66.92	67.42	67.92	68.42	50
4.1	68.921	69.43	69.93	70.44	70.96	71.47	71.99	72.51	73.03	73.56	53
4.2	74.088	74.62	75.15	75.69	76.23	76.77	77.31	77.85	78.40	78.95	56
4.3	79.507	80.06	80.62	81.18	81.75	82.31	82.88	83.45	84.03	84.60	58
4.4	85.184	85.77	86.35	86.94	87.53	88.12	88.72	89.31	89.92	90.52	61
4.5	91.125	91.73	92.35	92.96	93.58	94.20	94.82	95.44	96.07	96.70	64
4.6	97.336	97.97	98.61	99.25	99.90	100.5	101.2	101.8	102.5	103.2	6
4.7	103.823	104.5	105.2	105.8	106.5	107.2	107.9	108.5	109.2	109.9	7
4.8	110.592	111.3	112.0	112.7	113.4	114.1	114.8	115.5	116.2	116.9	7
4.9	117.649	118.4	119.1	119.8	120.6	121.3	122.0	122.8	123.5	124.3	7
5.0	125.000	125.8	126.5	127.3	128.0	128.8	129.6	130.3	131.1	131.9	8
5.1	132.651	133.4	134.2	135.0	135.8	136.6	137.4	138.2	139.0	139.8	8
5.2	140.608	141.4	142.2	143.1	143.9	144.7	145.5	146.4	147.2	148.0	9
5.3	148.877	149.7	150.6	151.4	152.3	153.1	154.0	154.9	155.7	156.6	9
5.4	157.464	158.3	159.2	160.1	161.0	161.9	162.8	163.7	164.6	165.5	9
5.5	166.375	167.3	168.2	169.1	170.0	171.0	171.9	172.8	173.7	174.7	9
5.6	175.616	176.6	177.5	178.5	179.4	180.4	181.3	182.3	183.3	184.2	10
5.7	185.193	186.2	187.1	188.1	189.1	190.1	191.1	192.1	193.1	194.1	10
5.8	195.112	196.1	197.1	198.2	199.2	200.2	201.2	202.3	203.3	204.3	11
5.9	205.379	206.4	207.5	208.5	209.6	210.6	211.7	212.8	213.8	214.9	11

n	0	1	2	3	4	5	6	7	8	9	d
6.0	216.000	217.1	218.2	219.3	220.3	221.4	222.5	223.6	224.8	225.9	11
6.1	226.981	228.1	229.2	230.3	231.5	232.6	233.7	234.9	236.0	237.2	11
6.2	238.328	239.5	240.6	241.8	243.0	244.1	245.3	246.5	247.7	248.9	11
6.3	250.047	251.2	252.4	253.6	254.8	256.0	257.3	258.5	259.7	260.9	12
6.4	262.144	263.4	264.6	265.8	267.1	268.3	269.6	270.8	272.1	273.4	12
6.5	274.625	275.9	277.2	278.4	279.7	281.0	282.3	283.6	284.9	286.2	13
6.6	287.496	288.8	290.1	291.4	292.8	294.1	295.4	296.7	298.1	299.4	14
6.7	300.763	302.1	303.5	304.8	306.2	307.5	308.9	310.3	311.7	313.0	14
6.8	314.432	315.8	317.2	318.6	320.0	321.4	322.8	324.2	325.7	327.1	14
6.9	328.509	329.9	331.4	332.8	334.3	335.7	337.2	338.6	340.1	341.5	15
7.0	343.000	344.5	345.9	347.4	348.9	350.4	351.9	353.4	354.9	356.4	15
7.1	357.911	359.4	360.9	362.5	364.0	365.5	367.1	368.6	370.1	371.7	15
7.2	373.248	374.8	376.4	377.9	379.5	381.1	382.7	384.2	385.8	387.4	16
7.3	389.017	390.6	392.2	393.8	395.4	397.1	398.7	400.3	401.9	403.6	16
7.4	405.224	406.9	408.5	410.2	411.8	413.5	415.2	416.8	418.5	420.2	17
7.5	421.875	423.6	425.3	427.0	428.7	430.4	432.1	433.8	435.5	437.2	18
7.6	438.976	440.7	442.5	444.2	445.9	447.7	449.5	451.2	453.0	454.8	17
7.7	456.533	458.3	460.1	461.9	463.7	465.5	467.3	469.1	470.9	472.7	19
7.8	474.552	476.4	478.2	480.0	481.9	483.7	485.6	487.4	489.3	491.2	18
7.9	493.039	494.9	496.8	498.7	500.6	502.5	504.4	506.3	508.2	510.1	19
8.0	512.000	513.9	515.8	517.8	519.7	521.7	523.6	525.6	527.5	529.5	19
8.1	531.441	533.4	535.4	537.4	539.4	541.3	543.3	545.3	547.3	549.4	20
8.2	551.368	553.4	555.4	557.4	559.5	561.5	563.6	565.6	567.7	569.7	21
8.3	571.787	573.9	575.9	578.0	580.1	582.2	584.3	586.4	588.5	590.6	21
8.4	592.704	594.8	596.9	599.1	601.2	603.4	605.5	607.6	609.8	612.0	21
8.5	614.125	616.3	618.5	620.7	622.8	625.0	627.2	629.4	631.6	633.8	23
8.6	636.056	638.3	640.5	642.7	645.0	647.2	649.5	651.7	654.0	656.2	23
8.7	658.503	660.8	663.1	665.3	667.6	669.9	672.2	674.5	676.8	679.2	23
8.8	681.472	683.8	686.1	688.5	690.8	693.2	695.5	697.9	700.2	702.6	24
8.9	704.969	707.3	709.7	712.1	714.5	716.9	719.3	721.7	724.2	726.6	24
9.0	729.000	731.4	733.9	736.3	738.8	741.2	743.7	746.1	748.6	751.1	25
9.1	753.571	756.1	758.6	761.0	763.6	766.1	768.6	771.1	773.6	776.2	25
9.2	778.688	781.2	783.8	786.3	788.9	791.5	794.0	796.6	799.2	801.8	26
9.3	804.357	807.0	809.6	812.2	814.8	817.4	820.0	822.7	825.3	827.9	27
9.4	830.584	833.2	835.9	838.6	841.2	843.9	846.6	849.3	852.0	854.7	27
9.5	857.375	860.1	862.8	865.5	868.3	871.0	873.7	876.5	879.2	882.0	27
9.6	884.736	887.5	890.3	893.1	895.8	898.6	901.4	904.2	907.0	909.9	28
9.7	912.673	915.5	918.3	921.2	924.0	926.9	929.7	932.6	935.4	938.3	29
9.8	941.192	944.1	947.0	949.9	952.8	955.7	958.6	961.5	964.4	967.4	29
9.9	970.299	973.2	976.2	979.1	982.1	985.1	988.0	991.0	994.0	997.0	30

n	.0	.1	.2	.3	.4	.5	.6	.7	.8	.9	d
1	1.000	*757	*579	*455	*364	*296	*244	*204	*171	*146	21
2	0.125	108	*939	*822	*723	*640	*569	*508	*456	*410	40
3	0.0 370	336	305	278	254	233	214	197	182	169	13
4	0.0 156	145	135	126	117	110	103	*963	*904	*850	50
5	0.00 800	754	711	672	635	601	569	540	513	487	24
6	0.00 463	441	420	400	381	364	348	332	318	304	12
7	0.00 292	279	268	257	247	237	228	219	211	203	8
8	0.00 195	188	181	175	169	163	157	152	147	142	5
9	0.00 137	133	129	124	120	117	113	110	106	103	3

n	0	1	2	3	4	5	6	7	8	9	d
1.0	1.0000	0050	0100	0149	0198	0247	0296	0344	0392	0440	48
1.1	0488	0536	0583	0630	0677	0724	0770	0817	0863	0909	45
1.2	0954	1000	1045	1091	1136	1180	1225	1269	1314	1358	44
1.3	1402	1446	1489	1533	1576	1619	1662	1705	1747	1790	42
1.4	1832	1874	1916	1958	2000	2042	2083	2124	2166	2207	40
1.5	2247	2288	2329	2369	2410	2450	2490	2530	2570	2610	39
1.6	2649	2689	2728	2767	2806	2845	2884	2923	2961	3000	38
1.7	3038	3077	3115	3153	3191	3229	3266	3304	3342	3379	37
1.8	3416	3454	3491	3528	3565	3601	3638	3675	3711	3748	36
1.9	3784	3820	3856	3892	3928	3964	4000	4036	4071	4107	35
2.0	1.4142	4177	4213	4248	4283	4318	4353	4387	4422	4457	34
2.1	4491	4526	4560	4595	4629	4663	4697	4731	4765	4799	33
2.2	4832	4866	4900	4933	4967	5000	5033	5067	5100	5133	33
2.3	5166	5199	5232	5264	5297	5330	5362	5395	5427	5460	32
2.4	5492	5524	5556	5588	5620	5652	5684	5716	5748	5780	31
2.5	5811	5843	5875	5906	5937	5969	6000	6031	6062	6093	32
2.6	6125	6155	6186	6217	6248	6279	6310	6340	6371	6401	31
2.7	6432	6462	6492	6523	6553	6583	6613	6643	6673	6703	30
2.8	6733	6763	6793	6823	6852	6882	6912	6941	6971	7000	29
2.9	7029	7059	7088	7117	7146	7176	7205	7234	7263	7292	29
3.0	1.7321	7349	7378	7407	7436	7464	7493	7521	7550	7578	29
3.1	7607	7635	7664	7692	7720	7748	7776	7804	7833	7861	28
3.2	7889	7916	7944	7972	8000	8028	8055	8083	8111	8138	28
3.3	8166	8193	8221	8248	8276	8303	8330	8358	8385	8412	27
3.4	8439	8466	8493	8520	8547	8574	8601	8628	8655	8682	26
3.5	8708	8735	8762	8788	8815	8841	8868	8894	8921	8947	27
3.6	8974	9000	9026	9053	9079	9105	9131	9157	9183	9209	26
3.7	9235	9261	9287	9313	9339	9365	9391	9416	9442	9468	26
3.8	9494	9519	9545	9570	9596	9621	9647	9672	9698	9723	25
3.9	9748	9774	9799	9824	9849	9875	9900	9925	9950	9975	25
4.0	2.0000	0025	0050	0075	0100	0125	0149	0174	0199	0224	24
4.1	0248	0273	0298	0322	0347	0372	0396	0421	0445	0469	25
4.2	0494	0518	0543	0567	0591	0616	0640	0664	0688	0712	24
4.3	0736	0761	0785	0809	0833	0857	0881	0905	0928	0952	24
4.4	0976	1000	1024	1048	1071	1095	1119	1142	1166	1190	23
4.5	1213	1237	1260	1284	1307	1331	1354	1378	1401	1424	24
4.6	1448	1471	1494	1517	1541	1564	1587	1610	1633	1656	23
4.7	1679	1703	1726	1749	1772	1794	1817	1840	1863	1886	23
4.8	1909	1932	1954	1977	2000	2023	2045	2068	2091	2113	23
4.9	2136	2159	2181	2204	2226	2249	2271	2293	2316	2338	23
5.0	2.2361	2383	2405	2428	2450	2472	2494	2517	2539	2561	22
5.1	2583	2605	2627	2650	2672	2694	2716	2738	2760	2782	22
5.2	2804	2825	2847	2869	2891	2913	2935	2956	2978	3000	22
5.3	3022	3043	3065	3087	3108	3130	3152	3173	3195	3216	22
5.4	3238	3259	3281	3302	3324	3345	3367	3388	3409	3431	21
5.5	3452	3473	3495	3516	3537	3558	3580	3601	3622	3643	21
5.6	3664	3685	3707	3728	3749	3770	3791	3812	3833	3854	21
5.7	3875	3896	3917	3937	3958	3979	4000	4021	4042	4062	21
5.8	4083	4104	4125	4145	4166	4187	4207	4228	4249	4269	21
5.9	4290	4310	4331	4352	4372	4393	4413	4434	4454	4474	21

n	0	1	2	3	4	5	6	7	8	9	d
6.0	2.4495	4515	4536	4556	4576	4597	4617	4637	4658	4678	20
6.1	4698	4718	4739	4759	4779	4799	4819	4839	4860	4880	20
6.2	4900	4920	4940	4960	4980	5000	5020	5040	5060	5080	20
6.3	5100	5120	5140	5159	5179	5199	5219	5239	5259	5278	20
6.4	5298	5318	5338	5357	5377	5397	5417	5436	5456	5475	20
6.5	5495	5515	5534	5554	5573	5593	5612	5632	5652	5671	19
6.6	5690	5710	5729	5749	5768	5788	5807	5826	5846	5865	19
6.7	5884	5904	5923	5942	5962	5981	6000	6019	6038	6058	19
6.8	6077	6096	6115	6134	6153	6173	6192	6211	6230	6249	19
6.9	6268	6287	6306	6325	6344	6363	6382	6401	6420	6439	19
7.0	2.6458	6476	6495	6514	6533	6552	6571	6589	6608	6627	19
7.1	6646	6665	6683	6702	6721	6739	6758	6777	6796	6814	19
7.2	6833	6851	6870	6889	6907	6926	6944	6963	6981	7000	19
7.3	7019	7037	7055	7074	7092	7111	7129	7148	7166	7185	18
7.4	7203	7221	7240	7258	7276	7295	7313	7331	7350	7368	18
7.5	7386	7404	7423	7441	7459	7477	7495	7514	7532	7550	18
7.6	7568	7586	7604	7622	7641	7659	7677	7695	7713	7731	18
7.7	7749	7767	7785	7803	7821	7839	7857	7875	7893	7911	17
7.8	7928	7946	7964	7982	8000	8018	8036	8054	8071	8089	18
7.9	8107	8125	8142	8160	8178	8196	8213	8231	8249	8267	17
8.0	2.8284	8302	8320	8337	8355	8373	8390	8408	8425	8443	17
8.1	8460	8478	8496	8513	8531	8548	8566	8583	8601	8618	18
8.2	8636	8653	8671	8688	8705	8723	8740	8758	8775	8792	18
8.3	8810	8827	8844	8862	8879	8896	8914	8931	8948	8965	18
8.4	8983	9000	9017	9034	9052	9069	9086	9103	9120	9138	17
8.5	9155	9172	9189	9206	9223	9240	9257	9275	9292	9309	17
8.6	9326	9343	9360	9377	9394	9411	9428	9445	9462	9479	17
8.7	9496	9513	9530	9547	9563	9580	9597	9614	9631	9648	17
8.8	9665	9682	9698	9715	9732	9749	9766	9783	9799	9816	17
8.9	9833	9850	9866	9883	9900	9917	9933	9950	9967	9983	17
9.0	3.0000	0017	0033	0050	0067	0083	0100	0116	0133	0150	16
9.1	0166	0183	0199	0216	0232	0249	0265	0282	0299	0315	17
9.2	0332	0348	0364	0381	0397	0414	0430	0447	0463	0480	16
9.3	0496	0512	0529	0545	0561	0578	0594	0610	0627	0643	16
9.4	0659	0676	0692	0708	0725	0741	0757	0773	0790	0806	16
9.5	0822	0838	0854	0871	0887	0903	0919	0935	0952	0968	16
9.6	0984	1000	1016	1032	1048	1064	1081	1097	1113	1129	16
9.7	1145	1161	1177	1193	1209	1225	1241	1257	1273	1289	16
9.8	1305	1321	1337	1353	1369	1385	1401	1417	1432	1448	16
9.9	1464	1480	1496	1512	1528	1544	1559	1575	1591	1607	16

n	.0	.1	.2	.3	.4	.5	.6	.7	.8	.9	d
1	1.000	*953	*913	*877	*845	*816	*791	*767	*745	*725	18
2	0.707	690	674	659	645	632	620	609	598	587	10
3	0.577	568	559	550	542	535	527	520	513	506	6
4	0.500	494	488	482	477	471	466	461	456	452	5
5	0.447	443	439	434	430	426	423	419	415	412	4
6	0.408	405	402	398	395	392	389	386	383	381	3
7	0.378	375	373	370	368	365	363	360	358	356	2
8	0.354	351	349	347	345	343	341	339	337	335	2
9	0.333	331	330	328	326	324	323	321	319	318	2

n	.0	.1	.2	.3	.4	.5	.6	.7	.8	.9	d
10	3.1623	1780	1937	2094	2249	2404	2558	2711	2863	3015	151
11	3166	3317	3466	3615	3764	3912	4059	4205	4351	4496	145
12	4641	4785	4928	5071	5214	5355	5496	5637	5777	5917	139
13	6056	6194	6332	6469	6606	6742	6878	7014	7148	7283	134
14	7417	7550	7683	7815	7947	8079	8210	8341	8471	8601	129
15	8730	8859	8987	9115	9243	9370	9497	9623	9749	9875	125
16	4.0000	0125	0249	0373	0497	0620	0743	0866	0988	1110	121
17	1231	1352	1473	1593	1713	1833	1952	2071	2190	2308	118
18	2426	2544	2661	2778	2895	3012	3128	3243	3359	3474	115
19	3589	3704	3818	3932	4045	4159	4272	4385	4497	4609	112
20	4.4721	4833	4944	5056	5166	5277	5387	5497	5607	5717	109
21	5826	5935	6043	6152	6260	6368	6476	6583	6690	6797	107
22	6904	7011	7117	7223	7329	7434	7539	7645	7749	7854	104
23	7958	8062	8166	8270	8374	8477	8580	8683	8785	8888	102
24	8990	9092	9193	9295	9396	9497	9598	9699	9800	9900	100
25	5.0000	0100	0200	0299	0398	0498	0596	0695	0794	0892	98
26	0990	1088	1186	1284	1381	1478	1575	1672	1769	1865	97
27	1962	2058	2154	2249	2345	2440	2536	2631	2726	2820	95
28	2915	3009	3104	3198	3292	3385	3479	3572	3666	3759	93
29	3852	3944	4037	4129	4222	4314	4406	4498	4589	4681	91
30	5.4772	4863	4955	5045	5136	5227	5317	5408	5498	5588	90
31	5678	5767	5857	5946	6036	6125	6214	6303	6391	6480	89
32	6569	6657	6745	6833	6921	7009	7096	7184	7271	7359	87
33	7446	7533	7619	7706	7793	7879	7966	8052	8138	8224'	86
34	8310	8395	8481	8566	8652	8737	8822	8907	8992	9076	85
35	9161	9245	9330	9414	9498	9582	9666	9749	9833	9917	83
36	6.0000	0083	0166	0249	0332	0415	0498	0581	0663	0745	83
37	0828	0910	0992	1074	1156	1237	1319	1400	1482	1563	81
38	1644	1725	1806	1887	1968	2048	2129	2209	2290	2370	80
39	2450	2530	2610	2690	2769	2849	2929	3008	3087	3166	80
40	6.3246	3325	3403	3482	3561	3640	3718	3797	3875	3953	78
41	4031	4109	4187	4265	4343	4420	4498	4576	4653	4730	77
42	4807	4885	4962	5038	5115	5192	5269	5345	5422	5498	76
43	5574	5651	5727	5803	5879	5955	6030	6106	6182	6257	75
44	6332	6408	6483	6558	6633	6708	6783	6858	6933	7007	75
45	7082	7157	7231	7305	7380	7454	7528	7602	7676	7750	73
46	7823	7897	7971	8044	8118	8191	8264	8337	8411	8484	73
47	8557	8629	8702	8775	8848	8920	8993	9065	9138	9210	72
48	9282	9354	9426	9498	9570	9642	9714	9785	9857	9929	71
49	7.0000	0071	0143	0214	0285	0356	0427	0498	0569	0640	71
50	7.0711	0781	0852	0922	0993	1063	1134	1204	1274	1344	70
51	1414	1484	1554	1624	1694	1764	1833	1903	1972	2042	69
52	2111	2180	2250	2319	2388	2457	2526	2595	2664	2732	69
53	2801	2870	2938	3007	3075	3144	3212	3280	3348	3417	68
54	3485	3553	3621	3689	3756	3824	3892	3959	4027	4095	67
55	4162	4229	4297	4364	4431	4498	4565	4632	4699	4766	67
56	4833	4900	4967	5033	5100	5166	5233	5299	5366	5432	66
57	5498	5565	5631	5697	5763	5829	5895	5961	6026	6092	66
58	6158	6223	6289	6354	6420	6485	6551	6616	6681	6746	65
59	6811	6877	6942	7006	7071	7136	7201	7266	7330	7395	65

n	.0	.1	.2	.3	.4	.5	.6	.7	.8	.9	d
60	7.7460	7524	7589	7653	7717	7782	7846	7910	7974	8038	64
61	8102	8166	8230	8294	8358	8422	8486	8549	8613	8677	63
62	8740	8804	8867	8930	8994	9057	9120	9183	9246	9310	63
63	9373	9436	9498	9561	9624	9687	9750	9812	9875	9937	63
64	8.0000	0062	0125	0187	0250	0312	0374	0436	0498	0561	62
65	0623	0685	0747	0808	0870	0932	0994	1056	1117	1179	61
66	1240	1302	1363	1425	1486	1548	1609	1670	1731	1792	62
67	1854	1915	1976	2037	2098	2158	2219	2280	2341	2401	61
68	2462	2523	2583	2644	2704	2765	2825	2885	2946	3006	60
69	3066	3126	3187	3247	3307	3367	3427	3487	3546	3606	60
70	8.3666	3726	3785	3845	3905	3964	4024	4083	4143	4202	59
71	4261	4321	4380	4439	4499	4558	4617	4676	4735	4794	59
72	4853	4912	4971	5029	5088	5147	5206	5264	5323	5381	59
73	5440	5499	5557	5615	5674	5732	5790	5849	5907	5965	58
74	6023	6081	6139	6197	6255	6313	6371	6429	6487	6545	58
75	6603	6660	6718	6776	6833	6891	6948	7006	7063	7121	57
76	7178	7235	7293	7350	7407	7464	7521	7579	7636	7693	57
77	7750	7807	7864	7920	7977	8034	8091	8148	8204	8261	57
78	8318	8374	8431	8487	8544	8600	8657	8713	8769	8826	56
79	8882	8938	8994	9051	9107	9163	9219	9275	9331	9387	56
80	8.9443	9499	9554	9610	9666	9722	9778	9833	9889	9944	56
81	9.0000	0056	0111	0167	0222	0277	0333	0388	0443	0499	55
82	0554	0609	0664	0719	0774	0830	0885	0940	0995	1049	55
83	1104	1159	1214	1269	1324	1378	1433	1488	1542	1597	55
84	1652	1706	1761	1815	1869	1924	1978	2033	2087	2141	54
85	2195	2250	2304	2358	2412	2466	2520	2574	2628	2682	54
86	2736	2790	2844	2898	2952	3005	3059	3113	3167	3220	54
87	3274	3327	3381	3434	3488	3541	3595	3648	3702	3755	53
88	3808	3862	3915	3968	4021	4074	4128	4181	4234	4287	53
89	4340	4393	4446	4499	4552	4604	4657	4710	4763	4816	52
90	9.4868	4921	4974	5026	5079	5131	5184	5237	5289	5341	53
91	5394	5446	5499	5551	5603	5656	5708	5760	5812	5864	53
92	5917	5969	6021	6073	6125	6177	6229	6281	6333	6385	52
93	6437	6488	6540	6592	6644	6695	6747	6799	6850	6902	52
94	6954	7005	7057	7108	7160	7211	7263	7314	7365	7417	51
95	7468	7519	7570	7622	7673	7724	7775	7826	7877	7929	51
96	7980	8031	8082	8133	8184	8234	8285	8336	8387	8438	51
97	8489	8539	8590	8641	8691	8742	8793	8843	8894	8944	51
98	8995	9045	9096	9146	9197	9247	9298	9348	9398	9448	51
99	9499	9549	9599	9649	9700	9750	9800	9850	9900	9950	50

n	0	1	2	3	4	5	6	7	8	9	d
1	0.316	302	289	277	267	258	250	243	236	229	5
2	0.224	219	213	209	204	200	196	192	189	186	3
3	0.183	180	177	174	171	169	167	164	162	160	2
4	0.158	156	154	152	151	149	147	146	144	143	2
5	0.141	140	139	137	136	135	134	132	131	130	1
6	0.129	128	127	126	125	124	123	122	121	120	0
7	0.120	119	118	117	116	115	115	114	113	113	1
8	0.112	111	110	110	109	108	108	107	107	106	1
9	0.105	105	104	104	103	103	102	102	101	101	1

n	0	1	2	3	4	5	6	7	8	9	d
1.0	1.0000	0033	0066	0099	0132	0164	0196	0228	0260	0291	32
1.1	0323	0354	0385	0416	0446	0477	0507	0537	0567	0597	30
1.2	0627	0656	0685	0714	0743	0772	0801	0829	0858	0886	28
1.3	0914	0942	0970	0997	1025	1052	1079	1106	1133	1160	27
1.4	1187	1213	1240	1266	1292	1319	1344	1370	1396	1422	25
1.5	1447	1473	1498	1523	1548	1573	1598	1623	1647	1672	24
1.6	1696	1720	1745	1769	1793	1817	1840	1864	1888	1911	24
1.7	1935	1958	1981	2005	2028	2051	2074	2096	2119	2142	22
1.8	2164	2187	2209	2232	2254	2276	2298	2320	2342	2364	22
1.9	2386	2407	2429	2450	2472	2493	2515	2536	2557	2578	21
2.0	1.2599	2620	2641	2662	2683	2703	2724	2745	2765	2785	21
2.1	2806	2826	2846	2866	2887	2907	2927	2947	2966	2986	20
2.2	3006	3026	3045	3065	3084	3104	3123	3142	3162	3181	19
2.3	3200	3219	3238	3257	3276	3295	3314	3333	3351	3370	19
2.4	3389	3407	3426	3444	3463	3481	3499	3518	3536	3554	18
2.5	3572	3590	3608	3626	3644	3662	3680	3698	3715	3733	18
2.6	3751	3768	3786	3803	3821	3838	3856	3873	3890	3908	17
2.7	3925	3942	3959	3976	3993	4010	4027	4044	4061	4078	17
2.8	4095	4111	4128	4145	4161	4178	4195	4211	4228	4244	16
2.9	4260	4277	4293	4309	4326	4342	4358	4374	4390	4406	16
3.0	1.4422	4439	4454	4470	4486	4502	4518	4534	4550	4565	16
3.1	4581	4597	4612	4628	4643	4659	4674	4690	4705	4721	15
3.2	4736	4751	4767	4782	4797	4812	4828	4843	4858	4873	15
3.3	4888	4903	4918	4933	4948	4963	4978	4993	5007	5022	15
3.4	5037	5052	5066	5081	5096	5110	5125	5139	5154	5168	15
3.5	5183	5197	5212	5226	5241	5255	5269	5283	5298	5312	14
3.6	5326	5340	5355	5369	5383	5397	5411	5425	5439	5453	14
3.7	5467	5481	5495	5508	5522	5536	5550	5564	5577	5591	14
3.8	5605	5619	5632	5646	5659	5673	5687	5700	5714	5727	14
3.9	5741	5754	5767	5781	5794	5808	5821	5834	5848	5861	13
4.0	1.5874	5887	5900	5914	5927	5940	5953	5966	5979	5992	13
4.1	6005	6018	6031	6044	6057	6070	6083	6096	6109	6121	13
4.2	6134	6147	6160	6173	6185	6198	6211	6223	6236	6249	12
4.3	6261	6274	6287	6299	6312	6324	6337	6349	6362	6374	12
4.4	6386	6399	6411	6424	6436	6448	6461	6473	6485	6497	13
4.5	6510	6522	6534	6546	6558	6571	6583	6595	6607	6619	12
4.6	6631	6643	6655	6667	6679	6691	6703	6715	6727	6739	12
4.7	6751	6763	6774	6786	6798	6810	6822	6833	6845	6857	12
4.8	6869	6880	6892	6904	6915	6927	6939	6950	6962	6973	12
4.9	6985	6997	7008	7020	7031	7043	7054	7065	7077	7088	12
5.0	1.7100	7111	7123	7134	7145	7157	7168	7179	7190	7202	11
5.1	7213	7224	7235	7247	7258	7269	7280	7291	7303	7314	11
5.2	7325	7336	7347	7358	7369	7380	7391	7402	7413	7424	11
5.3	7435	7446	7457	7468	7479	7490	7501	7512	7522	7533	11
5.4	7544	7555	7566	7577	7587	7598	7609	7620	7630	7641	11
5.5	7652	7662	7673	7684	7694	7705	7716	7726	7737	7748	10
5.6	7758	7769	7779	7790	7800	7811	7821	7832	7842	7853	10
5.7	7863	7874	7884	7894	7905	7915	7926	7936	7946	7957	10
5.8	7967	7977	7988	7998	8008	8018	8029	8039	8049	8059	11
5.9	8070	8080	8090	8100	8110	8121	8131	8141	8151	8161	10

n	0	1	2	3	4	5	6	7	8	9	d
6.0	1.8171	8181	8191	8201	8211	8222	8232	8242	8252	8262	10
6.1	8272	8282	8292	8302	8311	8321	8331	8341	8351	8361	10
6.2	8371	8381	8391	8400	8410	8420	8430	8440	8450	8459	10
6.3	8469	8479	8489	8498	8508	8518	8528	8537	8547	8557	9
6.4	8566	8576	8586	8595	8605	8615	8624	8634	8643	8653	10
6.5	8663	8672	8682	8691	8701	8710	8720	8729	8739	8748	10
6.6	8758	8767	8777	8786	8796	8805	8814	8824	8833	8843	9
6.7	8852	8861	8871	8880	8889	8899	8908	8917	8927	8936	9
6.8	8945	8955	8964	8973	8982	8992	9001	9010	9019	9029	9
6.9	9038	9047	9056	9065	9074	9084	9093	9102	9111	9120	9
7.0	1.9129	9138	9148	9157	9166	9175	9184	9193	9202	9211	9
7.1	9220	9229	9238	9247	9256	9265	9274	9283	9292	9301	9
7.2	9310	9319	9328	9337	9345	9354	9363	9372	9381	9390	9
7.3	9399	9408	9416	9425	9434	9443	9452	9461	9469	9478	9
7.4	9487	9496	9504	9513	9522	9531	9539	9548	9557	9566	8
7.5	9574	9583	9592	9600	9609	9618	9626	9635	9644	9652	9
7.6	9661	9670	9678	9687	9695	9704	9713	9721	9730	9738	9
7.7	9747	9755	9764	9772	9781	9789	9798	9806	9815	9823	9
7.8	9832	9840	9849	9857	9866	9874	9883	9891	9899	9908	8
7.9	9916	9925	9933	9941	9950	9958	9967	9975	9983	9992	8
8.0	2.0000	0008	0017	0025	0033	0042	0050	0058	0066	0075	8
8.1	0083	0091	0100	0108	0116	0124	0132	0141	0149	0157	8
8.2	0165	0173	0182	0190	0198	0206	0214	0223	0231	0239	8
8.3	0247	0255	0263	0271	0279	0288	0296	0304	0312	0320	8
8.4	0328	0336	0344	0352	0360	0368	0376	0384	0392	0400	8
8.5	0408	0416	0424	0432	0440	0448	0456	0464	0472	0480	8
8.6	0488	0496	0504	0512	0520	0528	0536	0543	0551	0559	8
8.7	0567	0575	0583	0591	0599	0606	0614	0622	0630	0638	8
8.8	0646	0653	0661	0669	0677	0685	0692	0700	0708	0716	8
8.9	0724	0731	0739	0747	0755	0762	0770	0778	0785	0793	8
9.0	2.0801	0809	0816	0824	0832	0839	0847	0855	0862	0870	8
9.1	0878	0885	0893	0901	0908	0916	0923	0931	0939	0946	8
9.2	0954	0961	0969	0977	0984	0992	0999	1007	1014	1022	7
9.3	1029	1037	1045	1052	1060	1067	1075	1082	1090	1097	8
9.4	1105	1112	1120	1127	1134	1142	1149	1157	1164	1172	7
9.5	1179	1187	1194	1201	1209	1216	1224	1231	1238	1246	7
9.6	1253	1261	1268	1275	1283	1290	1297	1305	1312	1319	8
9.7	1327	1334	1341	1349	1356	1363	1371	1378	1385	1392	8
9.8	1400	1407	1414	1422	1429	1436	1443	1451	1458	1465	7
9.9	1472	1480	1487	1494	1501	1508	1516	1523	1530	1537	7

n	.0	.1	.2	.3	.4	.5	.6	.7	.8	.9	d
1	1.000	*969	*941	*916	*894	*874	*855	*838	*822	*807	13
2	0.794	781	769	758	747	737	727	718	709	701	8
3	0.693	686	679	672	665	659	652	647	641	635	5
4	0.630	625	620	615	610	606	601	597	593	589	4
5	0.585	581	577	574	570	567	563	560	557	553	3
6	0.550	547	544	541	539	536	533	530	528	525	2
7	0.523	520	518	516	513	511	509	506	504	502	2
8	0.500	498	496	494	492	490	488	486	484	483	2
9	0.481	479	477	476	474	472	471	469	467	466	2

n	.0	.1	.2	.3	.4	.5	.6	.7	.8	.9	d
10	2.1544	1616	1687	1757	1828	1898	1967	2036	2104	2172	68
11	2240	2307	2374	2440	2506	2572	2637	2702	2766	2831	63
12	2894	2957	3021	3084	3146	3208	3270	3331	3392	3453	60
13	3513	3573	3633	3693	3752	3811	3870	3928	3986	4044	57
14	4101	4159	4216	4272	4329	4385	4441	4497	4552	4607	55
15	4662	4717	4771	4825	4879	4933	4987	5040	5093	5146	52
16	5198	5251	5303	5355	5407	5458	5509	5561	5612	5662	51
17	5713	5763	5813	5863	5913	5962	6012	6061	6110	6159	48
18	6207	6256	6304	6352	6400	6448	6495	6543	6590	6637	47
19	6684	6731	6777	6824	6870	6916	6962	7008	7053	7099	45
20	2.7144	7189	7234	7279	7324	7369	7413	7457	7501	7545	44
21	˙7589	7633	7677	7720	7763	7806	7850	7892	7935	7978	42
22	8020	8063	8105	8147	8189	8231	8273	8314	8356	8397	42
23	8439	8480	8521	8562	8603	8643	8684	8724	8765	8805	40
24	8845	8885	8925	8965	9004	9044	9083	9123	9162	9201	39
25	9240	9279	9318	9357	9395	9434	9472	9511	9549	9587	38
26	9625	9663	9701	9738	9776	9814	9851	9888	9926	9963	37
27	3.0000	0037	0074	0111	0147	0184	0221	0257	0293	0330	36
28	0366	0402	0438	0474	0510	0546	0581	0617	0652	0688	35
29	0723	0758	0794	0829	0864	0899	0934	0968	1003	1038	34
30	3.1072	1107	1141	1176	1210	1244	1278	1312	1346	1380	34
31	1414	1448	1481	1515	1548	1582	1615	1648	1682	1715	33
32	1748	1781	1814	1847	1880	1913	1945	1978	2010	2043	32
33	2075	2108	2140	2172	2204	2237	2269	2301	2332	2364	32
34	2396	2428	2460	2491	2523	2554	2586	2617	2648	2679	32
35	2711	2742	2773	2804	2835	2866	2897	2927	2958	2989	30
36	3019	3050	3080	3111	3141	3171	3202	3232	3262	3292	30
37	3322	3352	3382	3412	3442	3472	3501	3531	3561	3590	30
38	3620	3649	3679	3708	3737	3767	3796	3825	3854	3883	29
39	3912	3941	3970	3999	4028	4056	4085	4114	4142	4171	29
40	3.4200	4228	4256	4285	4313	4341	4370	4398	4426	4454	28
41	4482	4510	4538	4566	4594	4622	4650	4677	4705	4733	27
42	4760	4788	4815	4843	4870	4898	4925	4952	4980	5007	27
43	5034	5061	5088	5115	5142	5169	5196	5223	5250	5277	26
44	5303	5330	5357	5384	5410	5437	5463	5490	5516	5543	26
45	5569	5595	5622	5648	5674	5700	5726	5752	5778	5805	25
46	5830	5856	5882	5908	5934	5960	5986	6011	6037	6063	25
47	6088	6114	6139	6165	6190	6216	6241	6267	6292	6317	25
48	6342	6368	6393	6418	6443	6468	6493	6518	6543	6568	25
49	6593	6618	6643	6668	6692	6717	6742	6766	6791	6816	24
50	3.6840	6865	6889	6914	6938	6963	6987	7011	7036	7060	24
51	7084	7109	7133	7157	7181	7205	7229	7253	7277	7301	24
52	7325	7349	7373	7397	7421	7444	7468	7492	7516	7539	24
53	7563	7586	7610	7634	7657	7681	7704	7728	7751	7774	24
54	7798	7821	7844	7868	7891	7914	7937	7960	7983	8006	24
55	8030	8053	8076	8099	8121	8144	8167	8190	8213	8236	23
56	8259	8281	8304	8327	8349	8372	8395	8417	8440	8462	23
57	8485	8508	8530	8552	8575	8597	8620	8642	8664	8687	22
58	8709	8731	8753	8775	8798	8820	8842	8864	8886	8908	22
59	8930	8952	8974	8996	9018	9040	9061	9083	9105	9127	22

n	.0	.1	.2	.3	.4	.5	.6	.7	.8	.9	d
60	3.9149	9170	9192	9214	9235	9257	9279	9300	9322	9343	22
61	9365	9386	9408	9429	9451	9472	9494	9515	9536	9558	21
62	9579	9600	9621	9643	9664	9685	9706	9727	9748	9770	21
63	9791	9812	9833	9854	9875	9896	9916	9937	9958	9979	21
64	4.0000	0021	0042	0062	0083	0104	0125	0145	0166	0187	20
65	0207	0228	0248	0269	0290	0310	0331	0351	0372	0392	20
66	0412	0433	0453	0474	0494	0514	0534	0555	0575	0595	20
67	0615	0636	0656	0676	0696	0716	0736	0756	0776	0797	20
68	0817	0837	0857	0877	0896	0916	0936	0956	0976	0996	20
69	1016	1035	1055	1075	1095	1114	1134	1154	1174	1193	20
70	4.1213	1232	1252	1272	1291	1311	1330	1350	1369	1389	19
71	1408	1428	1447	1466	1486	1505	1524	1544	1563	1582	20
72	1602	1621	1640	1659	1679	1698	1717	1736	1755	1774	19
73	1793	1812	1832	1851	1870	1889	1908	1927	1946	1964	19
74	1983	2002	2021	2040	2059	2078	2097	2115	2134	2153	19
75	2172	2190	2209	2228	2246	2265	2284	2302	2321	2340	18
76	2358	2377	2395	2414	2432	2451	2469	2488	2506	2525	18
77	2543	2562	2580	2598	2617	2635	2653	2672	2690	2708	19
78	2727	2745	2763	2781	2799	2818	2836	2854	2872	2890	18
79	2908	2927	2945	2963	2981	2999	3017	3035	3053	3071	18
80	4.3089	3107	3125	3143	3160	3178	3196	3214	3232	3250	17
81	3267	3285	3303	3321	3339	3356	3374	3392	3409	3427	18
82	3445	3463	3480	3498	3515	3533	3551	3568	3586	3603	18
83	3621	3638	3656	3673	3691	3708	3726	3743	3760	3778	17
84	3795	3813	3830	3847	3865	3882	3899	3917	3934	3951	17
85	3968	3986	4003	4020	4037	4054	4072	4089	4106	4123	17
86	4140	4157	4174	4191	4208	4225	4242	4259	4276	4293	17
87	4310	4327	4344	4361	4378	4395	4412	4429	4446	4463	17
88	4480	4496	4513	4530	4547	4564	4580	4597	4614	4630	17
89	4647	4664	4681	4698	4714	4731	4748	4764	4781	4797	17
90	4.4814	4831	4847	4864	4880	4897	4913	4930	4946	4963	16
91	4979	4996	5012	5029	5045	5062	5078	5094	5111	5127	17
92	5144	5160	5176	5193	5209	5225	5241	5258	5274	5290	17
93	5307	5323	5339	5355	5371	5388	5404	5420	5436	5452	16
94	5468	5485	5501	5517	5533	5549	5565	5581	5597	5613	16
95	5629	5645	5661	5677	5693	5709	5725	5741	5757	5773	16
96	5789	5804	5820	5836	5852	5868	5884	5900	5915	5931	16
97	5947	5963	5979	5994	6010	6026	6042	6057	6073	6089	15
98	6104	6120	6136	6151	6167	6183	6198	6214	6229	6245	16
99	6261	6276	6292	6307	6323	6338	6354	6369	6385	6400	16

n	0	1	2	3	4	5	6	7	8	9	d
1	0.464	450	437	425	415	405	397	389	382	375	7
2	0.368	362	357	352	347	342	338	333	329	325	3
3	0.322	318	315	312	309	306	303	300	297	295	3
4	0.292	290	288	285	283	281	279	277	275	273	2
5	0.271	270	268	266	265	263	261	260	258	257	2
6	0.255	254	253	251	250	249	247	246	245	244	1
7	0.243	241	240	239	238	237	236	235	234	233	1
8	0.232	231	230	229	228	227	227	226	225	224	1
9	0.223	222	222	221	220	219	218	218	217	216	1

n	0	1	2	3	4	5	6	7	8	9	d
10	4.6416	6570	6723	6875	7027	7177	7326	7475	7622	7769	145
11	7914	8059	8203	8346	8488	8629	8770	8910	9049	9187	137
12	9324	9461	9597	9732	9866	*0000	*0133	*0265	*0397	*0528	130
13	5.0658	0788	0916	1045	1172	1299	1426	1551	1676	1801	124
14	1925	2048	2171	2293	2415	2536	2656	2776	2896	3015	118
15	3133	3251	3368	3485	3601	3717	3832	3947	4061	4175	113
16	4288	4401	4514	4626	4737	4848	4959	5069	5178	5288	109
17	5397	5505	5613	5721	5828	5934	6041	6147	6252	6357	105
18	6462	6567	6671	6774	6877	6980	7083	7185	7287	7388	101
19	7489	7590	7690	7790	7890	7989	8088	8186	8285	8383	97
20	5.8480	8578	8675	8771	8868	8964	9059	9155	9250	9345	94
21	9439	9533	9627	9721	9814	9907	*0000	*0092	*0185	*0277	91
22	6.0368	0459	0550	0641	0732	0822	0912	1002	1091	1180	89
23	1269	1358	1446	1534	1622	1710	1797	1885	1972	2058	87
24	2145	2231	2317	2403	2488	2573	2658	2743	2828	2912	84
25	2996	3080	3164	3247	3330	3413	3496	3579	3661	3743	82
26	3825	3907	3988	4070	4151	4232	4312	4393	4473	4553	80
27	4633	4713	4792	4872	4951	5030	5108	5187	5265	5343	78
28	5421	5499	5577	5654	5731	5808	5885	5962	6039	6115	76
29	6191	6267	6343	6419	6494	6569	6644	6719	6794	6869	74
30	6.6943	7018	7092	7166	7240	7313	7387	7460	7533	7606	73
31	7679	7752	7824	7897	7969	8041	8113	8185	8256	8328	71
32	8399	8470	8541	8612	8683	8753	8824	8894	8964	9034	70
33	9104	9174	9244	9313	9382	9451	9521	9589	9658	9727	68
34	9795	9864	9932	*0000	*0068	*0136	*0203	*0271	*0338	*0406	67
35	7.0473	0540	0607	0674	0740	0807	0873	0940	1006	1072	66
36	1138	1204	1269	1335	1400	1466	1531	1596	1661	1726	65
37	1791	1855	1920	1984	2048	2112	2177	2240	2304	2368	64
38	2432	2495	2558	2622	2685	2748	2811	2874	2936	2999	62
39	3061	3124	3186	3248	3310	3372	3434	3496	3558	3619	62
40	7.3681	3742	3803	3864	3925	3986	4047	4108	4169	4229	61
41	4290	4350	4410	4470	4530	4590	4650	4710	4770	4829	60
42	4889	4948	5007	5067	5126	5185	5244	5302	5361	5420	58
43	5478	5537	5595	5654	5712	5770	5828	5886	5944	6001	58
44	6059	6117	6174	6232	6289	6346	6403	6460	6517	6574	57
45	6631	6688	6744	6801	6857	6914	6970	7026	7082	7138	56
46	7194	7250	7306	7362	7418	7473	7529	7584	7639	7695	55
47	7750	7805	7860	7915	7970	8025	8079	8134	8188	8243	54
48	8297	8352	8406	8460	8514	8568	8622	8676	8730	8784	53
49	8837	8891	8944	8998	9051	9105	9158	9211	9264	9317	53
50	7.9370	9423	9476	9528	9581	9634	9686	9739	9791	9843	53
51	9896	9948	*0000	*0052	*0104	*0156	*0208	*0260	*0311	*0363	52
52	8.0415	0466	0517	0569	0620	0671	0723	0774	0825	0876	51
53	0927	0978	1028	1079	1130	1180	1231	1281	1332	1382	51
54	1433	1483	1533	1583	1633	1683	1733	1783	1833	1882	50
55	1932	1982	2031	2081	2130	2180	2229	2278	2327	2377	49
56	2426	2475	2524	2573	2621	2670	2719	2768	2816	2865	48
57	2913	2962	3010	3059	3107	3155	3203	3251	3300	3348	48
58	3396	3443	3491	3539	3587	3634	3682	3730	3777	3825	47
59	3872	3919	3967	4014	4061	4108	4155	4202	4249	4296	47

n	0	1	2	3	4	5	6	7	8	9	d
60	8.4343	4390	4437	4484	4530	4577	4623	4670	4716	4763	46
61	4809	4856	4902	4948	4994	5040	5086	5132	5178	5224	46
62	5270	5316	5362	5408	5453	5499	5544	5590	5635	5681	45
63	5726	5772	5817	5862	5907	5952	5997	6043	6088	6132	45
64	6177	6222	6267	6312	6357	6401	6446	6490	6535	6579	45
65	6624	6668	6713	6757	6801	6845	6890	6934	6978	7022	44
66	7066	7110	7154	7198	7241	7285	7329	7373	7416	7460	43
67	7503	7547	7590	7634	7677	7721	7764	7807	7850	7893	44
68	7937	7980	8023	8066	8109	8152	8194	8237	8280	8323	43
69	8366	8408	8451	8493	8536	8578	8621	8663	8706	8748	42
70	8.8790	8833	8875	8917	8959	9001	9043	9085	9127	9169	42
71	9211	9253	9295	9337	9378	9420	9462	9503	9545	9587	41
72	9628	9670	9711	9752	9794	9835	9876	9918	9959	*0000	41
73	9.0041	0082	0123	0164	0205	0246	0287	0328	0369	0410	40
74	0450	0491	0532	0572	0613	0654	0694	0735	0775	0816	40
75	0856	0896	0937	0977	1017	1057	1098	1138	1178	1218	40
76	1258	1298	1338	1378	1418	1458	1498	1537	1577	1617	40
77	1657	1696	1736	1775	1815	1855	1894	1933	1973	2012	40
78	2052	2091	2130	2170	2209	2248	2287	2326	2365	2404	39
79	2443	2482	2521	2560	2599	2638	2677	2716	2754	2793	39
80	9.2832	2870	2909	2948	2986	3025	3063	3102	3140	3179	38
81	3217	3255	3294	3332	3370	3408	3447	3485	3523	3561	38
82	3599	3637	3675	3713	3751	3789	3827	3865	3902	3940	38
83	3978	4016	4053	4091	4129	4166	4204	4241	4279	4316	38
84	4354	4391	4429	4466	4503	4541	4578	4615	4652	4690	37
85	4727	4764	4801	4838	4875	4912	4949	4986	5023	5060	37
86	5097	5134	5171	5207	5244	5281	5317	5354	5391	5427	37
87	5464	5501	5537	5574	5610	5647	5683	5719	5756	5792	36
88	5828	5865	5901	5937	5973	6010	6046	6082	6118	6154	36
89	6190	6226	6262	6298	6334	6370	6406	6442	6477	6513	36
90	9.6549	6585	6620	6656	6692	6727	6763	6799	6834	6870	35
91	6905	6941	6976	7012	7047	7082	7118	7153	7188	7224	35
92	7259	7294	7329	7364	7400	7435	7470	7505	7540	7575	35
93	7610	7645	7680	7715	7750	7785	7819	7854	7889	7924	35
94	7959	7993	8028	8063	8097	8132	8167	8201	8236	8270	35
95	8305	8339	8374	8408	8443	8477	8511	8546	8580	8614	34
96	8648	8683	8717	8751	8785	8819	8854	8888	8922	8956	34
97	8990	9024	9058	9092	9126	9160	9194	9227	9261	9295	34
98	9329	9363	9396	9430	9464	9497	9531	9565	9598	9632	34
99	9666	9699	9733	9766	9800	9833	9866	9900	9933	9967	33

n	0	1	2	3	4	5	6	7	8	9	d
.1	2.154	087	027	*974	*926	*882	*842	*805	*771	*739	29
.2	1.710	682	657	632	609	587	567	547	529	511	17
.3	1.494	478	462	447	433	419	406	393	381	369	12
.4	1.357	346	335	325	315	305	295	286	277	268	8
.5	1.260	252	244	236	228	221	213	206	199	192	6
.6	1.186	179	173	167	160	154	149	143	137	132	6
.7	1.126	121	116	111	106	101	096	091	086	082	5
.8	1.077	073	068	064	060	056	052	048	044	040	4
.9	1.036	032	028	025	021	017	014	010	007	003	3

	100	101	102	103	104	105	106	107	108	109
1	100	101	102	103	104	105	106	107	108	109
2	200	202	204	206	208	210	212	214	216	218
3	300	303	306	309	312	315	318	321	324	327
4	400	404	408	412	416	420	424	428	432	436
5	500	505	510	515	520	525	530	535	540	545
6	600	606	612	618	624	630	636	642	648	654
7	700	707	714	721	728	735	742	749	756	763
8	800	808	816	824	832	840	848	856	864	872
9	900	909	918	927	936	945	954	963	972	981

	110	111	112	113	114	115	116	117	118	119
1	110	111	112	113	114	115	116	117	118	119
2	220	222	224	226	228	230	232	234	236	238
3	330	333	336	339	342	345	348	351	354	357
4	440	444	448	452	456	460	464	468	472	476
5	550	555	560	565	570	575	580	585	590	595
6	660	666	672	678	684	690	696	702	708	714
7	770	777	784	791	798	805	812	819	826	833
8	880	888	896	904	912	920	928	936	944	952
9	990	999	1008	1017	1026	1035	1044	1053	1062	1071

	120	121	122	123	124	125	126	127	128	129
1	120	121	122	123	124	125	126	127	128	129
2	240	242	244	246	248	250	252	254	256	258
3	360	363	366	369	372	375	378	381	384	387
4	480	484	488	492	496	500	504	508	512	516
5	600	605	610	615	620	625	630	635	640	645
6	720	726	732	738	744	750	756	762	768	774
7	840	847	854	861	868	875	882	889	896	903
8	960	968	976	984	992	1000	1008	1016	1024	1032
9	1080	1089	1098	1107	1116	1125	1134	1143	1152	1161

	130	131	132	133	134	135	136	137	138	139
1	130	131	132	133	134	135	136	137	138	139
2	260	262	264	266	268	270	272	274	276	278
3	390	393	396	399	402	405	408	411	414	417
4	520	524	528	532	536	540	544	548	552	556
5	650	655	660	665	670	675	680	685	690	695
6	780	786	792	798	804	810	816	822	828	834
7	910	917	924	931	938	945	952	959	966	973
8	1040	1048	1056	1064	1072	1080	1088	1096	1104	1112
9	1170	1179	1188	1197	1206	1215	1224	1233	1242	1251

	140	141	142	143	144	145	146	147	148	149
1	140	141	142	143	144	145	146	147	148	149
2	280	282	284	286	288	290	292	294	296	298
3	420	423	426	429	432	435	438	441	444	447
4	560	564	568	572	576	580	584	588	592	596
5	700	705	710	715	720	725	730	735	740	745
6	840	846	852	858	864	870	876	882	888	894
7	980	987	994	1001	1008	1015	1022	1029	1036	1043
8	1120	1128	1136	1144	1152	1160	1168	1176	1184	1192
9	1260	1269	1278	1287	1296	1305	1314	1323	1332	1341

·	150	151	152	153	154	155	156	157	158	159
1	150	151	152	153	154	155	156	157	158	159
2	300	302	304	306	308	310	312	314	316	318
3	450	453	456	459	462	465	468	471	474	477
4	600	604	608	612	616	620	624	628	632	636
5	750	755	760	765	770	775	780	785	790	795
6	900	906	912	918	924	930	936	942	948	954
7	1050	1057	1064	1071	1078	1085	1092	1099	1106	1113
8	1200	1208	1216	1224	1232	1240	1248	1256	1264	1272
9	1350	1359	1368	1377	1386	1395	1404	1413	1422	1431

·	160	161	162	163	164	165	166	167	168	169
1	160	161	162	163	164	165	166	167	168	169
2	320	322	324	326	328	330	332	334	336	338
3	480	483	486	489	492	495	498	501	504	507
4	640	644	648	652	656	660	664	668	672	676
5	800	805	810	815	820	825	830	835	840	845
6	960	966	972	978	984	990	996	1002	1008	1014
7	1120	1127	1134	1141	1148	1155	1162	1169	1176	1183
8	1280	1288	1296	1304	1312	1320	1328	1336	1344	1352
9	1440	1449	1458	1467	1476	1485	1494	1503	1512	1521

·	170	171	172	173	174	175	176	177	178	179
1	170	171	172	173	174	175	176	177	178	179
2	340	342	344	346	348	350	352	354	356	358
3	510	513	516	519	522	525	528	531	534	537
4	680	684	688	692	696	700	704	708	712	716
5	850	855	860	865	870	875	880	885	890	895
6	1020	1026	1032	1038	1044	1050	1056	1062	1068	1074
7	1190	1197	1204	1211	1218	1225	1232	1239	1246	1253
8	1360	1368	1376	1384	1392	1400	1408	1416	1424	1432
9	1530	1539	1548	1557	1566	1575	1584	1593	1602	1611

·	180	181	182	183	184	185	186	187	188	189
1	180	181	182	183	184	185	186	187	188	189
2	360	362	364	366	368	370	372	374	376	378
3	540	543	546	549	552	555	558	561	564	567
4	720	724	728	732	736	740	744	748	752	756
5	900	905	910	915	920	925	930	935	940	945
6	1080	1086	1092	1098	1104	1110	1116	1122	1128	1134
7	1260	1267	1274	1281	1288	1295	1302	1309	1316	1323
8	1440	1448	1456	1464	1472	1480	1488	1496	1504	1512
9	1620	1629	1638	1647	1656	1665	1674	1683	1692	1701

·	190	191	192	193	194	195	196	197	198	199
1	190	191	192	193	194	195	196	197	198	199
2	380	382	384	386	388	390	392	394	396	398
3	570	573	576	579	582	585	588	591	594	597
4	760	764	768	772	776	780	784	788	792	796
5	950	955	960	965	970	975	980	985	990	995
6	1140	1146	1152	1158	1164	1170	1176	1182	1188	1194
7	1330	1337	1344	1351	1358	1365	1372	1379	1386	1393
8	1520	1528	1536	1544	1552	1560	1568	1576	1584	1592
9	1710	1719	1728	1737	1746	1755	1764	1773	1782	1791

	200	201	202	203	204	205	206	207	208	209
1	200	201	202	203	204	205	206	207	208	209
2	400	402	404	406	408	410	412	414	416	418
3	600	603	606	609	612	615	618	621	624	627
4	800	804	808	812	816	820	824	828	832	836
5	1000	1005	1010	1015	1020	1025	1030	1035	1040	1045
6	1200	1206	1212	1218	1224	1230	1236	1242	1248	1254
7	1400	1407	1414	1421	1428	1435	1442	1449	1456	1463
8	1600	1608	1616	1624	1632	1640	1648	1656	1664	1672
9	1800	1809	1818	1827	1836	1845	1854	1863	1872	1881

	210	211	212	213	214	215	216	217	218	219
1	210	211	212	213	214	215	216	217	218	219
2	420	422	424	426	428	430	432	434	436	438
3	630	633	636	639	642	645	648	651	654	657
4	840	844	848	852	856	860	864	868	872	876
5	1050	1055	1060	1065	1070	1075	1080	1085	1090	1095
6	1260	1266	1272	1278	1284	1290	1296	1302	1308	1314
7	1470	1477	1484	1491	1498	1505	1512	1519	1526	1533
8	1680	1688	1696	1704	1712	1720	1728	1736	1744	1752
9	1890	1899	1908	1917	1926	1935	1944	1953	1962	1971

	220	221	222	223	224	225	226	227	228	229
1	220	221	222	223	224	225	226	227	228	229
2	440	442	444	446	448	450	452	454	456	458
3	660	663	666	669	672	675	678	681	684	687
4	880	884	888	892	896	900	904	908	912	916
5	1100	1105	1110	1115	1120	1125	1130	1135	1140	1145
6	1320	1326	1332	1338	1344	1350	1356	1362	1368	1374
7	1540	1547	1554	1561	1568	1575	1582	1589	1596	1603
8	1760	1768	1776	1784	1792	1800	1808	1816	1824	1832
9	1980	1989	1998	2007	2016	2025	2034	2043	2052	2061

	230	231	232	233	234	235	236	237	238	239
1	230	231	232	233	234	235	236	237	238	239
2	460	462	464	466	468	470	472	474	476	478
3	690	693	696	699	702	705	708	711	714	717
4	920	924	928	932	936	940	944	948	952	956
5	1150	1155	1160	1165	1170	1175	1180	1185	1190	1195
6	1380	1386	1392	1398	1404	1410	1416	1422	1428	1434
7	1610	1617	1624	1631	1638	1645	1652	1659	1666	1673
8	1840	1848	1856	1864	1872	1880	1888	1896	1904	1912
9	2070	2079	2088	2097	2106	2115	2124	2133	2142	2151

	240	241	242	243	244	245	246	247	248	249
1	240	241	242	243	244	245	246	247	248	249
2	480	482	484	486	488	490	492	494	496	498
3	720	723	726	729	732	735	738	741	744	747
4	960	964	968	972	976	980	984	988	992	996
5	1200	1205	1210	1215	1220	1225	1230	1235	1240	1245
6	1440	1446	1452	1458	1464	1470	1476	1482	1488	1494
7	1680	1687	1694	1701	1708	1715	1722	1729	1736	1743
8	1920	1928	1936	1944	1952	1960	1968	1976	1984	1992
9	2160	2169	2178	2187	2196	2205	2214	2223	2232	2241

	250	251	252	253	254	255	256	257	258	259
1	250	251	252	253	254	255	256	257	258	259
2	500	502	504	506	508	510	512	514	516	518
3	750	753	756	759	762	765	768	771	774	777
4	1000	1004	1008	1012	1016	1020	1024	1028	1032	1036
5	1250	1255	1260	1265	1270	1275	1280	1285	1290	1295
6	1500	1506	1512	1518	1524	1530	1536	1542	1548	1554
7	1750	1757	1764	1771	1778	1785	1792	1799	1806	1813
8	2000	2008	2016	2024	2032	2040	2048	2056	2064	2072
9	2250	2259	2268	2277	2286	2295	2304	2313	2322	2331

	260	261	262	263	264	265	266	267	268	269
1	260	261	262	263	264	265	266	267	268	269
2	520	522	524	526	528	530	532	534	536	538
3	780	783	786	789	792	795	798	801	804	807
4	1040	1044	1048	1052	1056	1060	1064	1068	1072	1076
5	1300	1305	1310	1315	1320	1325	1330	1335	1340	1345
6	1560	1566	1572	1578	1584	1590	1596	1602	1608	1614
7	1820	1827	1834	1841	1848	1855	1862	1869	1876	1883
8	2080	2088	2096	2104	2112	2120	2128	2136	2144	2152
9	2340	2349	2358	2367	2376	2385	2394	2403	2412	2421

	270	271	272	273	274	275	276	277	278	279
1	270·	271	272	273	274	275	276	277	278	279
2	540	542	544	546	548	550	552	554	556	558
3	810	813	816	819	822	825	828	831	834	837
4	1080	1084	1088	1092	1096	1100	1104	1108	1112	1116
5	1350	1355	1360	1365	1370	1375	1380	1385	1390	1395
6	1620	1626	1632	1638	1644	1650	1656	1662	1668	1674
7	1890	1897	1904	1911	1918	1925	1932	1939	1946	1953
8	2160	2168	2176	2184	2192	2200	2208	2216	2224	2232
9	2430	2439	2448	2457	2466	2475	2484	2493	2502	2511

	280	281	282	283	284	285	286	287	288	289
1	280	281	282	283	284	285	286	287	288	289
2	560	562	564	566	568	570	572	574	576	578
3	840	843	846	849	852	855	858	861	864	867
4	1120	1124	1128	1132	1136	1140	1144	1148	1152	1156
5	1400	1405	1410	1415	1420	1425	1430	1435	1440	1445
6	1680	1686	1692	1698	1704	1710	1716	1722	1728	1734
7	1960	1967	1974	1981	1988	1995	2002	2009	2016	2023
8	2240	2248	2256	2264	2272	2280	2288	2296	2304	2312
9	2520	2529	2538	2547	2556	2565	2574	2583	2592	2601

	290	291	292	293	294	295	296	297	298	299
1	290	291	292	293	294	295	296	297	298	299
2	580	582	584	586	588	590	592	594	596	598
3	870	873	876	879	882	885	888	891	894	897
4	1160	1164	1168	1172	1176	1180	1184	1188	1192	1196
5	1450	1455	1460	1465	1470	1475	1480	1485	1490	1495
6	1740	1746	1752	1758	1764	1770	1776	1782	1788	1794
7	2030	2037	2044	2051	2058	2065	2072	2079	2086	2093
8	2320	2328	2336	2344	2352	2360	2368	2376	2384	2392
9	2610	2619	2628	2637	2646	2655	2664	2673	2682	2691

	300	301	302	303	304	305	306	307	308	309
1	300	301	302	303	304	305	306	307	308	309
2	600	602	604	606	608	610	612	614	616	618
3	900	903	906	909	912	915	918	921	924	927
4	1200	1204	1208	1212	1216	1220	1224	1228	1232	1236
5	1500	1505	1510	1515	1520	1525	1530	1535	1540	1545
6	1800	1806	1812	1818	1824	1830	1836	1842	1848	1854
7	2100	2107	2114	2121	2128	2135	2142	2149	2156	2163
8	2400	2408	2416	2424	2432	2440	2448	2456	2464	2472
9	2700	2709	2718	2727	2736	2745	2754	2763	2772	2781
	310	311	312	313	314	315	316	317	318	319
1	310	311	312	313	314	315	316	317	318	319
2	620	622	624	626	628	630	632	634	636	638
3	930	933	936	939	942	945	948	951	954	957
4	1240	1244	1248	1252	1256	1260	1264	1268	1272	1276
5	1550	1555	1560	1565	1570	1575	1580	1585	1590	1595
6	1860	1866	1872	1878	1884	1890	1896	1902	1908	1914
7	2170	2177	2184	2191	2198	2205	2212	2219	2226	2233
8	2480	2488	2496	2504	2512	2520	2528	2536	2544	2552
9	2790	2799	2808	2817	2826	2835	2844	2853	2862	2871
	320	321	322	323	324	325	326	327	328	329
1	320	321	322	323	324	325	326	327	328	329
2	640	642	644	646	648	650	652	654	656	658
3	960	963	966	969	972	975	978	981	984	987
4	1280	1284	1288	1292	1296	1300	1304	1308	1312	1316
5	1600	1605	1610	1615	1620	1625	1630	1635	1640	1645
6	1920	1926	1932	1938	1944	1950	1956	1962	1968	1974
7	2240	2247	2254	2261	2268	2275	2282	2289	2296	2303
8	2560	2568	2576	2584	2592	2600	2608	2616	2624	2632
9	2880	2889	2898	2907	2916	2925	2934	2943	2952	2961
	330	331	332	333	334	335	336	337	338	339
1	330	331	332	333	334	335	336	337	338	339
2	660	662	664	666	668	670	672	674	676	678
3	990	993	996	999	1002	1005	1008	1011	1014	1017
4	1320	1324	1328	1332	1336	1340	1344	1348	1352	1356
5	1650	1655	1660	1665	1670	1675	1680	1685	1690	1695
6	1980	1986	1992	1998	2004	2010	2016	2022	2028	2034
7	2310	2317	2324	2331	2338	2345	2352	2359	2366	2373
8	2640	2648	2656	2664	2672	2680	2688	2696	2704	2712
9	2970	2979	2988	2997	3006	3015	3024	3033	3042	3051
	340	341	342	343	344	345	346	347	348	349
1	340	341	342	343	344	345	346	347	348	349
2	680	682	684	686	688	690	692	694	696	698
3	1020	1023	1026	1029	1032	1035	1038	1041	1044	1047
4	1360	1364	1368	1372	1376	1380	1384	1388	1392	1396
5	1700	1705	1710	1715	1720	1725	1730	1735	1740	1745
6	2040	2046	2052	2058	2064	2070	2076	2082	2088	2094
7	2380	2387	2394	2401	2408	2415	2422	2429	2436	2443
8	2720	2728	2736	2744	2752	2760	2768	2776	2784	2792
9	3060	3069	3078	3087	3096	3105	3114	3123	3132	3141

	350	351	352	353	354	355	356	357	358	359
1	350	351	352	353	354	355	356	357	358	359
2	700	702	704	706	708	710	712	714	716	718
3	1050	1053	1056	1059	1062	1065	1068	1071	1074	1077
4	1400	1404	1408	1412	1416	1420	1424	1428	1432	1436
5	1750	1755	1760	1765	1770	1775	1780	1785	1790	1795
6	2100	2106	2112	2118	2124	2130	2136	2142	2148	2154
7	2450	2457	2464	2471	2478	2485	2492	2499	2506	2513
8	2800	2808	2816	2824	2832	2840	2848	2856	2864	2872
9	3150	3159	3168	3177	3186	3195	3204	3213	3222	3231
	360	361	362	363	364	365	366	367	368	369
1	360	361	362	363	364	365	366	367	368	369
2	720	722	724	726	728	730	732	734	736	738
3	1080	1083	1086	1089	1092	1095	1098	1101	1104	1107
4	1440	1444	1448	1452	1456	1460	1464	1468	1472	1476
5	1800	1805	1810	1815	1820	1825	1830	1835	1840	1845
6	2160	2166	2172	2178	2184	2190	2196	2202	2208	2214
7	2520	2527	2534	2541	2548	2555	2562	2569	2576	2583
8	2880	2888	2896	2904	2912	2920	2928	2936	2944	2952
9	3240	3249	3258	3267	3276	3285	3294	3303	3312	3321
	370	371	372	373	374	375	376	377	378	379
1	370	371	372	373	374	375	376	377	378	379
2	740	742	744	746	748	750	752	754	756	758
3	1110	1113	1116	1119	1122	1125	1128	1131	1134	1137
4	1480	1484	1488	1492	1496	1500	1504	1508	1512	1516
5	1850	1855	1860	1865	1870	1875	1880	1885	1890	1895
6	2220	2226	2232	2238	2244	2250	2256	2262	2268	2274
7	2590	2597	2604	2611	2618	2625	2632	2639	2646	2653
8	2960	2968	2976	2984	2992	3000	3008	3016	3024	3032
9	3330	3339	3348	3357	3366	3375	3384	3393	3402	3411
	380	381	382	383	384	385	386	387	388	389
1	380	381	382	383	384	385	386	387	388	389
2	760	762	764	766	768	770	772	774	776	778
3	1140	1143	1146	1149	1152	1155	1158	1161	1164	1167
4	1520	1524	1528	1532	1536	1540	1544	1548	1552	1556
5	1900	1905	1910	1915	1920	1925	1930	1935	1940	1945
6	2280	2286	2292	2298	2304	2310	2316	2322	2328	2334
7	2660	2667	2674	2681	2688	2695	2702	2709	2716	2723
8	3040	3048	3056	3064	3072	3080	3088	3096	3104	3112
9	3420	3429	3438	3447	3456	3465	3474	3483	3492	3501
	390	391	392	393	394	395	396	397	398	399
1	390	391	392	393	394	395	396	397	398	399
2	780	782	784	786	788	790	792	794	796	798
3	1170	1173	1176	1179	1182	1185	1188	1191	1194	1197
4	1560	1564	1568	1572	1576	1580	1584	1588	1592	1596
5	1950	1955	1960	1965	1970	1975	1980	1985	1990	1995
6	2340	2346	2352	2358	2364	2370	2376	2382	2388	2394
7	2730	2737	2744	2751	2758	2765	2772	2779	2786	2793
8	3120	3128	3136	3144	3152	3160	3168	3176	3184	3192
9	3510	3519	3528	3537	3546	3555	3564	3573	3582	3591

	400	401	402	403	404	405	406	407	408	409
1	400	401	402	403	404	405	406	407	408	409
2	800	802	804	806	808	810	812	814	816	818
3	1200	1203	1206	1209	1212	1215	1218	1221	1224	1227
4	1600	1604	1608	1612	1616	1620	1624	1628	1632	1636
5	2000	2005	2010	2015	2020	2025	2030	2035	2040	2045
6	2400	2406	2412	2418	2424	2430	2436	2442	2448	2454
7	2800	2807	2814	2821	2828	2835	2842	2849	2856	2863
8	3200	3208	3216	3224	3232	3240	3248	3256	3264	3272
9	3600	3609	3618	3627	3636	3645	3654	3663	3672	3681

	410	411	412	413	414	415	416	417	418	419
1	410	411	412	413	414	415	416	417	418	419
2	820	822	824	826	828	830	832	834	836	838
3	1230	1233	1236	1239	1242	1245	1248	1251	1254	1257
4	1640	1644	1648	1652	1656	1660	1664	1668	1672	1676
5	2050	2055	2060	2065	2070	2075	2080	2085	2090	2095
6	2460	2466	2472	2478	2484	2490	2496	2502	2508	2514
7	2870	2877	2884	2891	2898	2905	2912	2919	2926	2933
8	3280	3288	3296	3304	3312	3320	3328	3336	3344	3352
9	3690	3699	3708	3717	3726	3735	3744	3753	3762	3771

	420	421	422	423	424	425	426	427	428	429
1	420	421	422	423	424	425	426	427	428	429
2	840	842	844	846	848	850	852	854	856	858
3	1260	1263	1266	1269	1272	1275	1278	1281	1284	1287
4	1680	1684	1688	1692	1696	1700	1704	1708	1712	1716
5	2100	2105	2110	2115	2120	2125	2130	2135	2140	2145
6	2520	2526	2532	2538	2544	2550	2556	2562	2568	2574
7	2940	2947	2954	2961	2968	2975	2982	2989	2996	3003
8	3360	3368	3376	3384	3392	3400	3408	3416	3424	3432
9	3780	3789	3798	3807	3816	3825	3834	3843	3852	3861

	430	431	432	433	434	435	436	437	438	439
1	430	431	432	433	434	435	436	437	438	439
2	860	862	864	866	868	870	872	874	876	878
3	1290	1293	1296	1299	1302	1305	1308	1311	1314	1317
4	1720	1724	1728	1732	1736	1740	1744	1748	1752	1756
5	2150	2155	2160	2165	2170	2175	2180	2185	2190	2195
6	2580	2586	2592	2598	2604	2610	2616	2622	2628	2634
7	3010	3017	3024	3031	3038	3045	3052	3059	3066	3073
8	3440	3448	3456	3464	3472	3480	3488	3496	3504	3512
9	3870	3879	3888	3897	3906	3915	3924	3933	3942	3951

	440	441	442	443	444	445	446	447	448	449
1	440	441	442	443	444	445	446	447	448	449
2	880	882	884	886	888	890	892	894	896	898
3	1320	1323	1326	1329	1332	1335	1338	1341	1344	1347
4	1760	1764	1768	1772	1776	1780	1784	1788	1792	1796
5	2200	2205	2210	2215	2220	2225	2230	2235	2240	2245
6	2640	2646	2652	2658	2664	2670	2676	2682	2688	2694
7	3080	3087	3094	3101	3108	3115	3122	3129	3136	3143
8	3520	3528	3536	3544	3552	3560	3568	3576	3584	3592
9	3960	3969	3978	3987	3996	4005	4014	4023	4032	4041

	450	451	452	453	454	455	456	457	458	459
1	450	451	452	453	454	455	456	457	458	459
2	900	902	904	906	908	910	912	914	916	918
3	1350	1353	1356	1359	1362	1365	1368	1371	1374	1377
4	1800	1804	1808	1812	1816	1820	1824	1828	1832	1836
5	2250	2255	2260	2265	2270	2275	2280	2285	2290	2295
6	2700	2706	2712	2718	2724	2730	2736	2742	2748	2754
7	3150	3157	3164	3171	3178	3185	3192	3199	3206	3213
8	3600	3608	3616	3624	3632	3640	3648	3656	3664	3672
9	4050	4059	4068	4077	4086	4095	4104	4113	4122	4131

	460	461	462	463	464	465	466	467	468	469
1	460	461	462	463	464	465	466	467	468	469
2	920	922	924	926	928	930	932	934	936	938
3	1380	1383	1386	1389	1392	1395	1398	1401	1404	1407
4	1840	1844	1848	1852	1856	1860	1864	1868	1872	1876
5	2300	2305	2310	2315	2320	2325	2330	2335	2340	2345
6	2760	2766	2772	2778	2784	2790	2796	2802	2808	2814
7	3220	3227	3234	3241	3248	3255	3262	3269	3276	3283
8	3680	3688	3696	3704	3712	3720	3728	3736	3744	3752
9	4140	4149	4158	4167	4176	4185	4194	4203	4212	4221

	470	471	472	473	474	475	476	477	478	479
1	470	471	472	473	474	475	476	477	478	479
2	940	942	944	946	948	950	952	954	956	958
3	1410	1413	1416	1419	1422	1425	1428	1431	1434	1437
4	1880	1884	1888	1892	1896	1900	1904	1908	1912	1916
5	2350	2355	2360	2365	2370	2375	2380	2385	2390	2395
6	2820	2826	2832	2838	2844	2850	2856	2862	2868	2874
7	3290	3297	3304	3311	3318	3325	3332	3339	3346	3353
8	3760	3768	3776	3784	3792	3800	3808	3816	3824	3832
9	4230	4239	4248	4257	4266	4275	4284	4293	4302	4311

	480	481	482	483	484	485	486	487	488	489
1	480	481	482	483	484	485	486	487	488	489
2	960	962	964	966	968	970	972	974	976	978
3	1440	1443	1446	1449	1452	1455	1458	1461	1464	1467
4	1920	1924	1928	1932	1936	1940	1944	1948	1952	1956
5	2400	2405	2410	2415	2420	2425	2430	2435	2440	2445
6	2880	2886	2892	2898	2904	2910	2916	2922	2928	2934
7	3360	3367	3374	3381	3388	3395	3402	3409	3416	3423
8	3840	3848	3856	3864	3872	3880	3888	3896	3904	3912
9	4320	4329	4338	4347	4356	4365	4374	4383	4392	4401

	490	491	492	493	494	495	496	497	498	499
1	490	491	492	493	494	495	496	497	498	499
2	980	982	984	986	988	990	992	994	996	998
3	1470	1473	1476	1479	1482	1485	1488	1491	1494	1497
4	1960	1964	1968	1972	1976	1980	1984	1988	1992	1996
5	2450	2455	2460	2465	2470	2475	2480	2485	2490	2495
6	2940	2946	2952	2958	2964	2970	2976	2982	2988	2994
7	3430	3437	3444	3451	3458	3465	3472	3479	3486	3493
8	3920	3928	3936	3944	3952	3960	3968	3976	3984	3992
9	4410	4419	4428	4437	4446	4455	4464	4473	4482	4491

	500	501	502	503	504	505	506	507	508	509
1	500	501	502	503	504	505	506	507	508	509
2	1000	1002	1004	1006	1008	1010	1012	1014	1016	1018
3	1500	1503	1506	1509	1512	1515	1518	1521	1524	1527
4	2000	2004	2008	2012	2016	2020	2024	2028	2032	2036
5	2500	2505	2510	2515	2520	2525	2530	2535	2540	2545
6	3000	3006	3012	3018	3024	3030	3036	3042	3048	3054
7	3500	3507	3514	3521	3528	3535	3542	3549	3556	3563
8	4000	4008	4016	4024	4032	4040	4048	4056	4064	4072
9	4500	4509	4518	4527	4536	4545	4554	4563	4572	4581

	510	511	512	513	514	515	516	517	518	519
1	510	511	512	513	514	515	516	517	518	519
2	1020	1022	1024	1026	1028	1030	1032	1034	1036	1038
3	1530	1533	1536	1539	1542	1545	1548	1551	1554	1557
4	2040	2044	2048	2052	2056	2060	2064	2068	2072	2076
5	2550	2555	2560	2565	2570	2575	2580	2585	2590	2595
6	3060	3066	3072	3078	3084	3090	3096	3102	3108	3114
7	3570	3577	3584	3591	3598	3605	3612	3619	3626	3633
8	4080	4088	4096	4104	4112	4120	4128	4136	4144	4152
9	4590	4599	4608	4617	4626	4635	4644	4653	4662	4671

	520	521	522	523	524	525	526	527	528	529
1	520	521	522	523	524	525	526	527	528	529
2	1040	1042	1044	1046	1048	1050	1052	1054	1056	1058
3	1560	1563	1566	1569	1572	1575	1578	1581	1584	1587
4	2080	2084	2088	2092	2096	2100	2104	2108	2112	2116
5	2600	2605	2610	2615	2620	2625	2630	2635	2640	2645
6	3120	3126	3132	3138	3144	3150	3156	3162	3168	3174
7	3640	3647	3654	3661	3668	3675	3682	3689	3696	3703
8	4160	4168	4176	4184	4192	4200	4208	4216	4224	4232
9	4680	4689	4698	4707	4716	4725	4734	4743	4752	4761

	530	531	532	533	534	535	536	537	538	539
1	530	531	532	533	534	535	536	537	538	539
2	1060	1062	1064	1066	1068	1070	1072	1074	1076	1078
3	1590	1593	1596	1599	1602	1605	1608	1611	1614	1617
4	2120	2124	2128	2132	2136	2140	2144	2148	2152	2156
5	2650	2655	2660	2665	2670	2675	2680	2685	2690	2695
6	3180	3186	3192	3198	3204	3210	3216	3222	3228	3234
7	3710	3717	3724	3731	3738	3745	3752	3759	3766	3773
8	4240	4248	4256	4264	4272	4280	4288	4296	4304	4312
9	4770	4779	4788	4797	4806	4815	4824	4833	4842	4851

	540	541	542	543	544	545	546	547	548	549
1	540	541	542	543	544	545	546	547	548	549
2	1080	1082	1084	1086	1088	1090	1092	1094	1096	1098
3	1620	1623	1626	1629	1632	1635	1638	1641	1644	1647
4	2160	2164	2168	2172	2176	2180	2184	2188	2192	2196
5	2700	2705	2710	2715	2720	2725	2730	2735	2740	2745
6	3240	3246	3252	3258	3264	3270	3276	3282	3288	3294
7	3780	3787	3794	3801	3808	3815	3822	3829	3836	3843
8	4320	4328	4336	4344	4352	4360	4368	4376	4384	4392
9	4860	4869	4878	4887	4896	4905	4914	4923	4932	4941

	550	551	552	553	554	555	556	557	558	559
1	550	551	552	553	554	555	556	557	558	559
2	1100	1102	1104	1106	1108	1110	1112	1114	1116	1118
3	1650	1653	1656	1659	1662	1665	1668	1671	1674	1677
4	2200	2204	2208	2212	2216	2220	2224	2228	2232	2236
5	2750	2755	2760	2765	2770	2775	2780	2785	2790	2795
6	3300	3306	3312	3318	3324	3330	3336	3342	3348	3354
7	3850	3857	3864	3871	3878	3885	3892	3899	3906	3913
8	4400	4408	4416	4424	4432	4440	4448	4456	4464	4472
9	4950	4959	4968	4977	4986	4995	5004	5013	5022	5031

	560	561	562	563	564	565	566	567	568	569
1	560	561	562	563	564	565	566	567	568	569
2	1120	1122	1124	1126	1128	1130	1132	1134	1136	1138
3	1680	1683	1686	1689	1692	1695	1698	1701	1704	1707
4	2240	2244	2248	2252	2256	2260	2264	2268	2272	2276
5	2800	2805	2810	2815	2820	2825	2830	2835	2840	2845
6	3360	3366	3372	3378	3384	3390	3396	3402	3408	3414
7	3920	3927	3934	3941	3948	3955	3962	3969	3976	3983
8	4480	4488	4496	4504	4512	4520	4528	4536	4544	4552
9	5040	5049	5058	5067	5076	5085	5094	5103	5112	5121

	570	571	572	573	574	575	576	577	578	579
1	570	571	572	573	574	575	576	577	578	579
2	1140	1142	1144	1146	1148	1150	1152	1154	1156	1158
3	1710	1713	1716	1719	1722	1725	1728	1731	1734	1737
4	2280	2284	2288	2292	2296	2300	2304	2308	2312	2316
5	2850	2855	2860	2865	2870	2875	2880	2885	2890	2895
6	3420	3426	3432	3438	3444	3450	3456	3462	3468	3474
7	3990	3997	4004	4011	4018	4025	4032	4039	4046	4053
8	4560	4568	4576	4584	4592	4600	4608	4616	4624	4632
9	5130	5139	5148	5157	5166	5175	5184	5193	5202	5211

	580	581	582	583	584	585	586	587	588	589
1	580	581	582	583	584	585	586	587	588	589
2	1160	1162	1164	1166	1168	1170	1172	1174	1176	1178
3	1740	1743	1746	1749	1752	1755	1758	1761	1764	1767
4	2320	2324	2328	2332	2336	2340	2344	2348	2352	2356
5	2900	2905	2910	2915	2920	2925	2930	2935	2940	2945
6	3480	3486	3492	3498	3504	3510	3516	3522	3528	3534
7	4060	4067	4074	4081	4088	4095	4102	4109	4116	4123
8	4640	4648	4656	4664	4672	4680	4688	4696	4704	4712
9	5220	5229	5238	5247	5256	5265	5274	5283	5292	5301

	590	591	592	593	594	595	596	597	598	599
1	590	591	592	593	594	595	596	597	598	599
2	1180	1182	1184	1186	1188	1190	1192	1194	1196	1198
3	1770	1773	1776	1779	1782	1785	1788	1791	1794	1797
4	2360	2364	2368	2372	2376	2380	2384	2388	2392	2396
5	2950	2955	2960	2965	2970	2975	2980	2985	2990	2995
6	3540	3546	3552	3558	3564	3570	3576	3582	3588	3594
7	4130	4137	4144	4151	4158	4165	4172	4179	4186	4193
8	4720	4728	4736	4744	4752	4760	4768	4776	4784	4792
9	5310	5319	5328	5337	5346	5355	5364	5373	5382	5391

	600	601	602	603	604	605	606	607	608	609
1	600	601	602	603	604	605	606	607	608	609
2	1200	1202	1204	1206	1208	1210	1212	1214	1216	1218
3	1800	1803	1806	1809	1812	1815	1818	1821	1824	1827
4	2400	2404	2408	2412	2416	2420	2424	2428	2432	2436
5	3000	3005	3010	3015	3020	3025	3030	3035	3040	3045
6	3600	3606	3612	3618	3624	3630	3636	3642	3648	3654
7	4200	4207	4214	4221	4228	4235	4242	4249	4256	4263
8	4800	4808	4816	4824	4832	4840	4848	4856	4864	4872
9	5400	5409	5418	5427	5436	5445	5454	5463	5472	5481
	610	611	612	613	614	615	616	617	618	619
1	610	611	612	613	614	615	616	617	618	619
2	1220	1222	1224	1226	1228	1230	1232	1234	1236	1238
3	1830	1833	1836	1839	1842	1845	1848	1851	1854	1857
4	2440	2444	2448	2452	2456	2460	2464	2468	2472	2476
5	3050	3055	3060	3065	3070	3075	3080	3085	3090	3095
6	3660	3666	3672	3678	3684	3690	3696	3702	3708	3714
7	4270	4277	4284	4291	4298	4305	4312	4319	4326	4333
8	4880	4888	4896	4904	4912	4920	4928	4936	4944	4952
9	5490	5499	5508	5517	5526	5535	5544	5553	5562	5571
	620	621	622	623	624	625	626	627	628	629
1	620	621	622	623	624	625	626	627	628	629
2	1240	1242	1244	1246	1248	1250	1252	1254	1256	1258
3	1860	1863	1866	1869	1872	1875	1878	1881	1884	1887
4	2480	2484	2488	2492	2496	2500	2504	2508	2512	2516
5	3100	3105	3110	3115	3120	3125	3130	3135	3140	3145
6	3720	3726	3732	3738	3744	3750	3756	3762	3768	3774
7	4340	4347	4354	4361	4368	4375	4382	4389	4396	4403
8	4960	4968	4976	4984	4992	5000	5008	5016	5024	5032
9	5580	5589	5598	5607	5616	5625	5634	5643	5652	5661
	630	631	632	633	634	635	636	637	638	639
1	630	631	632	633	634	635	636	637	638	639
2	1260	1262	1264	1266	1268	1270	1272	1274	1276	1278
3	1890	1893	1896	1899	1902	1905	1908	1911	1914	1917
4	2520	2524	2528	2532	2536	2540	2544	2548	2552	2556
5	3150	3155	3160	3165	3170	3175	3180	3185	3190	3195
6	3780	3786	3792	3798	3804	3810	3816	3822	3828	3834
7	4410	4417	4424	4431	4438	4445	4452	4459	4466	4473
8	5040	5048	5056	5064	5072	5080	5088	5096	5104	5112
9	5670	5679	5688	5697	5706	5715	5724	5733	5742	5751
	640	641	642	643	644	645	646	647	648	649
1	640	641	642	643	644	645	646	647	648	649
2	1280	1282	1284	1286	1288	1290	1292	1294	1296	1298
3	1920	1923	1926	1929	1932	1935	1938	1941	1944	1947
4	2560	2564	2568	2572	2576	2580	2584	2588	2592	2596
5	3200	3205	3210	3215	3220	3225	3230	3235	3240	3245
6	3840	3846	3852	3858	3864	3870	3876	3882	3888	3894
7	4480	4487	4494	4501	4508	4515	4522	4529	4536	4543
8	5120	5128	5136	5144	5152	5160	5168	5176	5184	5192
9	5760	5769	5778	5787	5796	5805	5814	5823	5832	5841

	650	651	652	653	654	655	656	657	658	659
1	650	651	652	653	654	655	656	657	658	659
2	1300	1302	1304	1306	1308	1310	1312	1314	1316	1318
3	1950	1953	1956	1959	1962	1965	1968	1971	1974	1977
4	2600	2604	2608	2612	2616	2620	2624	2628	2632	2636
5	3250	3255	3260	3265	3270	3275	3280	3285	3290	3295
6	3900	3906	3912	3918	3924	3930	3936	3942	3948	3954
7	4550	4557	4564	4571	4578	4585	4592	4599	4606	4613
8	5200	5208	5216	5224	5232	5240	5248	5256	5264	5272
9	5850	5859	5868	5877	5886	5895	5904	5913	5922	5931

	660	661	662	663	664	665	666	667	668	669
1	660	661	662	663	664	665	666	667	668	669
2	1320	1322	1324	1326	1328	1330	1332	1334	1336	1338
3	1980	1983	1986	1989	1992	1995	1998	2001	2004	2007
4	2640	2644	2648	2652	2656	2660	2664	2668	2672	2676
5	3300	3305	3310	3315	3320	3325	3330	3335	3340	3345
6	3960	3966	3972	3978	3984	3990	3996	4002	4008	4014
7	4620	4627	4634	4641	4648	4655	4662	4669	4676	4683
8	5280	5288	5296	5304	5312	5320	5328	5336	5344	5352
9	5940	5949	5958	5967	5976	5985	5994	6003	6012	6021

	670	671	672	673	674	675	676	677	678	679
1	670	671	672	673	674	675	676	677	678	679
2	1340	1342	1344	1346	1348	1350	1352	1354	1356	1358
3	2010	2013	2016	2019	2022	2025	2028	2031	2034	2037
4	2680	2684	2688	2692	2696	2700	2704	2708	2712	2716
5	3350	3355	3360	3365	3370	3375	3380	3385	3390	3395
6	4020	4026	4032	4038	4044	4050	4056	4062	4068	4074
7	4690	4697	4704	4711	4718	4725	4732	4739	4746	4753
8	5360	5368	5376	5384	5392	5400	5408	5416	5424	5432
9	6030	6039	6048	6057	6066	6075	6084	6093	6102	6111

	680	681	682	683	684	685	686	687	688	689
1	680	681	682	683	684	685	686	687	688	689
2	1360	1362	1364	1366	1368	1370	1372	1374	1376	1378
3	2040	2043	2046	2049	2052	2055	2058	2061	2064	2067
4	2720	2724	2728	2732	2736	2740	2744	2748	2752	2756
5	3400	3405	3410	3415	3420	3425	3430	3435	3440	3445
6	4080	4086	4092	4098	4104	4110	4116	4122	4128	4134
7	4760	4767	4774	4781	4788	4795	4802	4809	4816	4823
8	5440	5448	5456	5464	5472	5480	5488	5496	5504	5512
9	6120	6129	6138	6147	6156	6165	6174	6183	6192	6201

	690	691	692	693	694	695	696	697	698	699
1	690	691	692	693	694	695	696	697	698	699
2	1380	1382	1384	1386	1388	1390	1392	1394	1396	1398
3	2070	2073	2076	2079	2082	2085	2088	2091	2094	2097
4	2760	2764	2768	2772	2776	2780	2784	2788	2792	2796
5	3450	3455	3460	3465	3470	3475	3480	3485	3490	3495
6	4140	4146	4152	4158	4164	4170	4176	4182	4188	4194
7	4830	4837	4844	4851	4858	4865	4872	4879	4886	4893
8	5520	5528	5536	5544	5552	5560	5568	5576	5584	5592
9	6210	6219	6228	6237	6246	6255	6264	6273	6282	6291

	700	701	702	703	704	705	706	707	708	709
1	700	701	702	703	704	705	706	707	708	709
2	1400	1402	1404	1406	1408	1410	1412	1414	1416	1418
3	2100	2103	2106	2109	2112	2115	2118	2121	2124	2127
4	2800	2804	2808	2812	2816	2820	2824	2828	2832	2836
5	3500	3505	3510	3515	3520	3525	3530	3535	3540	3545
6	4200	4206	4212	4218	4224	4230	4236	4242	4248	4254
7	4900	4907	4914	4921	4928	4935	4942	4949	4956	4963
8	5600	5608	5616	5624	5632	5640	5648	5656	5664	5672
9	6300	6309	6318	6327	6336	6345	6354	6363	6372	6381

	710	711	712	713	714	715	716	717	718	719
1	710	·711	712	713	714	715	716	717	718	719
2	1420	1422	1424	1426	1428	1430	1432	1434	1436	1438
3	2130	2133	2136	2139	2142	2145	2148	2151	2154	2157
4	2840	2844	2848	2852	2856	2860	2864	2868	2872	2876
5	3550	3555	3560	3565	3570	3575	3580	3585	3590	3595
6	4260	4266	4272	4278	4284	4290	4296	4302	4308	4314
7	4970	4977	4984	4991	4998	5005	5012	5019	5026	5033
8	5680	5688	5696	5704	5712	5720	5728	5736	5744	5752
9	6390	6399	6408	6417	6426	6435	6444	6453	6462	6471

	720	721	722	723	724	725	726	727	728	729
1	720	721	722	723	724	725	726	727	728	729
2	1440	1442	1444	1446	1448	1450	1452	1454	1456	1458
3	2160	2163	2166	2169	2172	2175	2178	2181	2184	2187
4	2880	2884	2888	2892	2896	2900	2904	2908	2912	2916
5	3600	3605	3610	3615	3620	3625	3630	3635	3640	3645
6	4320	4326	4332	4338	4344	4350	4356	4362	4368	4374
7	5040	5047	5054	5061	5068	5075	5082	5089	5096	5103
8	5760	5768	5776	5784	5792	5800	5808	5816	5824	5832
9	6480	6489	6498	6507	6516	6525	6534	6543	6552	6561

	730	731	732	733	734	735	736	737	738	739
1	730	731	732	733	734	735	736	737	738	739
2	1460	1462	1464	1466	1468	1470	1472	1474	1476	1478
3	2190	2193	2196	2199	2202	2205	2208	2211	2214	2217
4	2920	2924	2928	2932	2936	2940	2944	2948	2952	2956
5	3650	3655	3660	3665	3670	3675	3680	3685	3690	3695
6	4380	4386	4392	4398	4404	4410	4416	4422	4428	4434
7	5110	5117	5124	5131	5138	5145	5152	5159	5166	5173
8	5840	5848	5856	5864	5872	5880	5888	5896	5904	5912
9	6570	6579	6588	6597	6606	6615	6624	6633	6642	6651

	740	741	742	743	744	745	746	747	748	749
1	740	741	742	743	744	745	746	747	748	749
2	1480	1482	1484	1486	1488	1490	1492	1494	1496	1498
3	2220	2223	2226	2229	2232	2235	2238	2241	2244	2247
4	2960	2964	2968	2972	2976	2980	2984	2988	2992	2996
5	3700	3705	3710	3715	3720	3725	3730	3735	3740	3745
6	4440	4446	4452	4458	4464	4470	4476	4482	4488	4494
7	5180	5187	5194	5201	5208	5215	5222	5229	5236	5243
8	5920	5928	5936	5944	5952	5960	5968	5976	5984	5992
9	6660	6669	6678	6687	6696	6705	6714	6723	6732	6741

	750	751	752	753	754	755	756	757	758	759
1	750	751	752	753	754	755	756	757	758	759
2	1500	1502	1504	1506	1508	1510	1512	1514	1516	1518
3	2250	2253	2256	2259	2262	2265	2268	2271	2274	2277
4	3000	3004	3008	3012	3016	3020	3024	3028	3032	3036
5	3750	3755	3760	3765	3770	3775	3780	3785	3790	3795
6	4500	4506	4512	4518	4524	4530	4536	4542	4548	4554
7	5250	5257	5264	5271	5278	5285	5292	5299	5306	5313
8	6000	6008	6016	6024	6032	6040	6048	6056	6064	6072
9	6750	6759	6768	6777	6786	6795	6804	6813	6822	6831

	760	761	762	763	764	765	766	767	768	769
1	760	761	762	763	764	765	766	767	768	769
2	1520	1522	1524	1526	1528	1530	1532	1534	1536	1538
3	2280	2283	2286	2289	2292	2295	2298	2301	2304	2307
4	3040	3044	3048	3052	3056	3060	3064	3068	3072	3076
5	3800	3805	3810	3815	3820	3825	3830	3835	3840	3845
6	4560	4566	4572	4578	4584	4590	4596	4602	4608	4614
7	5320	5327	5334	5341	5348	5355	5362	5369	5376	5383
8	6080	6088	6096	6104	6112	6120	6128	6136	6144	6152
9	6840	6849	6858	6867	6876	6885	6894	6903	6912	6921

	770	771	772	773	774	775	776	777	778	779
1	770	771	772	773	774	775	776	777	778	779
2	1540	1542	1544	1546	1548	1550	1552	1554	1556	1558
3	2310	2313	2316	2319	2322	2325	2328	2331	2334	2337
4	3080	3084	3088	3092	3096	3100	3104	3108	3112	3116
5	3850	3855	3860	3865	3870	3875	3880	3885	3890	3895
6	4620	4626	4632	4638	4644	4650	4656	4662	4668	4674
7	5390	5397	5404	5411	5418	5425	5432	5439	5446	5453
8	6160	6168	6176	6184	6192	6200	6208	6216	6224	6232
9	6930	6939	6948	6957	6966	6975	6984	6993	7002	7011

	780	781	782	783	784	785	786	787	788	789
1	780	781	782	783	784	785	786	787	788	789
2	1560	1562	1564	1566	1568	1570	1572	1574	1576	1578
3	2340	2343	2346	2349	2352	2355	2358	2361	2364	2367
4	3120	3124	3128	3132	3136	3140	3144	3148	3152	3156
5	3900	3905	3910	3915	3920	3925	3930	3935	3940	3945
6	4680	4686	4692	4698	4704	4710	4716	4722	4728	4734
7	5460	5467	5474	5481	5488	5495	5502	5509	5516	5523
8	6240	6248	6256	6264	6272	6280	6288	6296	6304	6312
9	7020	7029	7038	7047	7056	7065	7074	7083	7092	7101

	790	791	792	793	794	795	796	797	798	799
1	790	791	792	793	794	795	796	797	798	799
2	1580	1582	1584	1586	1588	1590	1592	1594	1596	1598
3	2370	2373	2376	2379	2382	2385	2388	2391	2394	2397
4	3160	3164	3168	3172	3176	3180	3184	3188	3192	3196
5	3950	3955	3960	3965	3970	3975	3980	3985	3990	3995
6	4740	4746	4752	4758	4764	4770	4776	4782	4788	4794
7	5530	5537	5544	5551	5558	5565	5572	5579	5586	5593
8	6320	6328	6336	6344	6352	6360	6368	6376	6384	6392
9	7110	7119	7128	7137	7146	7155	7164	7173	7182	7191

	800	801	802	803	804	805	806	807	808	809
1	800	801	802	803	804	805	806	807	808	809
2	1600	1602	1604	1606	1608	1610	1612	1614	1616	1618
3	2400	2403	2406	2409	2412	2415	2418	2421	2424	2427
4	3200	3204	3208	3212	3216	3220	3224	3228	3232	3236
5	4000	4005	4010	4015	4020	4025	4030	4035	4040	4045
6	4800	4806	4812	4818	4824	4830	4836	4842	4848	4854
7	5600	5607	5614	5621	5628	5635	5642	5649	5656	5663
8	6400	6408	6416	6424	6432	6440	6448	6456	6464	6472
9	7200	7209	7218	7227	7236	7245	7254	7263	7272	7281
	810	**811**	**812**	**813**	**814**	**815**	**816**	**817**	**818**	**819**
1	810	811	812	813	814	815	816	817	818	819
2	1620	1622	1624	1626	1628	1630	1632	1634	1636	1638
3	2430	2433	2436	2439	2442	2445	2448	2451	2454	2457
4	3240	3244	3248	3252	3256	3260	3264	3268	3272	3276
5	4050	4055	4060	4065	4070	4075	4080	4085	4090	4095
6	4860	4866	4872	4878	4884	4890	4896	4902	4908	4914
7	5670	5677	5684	5691	5698	5705	5712	5719	5726	5733
8	6480	6488	6496	6504	6512	6520	6528	6536	6544	6552
9	7290	7299	7308	7317	7326	7335	7344	7353	7362	7371
	820	**821**	**822**	**823**	**824**	**825**	**826**	**827**	**828**	**829**
1	820	821	822	823	824	825	826	827	828	829
2	1640	1642	1644	1646	1648	1650	1652	1654	1656	1658
3	2460	2463	2466	2469	2472	2475	2478	2481	2484	2487
4	3280	3284	3288	3292	3296	3300	3304	3308	3312	3316
5	4100	4105	4110	4115	4120	4125	4130	4135	4140	4145
6	4920	4926	4932	4938	4944	4950	4956	4962	4968	4974
7	5740	5747	5754	5761	5768	5775	5782	5789	5796	5803
8	6560	6568	6576	6584	6592	6600	6608	6616	6624	6632
9	7380	7389	7398	7407	7416	7425	7434	7443	7452	7461
	830	**831**	**832**	**833**	**834**	**835**	**836**	**837**	**838**	**839**
1	830	831	832	833	834	835	836	837	838	839
2	1660	1662	1664 ·	1666	1668	1670	1672	1674	1676	1678
3	2490	2493	2496	2499	2502	2505	2508	2511	2514	2517
4	3320	3324	3328	3332	3336	3340	3344	3348	3352	3356
5	4150	4155	4160	4165	4170	4175	4180	4185	4190	4195
6	4980	4986	4992	4998	5004	5010	5016	5022	5028	5034
7	5810	5817	5824	5831	5838	5845	5852	5859	5866	5873
8	6640	6648	6656	6664	6672	6680	6688	6696	6704	6712
9	7470	7479	7488	7497	7506	7515	7524	7533	7542	7551
	840	**841**	**842**	**843**	**844**	**845**	**846**	**847**	**848**	**849**
1	840	841	842	843	844	845	846	847	848	849
2	1680	1682	1684	1686	1688	1690	1692	1694	1696	1698
3	2520	2523	2526	2529	2532	2535	2538	2541	2544	2547
4	3360	3364	3368	3372	3376	3380	3384	3388	3392	3396
5	4200	4205	4210	4215	4220	4225	4230	4235	4240	4245
6	5040	5046	5052	5058	5064	5070	5076	5082	5088	5094
7	5880	5887	5894	5901	5908	5915	5922	5929	5936	5943
8	6720	6728	6736	6744	6752	6760	6768	6776	6784	6792
9	7560	7569	7578	7587	7596	7605	7614	7623	7632	7641

	850	851	852	853	854	855	856	857	858	859
1	850	851	852	853	854	855	856	857	858	859
2	1700	1702	1704	1706	1708	1710	1712	1714	1716	1718
3	2550	2553	2556	2559	2562	2565	2568	2571	2574	2577
4	3400	3404	3408	3412	3416	3420	3424	3428	3432	3436
5	4250	4255	4260	4265	4270	4275	4280	4285	4290	4295
6	5100	5106	5112	5118	5124	5130	5136	5142	5148	5154
7	5950	5957	5964	5971	5978	5985	5992	5999	6006	6013
8	6800	6808	6816	6824	6832	6840	6848	6856	6864	6872
9	7650	7659	7668	7677	7686	7695	7704	7713	7722	7731

	860	861	862	863	864	865	866	867	868	869
1	860	861	862	863	864	865	866	867	868	869
2	1720	1722	1724	1726	1728	1730	1732	1734	1736	1738
3	2580	2583	2586	2589	2592	2595	2598	2601	2604	2607
4	3440	3444	3448	3452	3456	3460	3464	3468	3472	3476
5	4300	4305	4310	4315	4320	4325	4330	4335	4340	4345
6	5160	5166	5172	5178	5184	5190	5196	5202	5208	5214
7	6020	6027	6034	6041	6048	6055	6062	6069	6076	6083
8	6880	6888	6896	6904	6912	6920	6928	6936	6944	6952
9	7740	7749	7758	7767	7776	7785	7794	7803	7812	7821

	870	871	872	873	874	875	876	877	878	879
1	870	871	872	873	874	875	876	877	878	879
2	1740	1742	1744	1746	1748	1750	1752	1754	1756	1758
3	2610	2613	2616	2619	2622	2625	2628	2631	2634	2637
4	3480	3484	3488	3492	3496	3500	3504	3508	3512	3516
5	4350	4355	4360	4365	4370	4375	4380	4385	4390	4395
6	5220	5226	5232	5238	5244	5250	5256	5262	5268	5274
7	6090	6097	6104	6111	6118	6125	6132	6139	6146	6153
8	6960	6968	6976	6984	6992	7000	7008	7016	7024	7032
9	7830	7839	7848	7857	7866	7875	7884	7893	7902	7911

	880	881	882	883	884	885	886	887	888	889
1	880	881	882	883	884	885	886	887	888	889
2	1760	1762	1764	1766	1768	1770	1772	1774	1776	1778
3	2640	2643	2646	2649	2652	2655	2658	2661	2664	2667
4	3520	3524	3528	3532	3536	3540	3544	3548	3552	3556
5	4400	4405	4410	4415	4420	4425	4430	4435	4440	4445
6	5280	5286	5292	5298	5304	5310	5316	5322	5328	5334
7	6160	6167	6174	6181	6188	6195	6202	6209	6216	6223
8	7040	7048	7056	7064	7072	7080	7088	7096	7104	7112
9	7920	7929	7938	7947	7956	7965	7974	7983	7992	8001

	890	891	892	893	894	895	896	897	898	899
1	890	891	892	893	894	895	896	897	898	899
2	1780	1782	1784	1786	1788	1790	1792	1794	1796	1798
3	2670	2673	2676	2679	2682	2685	2688	2691	2694	2697
4	3560	3564	3568	3572	3576	3580	3584	3588	3592	3596
5	4450	4455	4460	4465	4470	4475	4480	4485	4490	4495
6	5340	5346	5352	5358	5364	5370	5376	5382	5388	5394
7	6230	6237	6244	6251	6258	6265	6272	6279	6286	6293
8	7120	7128	7136	7144	7152	7160	7168	7176	7184	7192
9	8010	8019	8028	8037	8046	8055	8064	8073	8082	8091

	900	901	902	903	904	905	906	907	908	909
1	900	901	902	903	904	905	906	907	908	909
2	1800	1802	1804	1806	1808	1810	1812	1814	1816	1818
3	2700	2703	2706	2709	2712	2715	2718	2721	2724	2727
4	3600	3604	3608	3612	3616	3620	3624	3628	3632	3636
5	4500	4505	4510	4515	4520	4525	4530	4535	4540	4545
6	5400	5406	5412	5418	5424	5430	5436	5442	5448	5454
7	6300	6307	6314	6321	6328	6335	6342	6349	6356	6363
8	7200	7208	7216	7224	7232	7240	7248	7256	7264	7272
9	8100	8109	8118	8127	8136	8145	8154	8163	8172	8181

	910	911	912	913	914	915	916	917	918	919
1	910	911	912	913	914	915	916	917	918	919
2	1820	1822	1824	1826	1828	1830	1832	1834	1836	1838
3	2730	2733	2736	2739	2742	2745	2748	2751	2754	2757
4	3640	3644	3648	3652	3656	3660	3664	3668	3672	3676
5	4550	4555	4560	4565	4570	4575	4580	4585	4590	4595
6	5460	5466	5472	5478	5484	5490	5496	5502	5508	5514
7	6370	6377	6384	6391	6398	6405	6412	6419	6426	6433
8	7280	7288	7296	7304	7312	7320	7328	7336	7344	7352
9	8190	8199	8208	8217	8226	8235	8244	8253	8262	8271

	920	921	922	923	924	925	926	927	928	929
1	920	921	922	923	924	925	926	927	928	929
2	1840	1842	1844	1846	1848	1850	1852	1854	1856	1858
3	2760	2763	2766	2769	2772	2775	2778	2781	2784	2787
4	3680	3684	3688	3692	3696	3700	3704	3708	3712	3716
5	4600	4605	4610	4615	4620	4625	4630	4635	4640	4645
6	5520	5526	5532	5538	5544	5550	5556	5562	5568	5574
7	6440	6447	6454	6461	6468	6475	6482	6489	6496	6503
8	7360	7368	7376	7384	7392	7400	7408	7416	7424	7432
9	8280	8289	8298	8307	8316	8325	8334	8343	8352	8361

	930	931	932	933	934	935	936	937	938	939
1	930	931	932	933	934	935	936	937	938	939
2	1860	1862	1864	1866	1868	1870	1872	1874	1876	1878
3	2790	2793	2796	2799	2802	2805	2808	2811	2814	2817
4	3720	3724	3728	3732	3736	3740	3744	3748	3752	3756
5	4650	4655	4660	4665	4670	4675	4680	4685	4690	4695
6	5580	5586	5592	5598	5604	5610	5616	5622	5628	5634
7	6510	6517	6524	6531	6538	6545	6552	6559	6566	6573
8	7440	7448	7456	7464	7472	7480	7488	7496	7504	7512
9	8370	8379	8388	8397	8406	8415	8424	8433	8442	8451

	940	941	942	943	944	945	946	947	948	949
1	940	941	942	943	944	945	946	947	948	949
2	1880	1882	1884	1886	1888	1890	1892	1894	1896	1898
3	2820	2823	2826	2829	2832	2835	2838	2841	2844	2847
4	3760	3764	3768	3772	3776	3780	3784	3788	3792	3796
5	4700	4705	4710	4715	4720	4725	4730	4735	4740	4745
6	5640	5646	5652	5658	5664	5670	5676	5682	5688	5694
7	6580	6587	6594	6601	6608	6615	6622	6629	6636	6643
8	7520	7528	7536	7544	7552	7560	7568	7576	7584	7592
9	8460	8469	8478	8487	8496	8505	8514	8523	8532	8541

	950	951	952	953	954	955	956	957	958	959
1	950	951	952	953	954	955	956	957	958	959
2	1900	1902	1904	1906	1908	1910	1912	1914	1916	1918
3	2850	2853	2856	2859	2862	2865	2868	2871	2874	2877
4	3800	3804	3808	3812	3816	3820	3824	3828	3832	3836
5	4750	4755	4760	4765	4770	4775	4780	4785	4790	4795
6	5700	5706	5712	5718	5724	5730	5736	5742	5748	5754
7	6650	6657	6664	6671	6678	6685	6692	6699	6706	6713
8	7600	7608	7616	7624	7632	7640	7648	7656	7664	7672
9	8550	8559	8568	8577	8586	8595	8604	8613	8622	8631

	960	961	962	963	964	965	966	967	968	969
1	960	961	962	963	964	965	966	967	968	969
2	1920	1922	1924	1926	1928	1930	1932	1934	1936	1938
3	2880	2883	2886	2889	2892	2895	2898	2901	2904	2907
4	3840	3844	3848	3852	3856	3860	3864	3868	3872	3876
5	4800	4805	4810	4815	4820	4825	4830	4835	4840	4845
6	5760	5766	5772	5778	5784	5790	5796	5802	5808	5814
7	6720	6727	6734	6741	6748	6755	6762	6769	6776	6783
8	7680	7688	7696	7704	7712	7720	7728	7736	7744	7752
9	8640	8649	8658	8667	8676	8685	8694	8703	8712	8721

	970	971	972	973	974	975	976	977	978	979
1	970	971	972	973	974	975	976	977	978	979
2	1940	1942	1944	1946	1948	1950	1952	1954	1956	1958
3	2910	2913	2916	2919	2922	2925	2928	2931	2934	2937
4	3880	3884	3888	3892	3896	3900	3904	3908	3912	3916
5	4850	4855	4860	4865	4870	4875	4880	4885	4890	4895
6	5820	5826	5832	5838	5844	5850	5856	5862	5868	5874
7	6790	6797	6804	6811	6818	6825	6832	6839	6846	6853
8	7760	7768	7776	7784	7792	7800	7808	7816	7824	7832
9	8730	8739	8748	8757	8766	8775	8784	8793	8802	8811

	980	981	982	983	984	985	986	987	988	989
1	980	981	982	983	984	985	986	987	988	989
2	1960	1962	1964	1966	1968	1970	1972	1974	1976	1978
3	2940	2943	2946	2949	2952	2955	2958	2961	2964	2967
4	3920	3924	3928	3932	3936	3940	3944	3948	3952	3956
5	4900	4905	4910	4915	4920	4925	4930	4935	4940	4945
6	5880	5886	5892	5898	5904	5910	5916	5922	5928	5934
7	6860	6867	6874	6881	6888	6895	6902	6909	6916	6923
8	7840	7848	7856	7864	7872	7880	7888	7896	7904	7912
9	8820	8829	8838	8847	8856	8865	8874	8883	8892	8901

	990	991	992	993	994	995	996	997	998	999
1	990	991	992	993	994	995	996	997	998	999
2	1980	1982	1984	1986	1988	1990	1992	1994	1996	1998
3	2970	2973	2976	2979	2982	2985	2988	2991	2994	2997
4	3960	3964	3968	3972	3976	3980	3984	3988	3992	3996
5	4950	4955	4960	4965	4970	4975	4980	4985	4990	4995
6	5940	5946	5952	5958	5964	5970	5976	5982	5988	5994
7	6930	6937	6944	6951	6958	6965	6972	6979	6986	6993
8	7920	7928	7936	7944	7952	7960	7968	7976	7984	7992
9	8910	8919	8928	8937	8946	8955	8964	8973	8982	8991

n	0	1	2	3	4	5	6	7	8	9	pp
1.0	3.142	3.173	3.204	3.236	3.267	3.299	3.330	3.362	3.393	3.424	32
1.1	3.456	3.487	3.519	3.550	3.581	3.613	3.644	3.676	3.707	3.738	3
1.2	3.770	3.801	3.833	3.864	3.896	3.927	3.958	3.990	4.021	4.053	6
1.3	4.084	4.115	4.147	4.178	4.210	4.241	4.273	4.304	4.335	4.367	10
1.4	4.398	4.430	4.461	4.492	4.524	4.555	4.587	4.618	4.650	4.681	13
1.5	4.712	4.744	4.775	4.807	4.838	4.869	4.901	4.932	4.964	4.995	16
1.6	5.027	5.058	5.089	5.121	5.152	5.184	5.215	5.246	5.278	5.309	19
1.7	5.341	5.372	5.404	5.435	5.466	5.498	5.529	5.561	5.592	5.623	22
1.8	5.655	5.686	5.718	5.749	5.781	5.812	5.843	5.875	5.906	5.938	26
1.9	5.969	6.000	6.032	6.063	6.095	6.126	6.158	6.189	6.220	6.252	29
2.0	6.283	6.315	6.346	6.377	6.409	6.440	6.472	6.503	6.535	6.566	31
2.1	6.597	6.629	6.660	6.692	6.723	6.754	6.786	6.817	6.849	6.880	3
2.2	6.912	6.943	6.974	7.006	7.037	7.069	7.100	7.131	7.163	7.194	6
2.3	7.226	7.257	7.288	7.320	7.351	7.383	7.414	7.446	7.477	7.508	9
2.4	7.540	7.571	7.603	7.634	7.665	7.697	7.728	7.760	7.791	7.823	12
2.5	7.854	7.885	7.917	7.948	7.980	8.011	8.042	8.074	8.105	8.137	16
2.6	8.168	8.200	8.231	8.262	8.294	8.325	8.357	8.388	8.419	8.451	19
2.7	8.482	8.514	8.545	8.577	8.608	8.639	8.671	8.702	8.734	8.765	22
2.8	8.796	8.828	8.859	8.891	8.922	8.954	8.985	9.016	9.048	9.079	25
2.9	9.111	9.142	9.173	9.205	9.236	9.268	9.299	9.331	9.362	9.393	28
3.0	9.425	9.456	9.488	9.519	9.550	9.582	9.613	9.645	9.676	9.708	4
3.1	9.739	9.770	9.802	9.833	9.865	9.896	9.927	9.959	9.990	10.02	0
3.2	10.05	10.08	10.12	10.15	10.18	10.21	10.24	10.27	10.30	10.34	1
3.3	10.37	10.40	10.43	10.46	10.49	10.52	10.56	10.59	10.62	10.65	1
3.4	10.68	10.71	10.74	10.78	10.81	10.84	10.87	10.90	10.93	10.96	2
3.5	11.00	11.03	11.06	11.09	11.12	11.15	11.18	11.22	11.25	11.28	2
3.6	11.31	11.34	11.37	11.40	11.44	11.47	11.50	11.53	11.56	11.59	2
3.7	11.62	11.66	11.69	11.72	11.75	11.78	11.81	11.84	11.88	11.91	3
3.8	11.94	11.97	12.00	12.03	12.06	12.10	12.13	12.16	12.19	12.22	3
3.9	12.25	12.28	12.32	12.35	12.38	12.41	12.44	12.47	12.50	12.53	4
4.0	12.57	12.60	12.63	12.66	12.69	12.72	12.75	12.79	12.82	12.85	3
4.1	12.88	12.91	12.94	12.97	13.01	13.04	13.07	13.10	13.13	13.16	0
4.2	13.19	13.23	13.26	13.29	13.32	13.35	13.38	13.41	13.45	13.48	1
4.3	13.51	13.54	13.57	13.60	13.63	13.67	13.70	13.73	13.76	13.79	1
4.4	13.82	13.85	13.89	13.92	13.95	13.98	14.01	14.04	14.07	14.11	1
4.5	14.14	14.17	14.20	14.23	14.26	14.29	14.33	14.36	14.39	14.42	2
4.6	14.45	14.48	14.51	14.55	14.58	14.61	14.64	14.67	14.70	14.73	2
4.7	14.77	14.80	14.83	14.86	14.89	14.92	14.95	14.99	15.02	15.05	2
4.8	15.08	15.11	15.14	15.17	15.21	15.24	15.27	15.30	15.33	15.36	2
4.9	15.39	15.43	15.46	15.49	15.52	15.55	15.58	15.61	15.65	15.68	3
5.0	15.71	15.74	15.77	15.80	15.83	15.87	15.90	15.93	15.96	15.99	
5.1	16.02	16.05	16.08	16.12	16.15	16.18	16.21	16.24	16.27	16.30	
5.2	16.34	16.37	16.40	16.43	16.46	16.49	16.52	16.56	16.59	16.62	
5.3	16.65	16.68	16.71	16.74	16.78	16.81	16.84	16.87	16.90	16.93	
5.4	16.96	17.00	17.03	17.06	17.09	17.12	17.15	17.18	17.22	17.25	
5.5	17.28	17.31	17.34	17.37	17.40	17.44	17.47	17.50	17.53	17.56	
5.6	17.59	17.62	17.66	17.69	17.72	17.75	17.78	17.81	17.84	17.88	
5.7	17.91	17.94	17.97	18.00	18.03	18.06	18.10	18.13	18.16	18.19	
5.8	18.22	18.25	18.28	18.32	18.35	18.38	18.41	18.44	18.47	18.50	
5.9	18.54	18.57	18.60	18.63	18.66	18.69	18.72	18.76	18.79	18.82	

n	0	1	2	3	4	5	6	7	8	9	pp
6.0	18.85	18.88	18.91	18.94	18.98	19.01	19.04	19.07	19.10	19.13	4
6.1	19.16	19.20	19.23	19.26	19.29	19.32	19.35	19.38	19.42	19.45	0
6.2	19.48	19.51	19.54	19.57	19.60	19.63	19.67	19.70	19.73	19.76	1
6.3	19.79	19.82	19.85	19.89	19.92	19.95	19.98	20.01	20.04	20.07	1
6.4	20.11	20.14	20.17	20.20	20.23	20.26	20.29	20.33	20.36	20.39	2
6.5	20.42	20.45	20.48	20.51	20.55	20.58	20.61	20.64	20.67	20.70	2
6.6	20.73	20.77	20.80	20.83	20.86	20.89	20.92	20.95	20.99	21.02	2
6.7	21.05	21.08	21.11	21.14	21.17	21.21	21.24	21.27	21.30	21.33	3
6.8	21.36	21.39	21.43	21.46	21.49	21.52	21.55	21.58	21.61	21.65	3
6.9	21.68	21.71	21.74	21.77	21.80	21.83	21.87	21.90	21.93	21.96	4
7.0	21.99	22.02	22.05	22.09	22.12	22.15	22.18	22.21	22.24	22.27	
7.1	22.31	22.34	22.37	22.40	22.43	22.46	22.49	22.53	22.56	22.59	
7.2	22.62	22.65	22.68	22.71	22.75	22.78	22.81	22.84	22.87	22.90	
7.3	22.93	22.97	23.00	23.03	23.06	23.09	23.12	23.15	23.18	23.22	
7.4	23.25	23.28	23.31	23.34	23.37	23.40	23.44	23.47	23.50	23.53	
7.5	23.56	23.59	23.62	23.66	23.69	23.72	23.75	23.78	23.81	23.84	
7.6	23.88	23.91	23.94	23.97	24.00	24.03	24.06	24.10	24.13	24.16	
7.7	24.19	24.22	24.25	24.28	24.32	24.35	24.38	24.41	24.44	24.47	
7.8	24.50	24.54	24.57	24.60	24.63	24.66	24.69	24.72	24.76	24.79	
7.9	24.82	24.85	24.88	24.91	24.94	24.98	25.01	25.04	25.07	25.10	
8.0	25.13	25.16	25.20	25.23	25.26	25.29	25.32	25.35	25.38	25.42	3
8.1	25.45	25.48	25.51	25.54	25.57	25.60	25.64	25.67	25.70	25.73	0
8.2	25.76	25.79	25.82	25.86	25.89	25.92	25.95	25.98	26.01	26.04	1
8.3	26.08	26.11	26.14	26.17	26.20	26.23	26.26	26.30	26.33	26.36	1
8.4	26.39	26.42	26.45	26.48	26.52	26.55	26.58	26.61	26.64	26.67	1
8.5	26.70	26.73	26.77	26.80	26.83	26.86	26.89	26.92	26.95	26.99	2
8.6	27.02	27.05	27.08	27.11	27.14	27.17	27.21	27.24	27.27	27.30	2
8.7	27.33	27.36	27.39	27.43	27.46	27.49	27.52	27.55	27.58	27.61	2
8.8	27.65	27.68	27.71	27.74	27.77	27.80	27.83	27.87	27.90	27.93	2
8.9	27.96	27.99	28.02	28.05	28.09	28.12	28.15	28.18	28.21	28.24	3
9.0	28.27	28.31	28.34	28.37	28.40	28.43	28.46	28.49	28.53	28.56	
9.1	28.59	28.62	28.65	28.68	28.71	28.75	28.78	28.81	28.84	28.87	
9.2	28.90	28.93	28.97	29.00	29.03	29.06	29.09	29.12	29.15	29.19	
9.3	29.22	29.25	29.28	29.31	29.34	29.37	29.41	29.44	29.47	29.50	
9.4	29.53	29.56	29.59	29.63	29.66	29.69	29.72	29.75	29.78	29.81	
9.5	29.85	29.88	29.91	29.94	29.97	30.00	30.03	30.07	30.10	30.13	
9.6	30.16	30.19	30.22	30.25	30.28	30.32	30.35	30.38	30.41	30.44	
9.7	30.47	30.50	30.54	30.57	30.60	30.63	30.66	30.69	30.72	30.76	
9.8	30.79	30.82	30.85	30.88	30.91	30.94	30.98	31.01	31.04	31.07	
9.9	31.10	31.13	31.16	31.20	31.23	31.26	31.29	31.32	31.35	31.38	

	value	log	recip.		value	log	recip.
π	3.1416	0.4971	0.3183	$\frac{\pi}{180}$	0.0175	$\bar{2}.2419$	57.2958
2π	6.2832	0.7982	0.1592	$\frac{\pi}{360}$	0.0087	$\bar{3}.9408$	114.5916
4π	12.5664	1.0992	0.0796	π^2	9.8696	0.9943	0.1013
$\frac{\pi}{2}$	1.5708	0.1961	0.6366	$\sqrt{\pi}$	1.7725	0.2486	0.5642
$\frac{\pi}{4}$	0.7854	$\bar{1}.8951$	1.2732	π^3	31.006	1.4914	0.0323
$\frac{\pi}{6}$	0.5236	$\bar{1}.7190$	1.9099	$\sqrt[3]{\pi}$	1.4646	0.1657	0.6828
$\frac{4\pi}{3}$	4.1888	0.6221	0.2387	$\sqrt[3]{\frac{\pi}{6}}$	0.8060	$\bar{1}.9063$	1.2407
				$\sqrt[3]{\frac{4\pi}{3}}$	1.6120	0.2074	0.6204

$\pi = 3.1415926536$

n	0	1	2	3	4	5	6	7	8	9	d
1.0	0.785	0.801	0.817	0.833	0.849	0.866	0.882	0.899	0.916	0.933	17
1.1	0.950	0.968	0.985	1.003	1.021	1.039	1.057	1.075	1.094	1.112	19
1.2	1.131	1.150	1.169	1.188	1.208	1.227	1.247	1.267	1.287	1.307	20
1.3	1.327	1.348	1.368	1.389	1.410	1.431	1.453	1.474	1.496	1.517	22
1.4	1.539	1.561	1.584	1.606	1.629	1.651	1.674	1.697	1.720	1.744	23
1.5	1.767	1.791	1.815	1.839	1.863	1.887	1.911	1.936	1.961	1.986	25
1.6	2.011	2.036	2.061	2.087	2.112	2.138	2.164	2.190	2.217	2.243	27
1.7	2.270	2.297	2.324	2.351	2.378	2.405	2.433	2.461	2.488	2.516	29
1.8	2.545	2.573	2.602	2.630	2.659	2.688	2.717	2.746	2.776	2.806	29
1.9	2.835	2.865	2.895	2.926	2.956	2.986	3.017	3.048	3.079	3.110	32
2.0	3.142	3.173	3.205	3.237	3.269	3.301	3.333	3.365	3.398	3.431	33
2.1	3.464	3.497	3.530	3.563	3.597	3.631	3.664	3.698	3.733	3.767	34
2.2	3.801	3.836	3.871	3.906	3.941	3.976	4.011	4.047	4.083	4.119	36
2.3	4.155	4.191	4.227	4.264	4.301	4.337	4.374	4.412	4.449	4.486	38
2.4	4.524	4.562	4.600	4.638	4.676	4.714	4.753	4.792	4.831	4.870	39
2.5	4.909	4.948	4.988	5.027	5.067	5.107	5.147	5.187	5.228	5.269	40
2.6	5.309	5.350	5.391	5.433	5.474	5.515	5.557	5.599	5.641	5.683	43
2.7	5.726	5.768	5.811	5.853	5.896	5.940	5.983	6.026	6.070	6.114	44
2.8	6.158	6.202	6.246	6.290	6.335	6.379	6.424	6.469	6.514	6.560	45
2.9	6.605	6.651	6.697	6.743	6.789	6.835	6.881	6.928	6.975	7.022	47
3.0	7.069	7.116	7.163	7.211	7.258	7.306	7.354	7.402	7.451	7.499	49
3.1	7.548	7.596	7.645	7.694	7.744	7.793	7.843	7.892	7.942	7.992	50
3.2	8.042	8.093	8.143	8.194	8.245	8.296	8.347	8.398	8.450	8.501	52
3.3	8.553	8.605	8.657	8.709	8.762	8.814	8.867	8.920	8.973	9.026	53
3.4	9.079	9.133	9.186	9.240	9.294	9.348	9.402	9.457	9.511	9.566	55
3.5	9.621	9.676	9.731	9.787	9.842	9.898	9.954	10.01	10.07	10.12	6
3.6	10.18	10.24	10.29	10.35	10.41	10.46	10.52	10.58	10.64	10.69	6
3.7	10.75	10.81	10.87	10.93	10.99	11.04	11.10	11.16	11.22	11.28	6
3.8	11.34	11.40	11.46	11.52	11.58	11.64	11.70	11.76	11.82	11.88	7
3.9	11.95	12.01	12.07	12.13	12.19	12.25	12.32	12.38	12.44	12.50	7
4.0	12.57	12.63	12.69	12.76	12.82	12.88	12.95	13.01	13.07	13.14	6
4.1	13.20	13.27	13.33	13.40	13.46	13.53	13.59	13.66	13.72	13.79	6
4.2	13.85	13.92	13.99	14.05	14.12	14.19	14.25	14.32	14.39	14.45	7
4.3	14.52	14.59	14.66	14.73	14.79	14.86	14.93	15.00	15.07	15.14	7
4.4	15.21	15.27	15.34	15.41	15.48	15.55	15.62	15.69	15.76	15.83	7
4.5	15.90	15.98	16.05	16.12	16.19	16.26	16.33	16.40	16.47	16.55	7
4.6	16.62	16.69	16.76	16.84	16.91	16.98	17.06	17.13	17.20	17.28	7
4.7	17.35	17.42	17.50	17.57	17.65	17.72	17.80	17.87	17.95	18.02	8
4.8	18.10	18.17	18.25	18.32	18.40	18.47	18.55	18.63	18.70	18.78	8
4.9	18.86	18.93	19.01	19.09	19.17	19.24	19.32	19.40	19.48	19.56	7
5.0	19.63	19.71	19.79	19.87	19.95	20.03	20.11	20.19	20.27	20.35	8
5.1	20.43	20.51	20.59	20.67	20.75	20.83	20.91	20.99	21.07	21.16	8
5.2	21.24	21.32	21.40	21.48	21.57	21.65	21.73	21.81	21.90	21.98	8
5.3	22.06	22.15	22.23	22.31	22.40	22.48	22.56	22.65	22.73	22.82	8
5.4	22.90	22.99	23.07	23.16	23.24	23.33	23.41	23.50	23.59	23.67	9
5.5	23.76	23.84	23.93	24.02	24.11	24.19	24.28	24.37	24.45	24.54	9
5.6	24.63	24.72	24.81	24.89	24.98	25.07	25.16	25.25	25.34	25.43	9
5.7	25.52	25.61	25.70	25.79	25.88	25.97	26.06	26.15	26.24	26.33	9
5.8	26.42	26.51	26.60	26.69	26.79	26.88	26.97	27.06	27.15	27.25	9
5.9	27.34	27.43	27.53	27.62	27.71	27.81	27.90	27.99	28.09	28.18	9

n	0	1	2	3	4	5	6	7	8	9	d
6.0	28.27	28.37	28.46	28.56	28.65	28.75	28.84	28.94	29.03	29.13	9
6.1	29.22	29.32	29.42	29.51	29.61	29.71	29.80	29.90	30.00	30.09	10
6.2	30.19	30.29	30.39	30.48	30.58	30.68	30.78	30.88	30.97	31.07	10
6.3	31.17	31.27	31.37	31.47	31.57	31.67	31.77	31.87	31.97	32.07	10
6.4	32.17	32.27	32.37	32.47	32.57	32.67	32.78	32.88	32.98	33.08	10
6.5	33.18	33.29	33.39	33.49	33.59	33.70	33.80	33.90	34.00	34.11	10
6.6	34.21	34.32	34.42	34.52	34.63	34.73	34.84	34.94	35.05	35.15	11
6.7	35.26	35.36	35.47	35.57	35.68	35.78	35.89	36.00	36.10	36.21	11
6.8	36.32	36.42	36.53	36.64	36.75	36.85	36.96	37.07	37.18	37.28	11
6.9	37.39	37.50	37.61	37.72	37.83	37.94	38.05	38.16	38.26	38.37	11
7.0	38.48	38.59	38.70	38.82	38.93	39.04	39.15	39.26	39.37	39.48	11
7.1	39.59	39.70	39.82	39.93	40.04	40.15	40.26	40.38	40.49	40.60	12
7.2	40.72	40.83	40.94	41.06	41.17	41.28	41.40	41.51	41.62	41.74	11
7.3	41.85	41.97	42.08	42.20	42.31	42.43	42.54	42.66	42.78	42.89	12
7.4	43.01	43.12	43.24	43.36	43.47	43.59	43.71	43.83	43.94	44.06	12
7.5	44.18	44.30	44.41	44.53	44.65	44.77	44.89	45.01	45.13	45.25	11
7.6	45.36	45.48	45.60	45.72	45.84	45.96	46.08	46.20	46.32	46.45	12
7.7	46.57	46.69	46.81	46.93	47.05	47.17	47.29	47.42	47.54	47.66	12
7.8	47.78	47.91	48.03	48.15	48.27	48.40	48.52	48.65	48.77	48.89	13
7.9	49.02	49.14	49.27	49.39	49.51	49.64	49.76	49.89	50.01	50.14	13
8.0	50.27	50.39	50.52	50.64	50.77	50.90	51.02	51.15	51.28	51.40	13
8.1	51.53	51.66	51.78	51.91	52.04	52.17	52.30	52.42	52.55	52.68	13
8.2	52.81	52.94	53.07	53.20	53.33	53.46	53.59	53.72	53.85	53.98	13
8.3	54.11	54.24	54.37	54.50	54.63	54.76	54.89	55.02	55.15	55.29	13
8.4	55.42	55.55	55.68	55.81	55.95	56.08	56.21	56.35	56.48	56.61	14
8.5	56.75	56.88	57.01	57.15	57.28	57.41	57.55	57.68	57.82	57.95	14
8.6	58.09	58.22	58.36	58.49	58.63	58.77	58.90	59.04	59.17	59.31	14
8.7	59.45	59.58	59.72	59.86	59.99	60.13	60.27	60.41	60.55	60.68	14
8.8	60.82	60.96	61.10	61.24	61.38	61.51	61.65	61.79	61.93	62.07	14
8.9	62.21	62.35	62.49	62.63	62.77	62.91	63.05	63.19	63.33	63.48	14
9.0	63.62	63.76	63.90	64.04	64.18	64.33	64.47	64.61	64.75	64.90	14
9.1	65.04	65.18	65.33	65.47	65.61	65.76	65.90	66.04	66.19	66.33	15
9.2	66.48	66.62	66.77	66.91	67.06	67.20	67.35	67.49	67.64	67.78	15
9.3	67.93	68.08	68.22	68.37	68.51	68.66	68.81	68.96	69.10	69.25	15
9.4	69.40	69.55	69.69	69.84	69.99	70.14	70.29	70.44	70.58	70.73	15
9.5	70.88	71.03	71.18	71.33	71.48	71.63	71.78	71.93	72.08	72.23	15
9.6	72.38	72.53	72.68	72.84	72.99	73.14	73.29	73.44	73.59	73.75	15
9.7	73.90	74.05	74.20	74.36	74.51	74.66	74.82	74.97	75.12	75.28	15
9.8	75.43	75.58	75.74	75.89	76.05	76.20	76.36	76.51	76.67	76.82	16
9.9	76.98	77.13	77.29	77.44	77.60	77.76	77.91	78.07	78.23	78.38	16

	32nds	36ths								
1	.03125	.02(7)	10	.3125	.2(7)	20	.625	.(5)	30	.9375	.8(3)
2	.0625	.0(5)	11	.34375	.30(5)	21	.65625	.58(3)	31	.96875	.86(1)
3	.09375	.08(3)	12	.375	.(3)	22	.6875	.6(1)	32		.(8)
4	.125	.(1)	13	.40625	.36(1)	23	.71875	.63(8)	33		.91(6)
5	.15625	.13(8)	14	.4375	.3(8)	24	.75	.(6)	34		.9(4)
6	.1875	.1(6)	15	.46875	.41(6)	25	.78125	.69(4)	35		.97(2)
7	.21875	.19(4)	16	.5	.(4)	26	.8125	.7(2)	36		
8	.25	.(2)	17	.53125	.47(2)	27	.84375	.75			
9	.28125	.25	18	.5625	.5	28	.875	.(7)			
			19	.59375	.52(7)	29	.90625	.80(5)			

n	0	1	2	3	4	5	6	7	8	9	d
1.0	.5236	.5395	.5556	.5722	.5890	.6061	.6236	.6414	.6596	.6781	188
1.1	.6969	.7161	.7356	.7555	.7757	.7963	.8173	.8386	.8603	.8823	225
1.2	.9048	.9276	.9508	.9743	.9983	1.023	1.047	1.073	1.098	1.124	26
1.3	1.150	1.177	1.204	1.232	1.260	1.288	1.317	1.346	1.376	1.406	31
1.4	1.437	1.468	1.499	1.531	1.563	1.596	1.630	1.663	1.697	1.732	35
1.5	1.767	1.803	1.839	1.875	1.912	1.950	1.988	2.026	2.065	2.105	40
1.6	2.145	2.185	2.226	2.268	2.310	2.352	2.395	2.439	2.483	2.527	45
1.7	2.572	2.618	2.664	2.711	2.758	2.806	2.855	2.903	2.953	3.003	51
1.8	3.054	3.105	3.157	3.209	3.262	3.315	3.369	3.424	3.479	3.535	56
1.9	3.591	3.648	3.706	3.764	3.823	3.882	3.942	4.003	4.064	4.126	63
2.0	4.189	4.252	4.316	4.380	4.445	4.511	4.577	4.644	4.712	4.780	69
2.1	4.849	4.919	4.989	5.060	5.131	5.204	5.277	5.350	5.425	5.500	75
2.2	5.575	5.652	5.729	5.806	5.885	5.964	6.044	6.125	6.206	6.288	83
2.3	6.371	6.454	6.538	6.623	6.709	6.795	6.882	6.970	7.059	7.148	90
2.4	7.238	7.329	7.421	7.513	7.606	7.700	7.795	7.890	7.986	8.083	98
2.5	8.181	8.280	8.379	8.479	8.580	8.682	8.785	8.888	8.992	9.097	106
2.6	9.203	9.309	9.417	9.525	9.634	9.744	9.855	9.966	10.08	10.19	12
2.7	10.31	10.42	10.54	10.65	10.77	10.89	11.01	11.13	11.25	11.37	12
2.8	11.49	11.62	11.74	11.87	11.99	12.12	12.25	12.38	12.51	12.64	13
2.9	12.77	12.90	13.04	13.17	13.31	13.44	13.58	13.72	13.86	14.00	14
3.0	14.14	14.28	14.42	14.57	14.71	14.86	15.00	15.15	15.30	15.45	15
3.1	15.60	15.75	15.90	16.06	16.21	16.37	16.52	16.68	16.84	17.00	16
3.2	17.16	17.32	17.48	17.64	17.81	17.97	18.14	18.31	18.48	18.65	17
3.3	18.82	18.99	19.16	19.33	19.51	19.68	19.86	20.04	20.22	20.40	18
3.4	20.58	20.76	20.94	21.13	21.31	21.50	21.69	21.88	22.07	22.26	19
3.5	22.45	22.64	22.84	23.03	23.23	23.43	23.62	23.82	24.02	24.23	20
3.6	24.43	24.63	24.84	25.04	25.25	25.46	25.67	25.88	26.09	26.31	21
3.7	26.52	26.74	26.95	27.17	27.39	27.61	27.83	28.06	28.28	28.50	23
3.8	28.73	28.96	29.19	29.42	29.65	29.88	30.11	30.35	30.58	30.82	24
3.9	31.06	31.30	31.54	31.78	32.02	32.27	32.52	32.76	33.01	33.26	25
4.0	33.51	33.76	34.02	34.27	34.53	34.78	35.04	35.30	35.56	35.82	27
4.1	36.09	36.35	36.62	36.88	37.15	37.42	37.69	37.97	38.24	38.52	27
4.2	38.79	39.07	39.35	39.63	39.91	40.19	40.48	40.76	41.05	41.34	29
4.3	41.63	41.92	42.21	42.51	42.80	43.10	43.40	43.70	44.00	44.30	30
4.4	44.60	44.91	45.21	45.52	45.83	46.14	46.45	46.77	47.08	47.40	31
4.5	47.71	48.03	48.35	48.67	49.00	49.32	49.65	49.97	50.30	50.63	34
4.6	50.97	51.30	51.63	51.97	52.31	52.65	52.99	53.33	53.67	54.02	34
4.7	54.36	54.71	55.06	55.41	55.76	56.12	56.47	56.83	57.19	57.54	37
4.8	57.91	58.27	58.63	59.00	59.37	59.73	60.10	60.48	60.85	61.22	38
4.9	61.60	61.98	62.36	62.74	63.12	63.51	63.89	64.28	64.67	65.06	39
5.0	65.45	65.84	66.24	66.64	67.03	67.43	67.83	68.24	68.64	69.05	41
5.1	69.46	69.87	70.28	70.69	71.10	71.52	71.94	72.36	72.78	73.20	42
5.2	73.62	74.05	74.47	74.90	75.33	75.77	76.20	76.64	77.07	77.51	44
5.3	77.95	78.39	78.84	79.28	79.73	80.18	80.63	81.08	81.54	81.99	46
5.4	82.45	82.91	83.37	83.83	84.29	84.76	85.23	85.70	86.17	86.64	47
5.5	87.11	87.59	88.07	88.55	89.03	89.51	90.00	90.48	90.97	91.46	49
5.6	91.95	92.45	92.94	93.44	93.94	94.44	94.94	95.44	95.95	96.46	51
5.7	96.97	97.48	97.99	98.51	99.02	99.54	100.1	100.6	101.1	101.6	6
5.8	102.2	102.7	103.2	103.8	104.3	104.8	105.4	105.9	106.4	107.0	5
5.9	107.5	108.1	108.6	109.2	109.7	110.3	110.9	111.4	112.0	112.5	6

n	0	1	2	3	4	5	6	7	8	9	d
6.0	113.1	113.7	114.2	114.8	115.4	115.9	116.5	117.1	117.7	118.3	5
6.1	118.8	119.4	120.0	120.6	121.2	121.8	122.4	123.0	123.6	124.2	6
6.2	124.8	125.4	126.0	126.6	127.2	127.8	128.4	129.1	129.7	130.3	6
6.3	130.9	131.5	132.2	132.8	133.4	134.1	134.7	135.3	136.0	136.6	7
6.4	137.3	137.9	138.5	139.2	139.8	140.5	141.2	141.8	142.5	143.1	7
6.5	143.8	144.5	145.1	145.8	146.5	147.1	147.8	148.5	149.2	149.8	7
6.6	150.5	151.2	151.9	152.6	153.3	154.0	154.7	155.4	156.1	156.8	7
6.7	157.5	158.2	158.9	159.6	160.3	161.0	161.7	162.5	163.2	163.9	7
6.8	164.6	165.4	166.1	166.8	167.6	168.3	169.0	169.8	170.5	171.3	7
6.9	172.0	172.8	173.5	174.3	175.0	175.8	176.5	177.3	178.1	178.8	8
7.0	179.6	180.4	181.1	181.9	182.7	183.5	184.3	185.0	185.8	186.6	8
7.1	187.4	188.2	189.0	189.8	190.6	191.4	192.2	193.0	193.8	194.6	8
7.2	195.4	196.2	197.1	197.9	198.7	199.5	200.4	201.2	202.0	202.9	8
7.3	203.7	204.5	205.4	206.2	207.1	207.9	208.8	209.6	210.5	211.3	9
7.4	212.2	213.0	213.9	214.8	215.6	216.5	217.4	218.3	219.1	220.0	9
7.5	220.9	221.8	222.7	223.6	224.4	225.3	226.2	227.1	228.0	228.9	9
7.6	229.8	230.8	231.7	232.6	233.5	234.4	235.3	236.3	237.2	238.1	9
7.7	239.0	240.0	240.9	241.8	242.8	243.7	244.7	245.6	246.6	247.5	10
7.8	248.5	249.4	250.4	251.4	252.3	253.3	254.3	255.2	256.2	257.2	10
7.9	258.2	259.1	260.1	261.1	262.1	263.1	264.1	265.1	266.1	267.1	10
8.0	268.1	269.1	270.1	271.1	272.1	273.1	274.2	275.2	276.2	277.2	11
8.1	278.3	279.3	280.3	281.4	282.4	283.4	284.5	285.5	286.6	287.6	11
8.2	288.7	289.8	290.8	291.9	292.9	294.0	295.1	296.2	297.2	298.3	11
8.3	299.4	300.5	301.6	302.6	303.7	304.8	305.9	307.0	308.1	309.2	11
8.4	310.3	311.4	312.6	313.7	314.8	315.9	317.0	318.2	319.3	320.4	12
8.5	321.6	322.7	323.8	325.0	326.1	327.3	328.4	329.6	330.7	331.9	11
8.6	333.0	334.2	335.4	336.5	337.7	338.9	340.1	341.2	342.4	343.6	12
8.7	344.8	346.0	347.2	348.4	349.6	350.8	352.0	353.2	354.4	355.6	12
8.8	356.8	358.0	359.3	360.5	361.7	362.9	364.2	365.4	366.6	367.9	12
8.9	369.1	370.4	371.6	372.9	374.1	375.4	376.6	377.9	379.2	380.4	13
9.0	381.7	383.0	384.3	385.5	386.8	388.1	389.4	390.7	392.0	393.3	13
9.1	394.6	395.9	397.2	398.5	399.8	401.1	402.4	403.7	405.1	406.4	13
9.2	407.7	409.1	410.4	411.7	413.1	414.4	415.7	417.1	418.4	419.8	14
9.3	421.2	422.5	423.9	425.2	426.6	428.0	429.4	430.7	432.1	433.5	14
9.4	434.9	436.3	437.7	439.1	440.5	441.9	443.3	444.7	446.1	447.5	14
9.5	448.9	450.3	451.8	453.2	454.6	456.0	457.5	458.9	460.4	461.8	14
9.6	463.2	464.7	466.1	467.6	469.1	470.5	472.0	473.5	474.9	476.4	15
9.7	477.9	479.4	480.8	482.3	483.8	485.3	486.8	488.3	489.8	491.3	15
9.8	492.8	494.3	495.8	497.3	498.9	500.4	501.9	503.4	505.0	506.5	15
9.9	508.0	509.6	511.1	512.7	514.2	515.8	517.3	518.9	520.5	522.0	16

n	log n!	log 2n						
1	0.0000	0.3010	**10**	6.5598	3.0103	**20**	18.3861	6.0206
2	0.3010	0.6021	**11**	7.6012	3.3113	**21**	19.7083	6.3216
3	0.7782	0.9031	**12**	8.6803	3.6124	**22**	21.0508	6.6227
4	1.3802	1.2041	**13**	9.7943	3.9134	**23**	22.4125	6.9237
5	2.0792	1.5051	**14**	10.9404	4.2144	**24**	23.7927	7.2247
6	2.8573	1.8062	**15**	12.1165	4.5154	**25**	25.1906	7.5257
7	3.7024	2.1072	**16**	13.3206	4.8165	**26**	26.6056	7.8268
8	4.6055	2.4082	**17**	14.5511	5.1175	**27**	28.0370	8.1278
9	5.5598	2.7093	**18**	15.8063	5.4185	**28**	29.4841	8.4288
			19	17.0851	5.7196	**29**	30.9465	8.7299

n	0	1	2	3	4	5	6	7	8	9	d
1.0	0.0000	0100	0198	0296	0392	0488	0583	0677	0770	0862	91
1.1	0953	1044	1133	1222	1310	1398	1484	1570	1655	1740	83
1.2	1823	1906	1989	2070	2151	2231	2311	2390	2469	2546	78
1.3	2624	2700	2776	2852	2927	3001	3075	3148	3221	3293	72
1.4	3365	3436	3507	3577	3646	3716	3784	3853	3920	3988	67
1.5	4055	4121	4187	4253	4318	4383	4447	4511	4574	4637	63
1.6	4700	4762	4824	4886	4947	5008	5068	5128	5188	5247	59
1.7	5306	5365	5423	5481	5539	5596	5653	5710	5766	5822	56
1.8	5878	5933	5988	6043	6098	6152	6206	6259	6313	6366	53
1.9	6419	6471	6523	6575	6627	6678	6729	6780	6831	6881	50
2.0	0.6931	6981	7031	7080	7129	7178	7227	7275	7324	7372	47
2.1	7419	7467	7514	7561	7608	7655	7701	7747	7793	7839	46
2.2	7885	7930	7975	8020	8065	8109	8154	8198	8242	8286	43
2.3	8329	8372	8416	8459	8502	8544	8587	8629	8671	8713	42
2.4	8755	8796	8838	8879	8920	8961	9002	9042	9083	9123	40
2.5	9163	9203	9243	9282	9322	9361	9400	9439	9478	9517	38
2.6	9555	9594	9632	9670	9708	9746	9783	9821	9858	9895	38
2.7	9933	9969	*0006	*0043	*0080	*0116	*0152	*0188	*0225	*0260	36
2.8	1.0296	0332	0367	0403	0438	0473	0508	0543	0578	0613	34
2.9	0647	0682	0716	0750	0784	0818	0852	0886	0919	0953	33
3.0	1.0986	1019	1053	1086	1119	1151	1184	1217	1249	1282	32
3.1	1314	1346	1378	1410	1442	1474	1506	1537	1569	1600	32
3.2	1632	1663	1694	1725	1756	1787	1817	1848	1878	1909	30
3.3	1939	1969	2000	2030	2060	2090	2119	2149	2179.	2208	30
3.4	2238	2267	2296	2326	2355	2384	2413	2442	2470	2499	29
3.5	2528	2556	2585	2613	2641	2669	2698	2726	2754	2782	27
3.6	2809	2837	2865	2892	2920	2947	2975	3002	3029	3056	27
3.7	3083	3110	3137	3164	3191	3218	3244	3271	3297	3324	26
3.8	3350	3376	3403	3429	3455	3481	3507	3533	3558	3584	26
3.9	3610	3635	3661	3686	3712	3737	3762	3788	3813	3838	25
4.0	1.3863	3888	3913	3938	3962	3987	4012	4036	4061	4085	25
4.1	4110	4134	4159	4183	4207	4231	4255	4279	4303	4327	24
4.2	4351	4375	4398	4422	4446	4469	4493	4516	4540	4563	23
4.3	4586	4609	4633	4656	4679	4702	4725	4748	4770	4793	23
4.4	4816	4839	4861	4884	4907	4929	4951	4974	4996	5019	22
4.5	5041	5063	5085	5107	5129	5151	5173	5195	5217	5239	22
4.6	5261	5282	5304	5326	5347	5369	5390	5412	5433	5454	22
4.7	5476	5497	5518	5539	5560	5581	5602	5623	5644	5665	21
4.8	5686	5707	5728	5748	5769	5790	5810	5831	5851	5872	20
4.9	5892	5913	5933	5953	5974	5994	6014	6034	6054	6074	20
5.0	1.6094	6114	6134	6154	6174	6194	6214	6233	6253	6273	19
5.1	6292	6312	6332	6351	6371	6390	6409	6429	6448	6467	20
5.2	6487	6506	6525	6544	6563	6582	6601	6620	6639	6658	19
5.3	6677	6696	6715	6734	6752	6771	6790	6808	6827	6845	19
5.4	6864	6882	6901	6919	6938	6956	6974	6993	7011	7029	18
5.5	7047	7066	7084	7102	7120	7138	7156	7174	7192	7210	18
5.6	7228	7246	7263	7281	7299	7317	7334	7352	7370	7387	18
5.7	7405	7422	7440	7457	7475	7492	7509	7527	7544	7561	18
5.8	7579	7596	7613	7630	7647	7664	7681	7699	7716	7733	17
5.9	7750	7766	7783	7800	7817	7834	7851	7867	7884	7901	17

n	0	1	2	3	4	5	6	7	8	9	d
6.0	1.7918	7934	7951	7967	7984	8001	8017	8034	8050	8066	17
6.1	8083	8099	8116	8132	8148	8165	8181	8197	8213	8229	16
6.2	8245	8262	8278	8294	8310	8326	8342	8358	8374	8390	15
6.3	8405	8421	8437	8453	8469	8485	8500	8516	8532	8547	16
6.4	8563	8579	8594	8610	8625	8641	8656	8672	8687	8703	15
6.5	8718	8733	8749	8764	8779	8795	8810	8825	8840	8856	15
6.6	8871	8886	8901	8916	8931	8946	8961	8976	8991	9006	15
6.7	9021	9036	9051	9066	9081	9095	9110	9125	9140	9155	14
6.8	9169	9184	9199	9213	9228	9242	9257	9272	9286	9301	14
6.9	9315	9330	9344	9359	9373	9387	9402	9416	9430	9445	14
7.0	1.9459	9473	9488	9502	9516	9530	9544	9559	9573	9587	14
7.1	9601	9615	9629	9643	9657	9671	9685	9699	9713	9727	14
7.2	9741	9755	9769	9782	9796	9810	9824	9838	9851	9865	14
7.3	9879	9892	9906	9920	9933	9947	9961	9974	9988	*0001	14
7.4	2.0015	0028	0042	0055	0069	0082	0096	0109	0122	0136	13
7.5	0149	0162	0176	0189	0202	0215	0229	0242	0255	0268	13
7.6	0281	0295	0308	0321	0334	0347	0360	0373	0386	0399	13
7.7	0412	0425	0438	0451	0464	0477	0490	0503	0516	0528	13
7.8	0541	0554	0567	0580	0592	0605	0618	0631	0643	0656	13
7.9	0669	0681	0694	0707	0719	0732	0744	0757	0769	0782	12
8.0	2.0794	0807	0819	0832	0844	0857	0869	0882	0894	0906	13
8.1	0919	0931	0943	0956	0968	0980	0992	1005	1017	1029	12
8.2	1041	1054	1066	1078	1090	1102	1114	1126	1138	1150	13
8.3	1163	1175	1187	1199	1211	1223	1235	1247	1258	1270	12
8.4	1282	1294	1306	1318	1330	1342	1353	1365	1377	1389	12
8.5	1401	1412	1424	1436	1448	1459	1471	1483	1494	1506	12
8.6	1518	1529	1541	1552	1564	1576	1587	1599	1610	1622	11
8.7	1633	1645	1656	1668	1679	1691	1702	1713	1725	1736	12
8.8	1748	1759	1770	1782	1793	1804	1815	1827	1838	1849	12
8.9	1861	1872	1883	1894	1905	1917	1928	1939	1950	1961	11
9.0	2.1972	1983	1994	2006	2017	2028	2039	2050	2061	2072	11
9.1	2083	2094	2105	2116	2127	2138	2148	2159	2170	2181	11
9.2	2192	2203	2214	2225	2235	2246	2257	2268	2279	2289	11
9.3	2300	2311	2322	2332	2343	2354	2364	2375	2386	2396	11
9.4	2407	2418	2428	2439	2450	2460	2471	2481	2492	2502	11
9.5	2513	2523	2534	2544	2555	2565	2576	2586	2597	2607	11
9.6	2618	2628	2638	2649	2659	2670	2680	2690	2701	2711	10
9.7	2721	2732	2742	2752	2762	2773	2783	2793	2803	2814	10
9.8	2824	2834	2844	2854	2865	2875	2885	2895	2905	2915	10
9.9	2925	2935	2946	2956	2966	2976	2986	2996	3006	3016	10

n	$\frac{1}{m}$	1st	2d	3d	4th	m	$\log_e 10^n$	$\log_e 10^{-n}$
1	2.3026	0.2303	0.0230	0.0023	0.0002	0.4343	2.3026	$\bar{3}$.6974
2	4.6052	0.4605	0.0461	0.0046	0.0005	0.8686	4.6052	$\bar{5}$.3948
3	6.9078	0.6908	0.0691	0.0069	0.0007	1.3029	6.9078	$\bar{7}$.0922
4	9.2103	0.9210	0.0921	0.0092	0.0009	1.7372	9.2103	$\overline{10}$.7897
5	11.5129	1.1513	0.1151	0.0115	0.0012	2.1715	11.5129	$\overline{12}$.4871
6	13.8155	1.3816	0.1382	0.0138	0.0014	2.6058	13.8155	$\overline{14}$.1845
7	16.1181	1.6118	0.1612	0.0161	0.0016	3.0401	16.1181	$\overline{17}$.8819
8	18.4207	1.8421	0.1842	0.0184	0.0018	3.4744	18.4207	$\overline{19}$.5793
9	20.7233	2.0723	0.2072	0.0207	0.0021	3.9087	20.7233	$\overline{21}$.2767

n	3	3½	4	4½	5	6	7	8	9	10
0	1.000	1.000	1.000	1.000	1.000	1.000	1.000	1.000	1.000	1.000
1	1.030	1.035	1.040	1.045	1.050	1.060	1.070	1.080	1.090	1.100
2	1.061	1.071	1.082	1.092	1.103	1.124	1.145	1.166	1.188	1.210
3	1.093	1.109	1.125	1.141	1.158	1.191	1.225	1.260	1.295	1.331
4	1.126	1.148	1.170	1.193	1.216	1.262	1.311	1.360	1.412	1.464
5	1.159	1.188	1.217	1.246	1.276	1.338	1.403	1.469	1.539	1.611
6	1.194	1.229	1.265	1.302	1.340	1.419	1.501	1.587	1.677	1.772
7	1.230	1.272	1.316	1.361	1.407	1.504	1.606	1.714	1.828	1.949
8	1.267	1.317	1.369	1.422	1.477	1.594	1.718	1.851	1.993	2.144
9	1.305	1.363	1.423	1.486	1.551	1.689	1.838	1.999	2.172	2.358
10	1.344	1.411	1.480	1.553	1.629	1.791	1.967	2.159	2.367	2.594
11	1.384	1.460	1.539	1.623	1.710	1.898	2.105	2.332	2.580	2.853
12	1.426	1.511	1.601	1.696	1.796	2.012	2.252	2.518	2.813	3.138
13	1.469	1.564	1.665	1.772	1.886	2.133	2.410	2.720	3.066	3.452
14	1.513	1.619	1.732	1.852	1.980	2.261	2.579	2.937	3.342	3.797
15	1.558	1.675	1.801	1.935	2.079	2.397	2.759	3.172	3.642	4.177
16	1.605	1.734	1.873	2.022	2.183	2.540	2.952	3.426	3.970	4.595
17	1.653	1.795	1.948	2.113	2.292	2.693	3.159	3.700	4.328	5.054
18	1.702	1.857	2.026	2.208	2.407	2.854	3.380	3.996	4.717	5.560
19	1.754	1.923	2.107	2.308	2.527	3.026	3.617	4.316	5.142	6.116
20	1.806	1.990	2.191	2.412	2.653	3.207	3.870	4.661	5.604	6.727
21	1.860	2.059	2.279	2.520	2.786	3.400	4.141	5.034	6.109	7.400
22	1.916	2.132	2.370	2.634	2.925	3.604	4.430	5.437	6.659	8.140
23	1.974	2.206	2.465	2.752	3.072	3.820	4.741	5.871	7.258	8.954
24	2.033	2.283	2.563	2.876	3.225	4.049	5.072	6.341	7.911	9.850
25	2.094	2.363	2.666	3.005	3.386	4.292	5.427	6.848	8.623	10.83
26	2.157	2.446	2.772	3.141	3.556	4.549	5.807	7.396	9.399	11.92
27	2.221	2.532	2.883	3.282	3.733	4.822	6.214	7.988	10.25	13.11
28	2.288	2.620	2.999	3.430	3.920	5.112	6.649	8.627	11.17	14.42
29	2.357	2.712	3.119	3.584	4.116	5.418	7.114	9.317	12.17	15.86
30	2.427	2.807	3.243	3.745	4.322	5.743	7.612	10.06	13.27	17.45
31	2.500	2.905	3.373	3.914	4.538	6.088	8.145	10.87	14.46	19.19
32	2.575	3.007	3.508	4.090	4.765	6.453	8.715	11.74	15.76	21.11
33	2.652	3.112	3.648	4.274	5.003	6.841	9.325	12.68	17.18	23.23
34	2.732	3.221	3.794	4.466	5.253	7.251	9.978	13.69	18.73	25.55
35	2.814	3.334	3.946	4.667	5.516	7.686	10.68	14.79	20.41	28.10
36	2.898	3.450	4.104	4.877	5.792	8.147	11.42	15.97	22.25	30.91
37	2.985	3.571	4.268	5.097	6.081	8.636	12.22	17.25	24.25	34.00
38	3.075	3.696	4.439	5.326	6.385	9.154	13.08	18.63	26.44	37.40
39	3.167	3.825	4.616	5.566	6.705	9.704	13.99	20.12	28.82	41.14
40	3.262	3.959	4.801	5.816	7.040	10.29	14.97	21.72	31.41	45.26
41	3.360	4.098	4.993	6.078	7.392	10.90	16.02	23.46	34.24	49.79
42	3.461	4.241	5.193	6.352	7.762	11.56	17.14	25.34	37.32	54.76
43	3.565	4.390	5.400	6.637	8.150	12.25	18.34	27.37	40.68	60.24
44	3.671	4.543	5.617	6.936	8.557	12.99	19.63	29.56	44.34	66.26
45	3.782	4.702	5.841	7.248	8.985	13.76	21.00	31.92	48.33	72.89
46	3.895	4.867	6.075	7.574	9.434	14.59	22.47	34.47	52.68	80.18
47	4.012	5.037	6.318	7.915	9.906	15.47	24.05	37.23	57.42	88.20
48	4.132	5.214	6.571	8.271	10.40	16.39	25.73	40.21	62.59	97.02
49	4.256	5.396	6.833	8.644	10.92	17.38	27.53	43.43	68.22	106.7

n	3	3½	4	4½	5	6	7	8	9	10
0	1000	1000	1000	1000	1000	1000	1000	1000	1000	1000
1	970.9	966.2	961.5	956.9	952.4	943.4	934.6	925.9	917.4	909.1
2	942.6	933.5	924.6	915.7	907.0	890.0	873.4	857.3	841.7	826.4
3	915.1	901.9	889.0	876.3	863.8	839.6	816.3	793.8	772.2	751.3
4	888.5	871.4	854.8	838.6	822.7	792.1	762.9	735.0	708.4	683.0
5	862.6	842.0	821.9	802.5	783.5	747.3	713.0	680.6	649.9	620.9
6	837.5	813.5	790.3	767.9	746.2	705.0	666.3	630.2	596.3	564.5
7	813.1	786.0	759.9	734.8	710.7	665.1	622.7	583.5	547.0	513.2
8	789.4	759.4	730.7	703.2	676.8	627.4	582.0	540.3	501.9	466.5
9	766.4	733.7	702.6	672.9	644.6	591.9	543.9	500.2	460.4	424.1
10	744.1	708.9	675.6	643.9	613.9	558.4	508.3	463.2	422.4	385.5
11	722.4	684.9	649.6	616.2	584.7	526.8	475.1	428.9	387.5	350.5
12	701.4	661.8	624.6	589.7	556.8	497.0	444.0	397.1	355.5	318.6
13	681.0	639.4	600.6	564.3	530.3	468.8	415.0	367.7	326.2	289.7
14	661.1	617.8	577.5	540.0	505.1	442.3	387.8	340.5	299.2	263.3
15	641.9	596.9	555.3	516.7	481.0	417.3	362.4	315.2	274.5	239.4
16	623.2	576.7	533.9	494.5	458.1	393.6	338.7	291.9	251.9	217.6
17	605.0	557.2	513.4	473.2	436.3	371.4	316.6	270.3	231.1	197.8
18	587.4	538.4	493.6	452.8	415.5	350.3	295.9	250.2	212.0	179.9
19	570.3	520.2	474.6	433.3	395.7	330.5	276.5	231.7	194.5	163.5
20	553.7	502.6	456.4	414.6	376.9	311.8	258.4	214.5	178.4	148.6
21	537.5	485.6	438.8	396.8	358.9	294.2	241.5	198.7	163.7	135.1
22	521.9	469.2	422.0	379.7	341.8	277.5	225.7	183.9	150.2	122.8
23	506.7	453.3	405.7	363.4	325.6	261.8	210.9	170.3	137.8	111.7
24	491.9	438.0	390.1	347.7	310.1	247.0	197.1	157.7	126.4	101.5
25	477.6	423.1	375.1	332.7	295.3	233.0	184.2	146.0	116.0	92.30
26	463.7	408.8	360.7	318.4	281.2	219.8	172.2	135.2	106.4	83.91
27	450.2	395.0	346.8	304.7	267.8	207.4	160.9	125.2	97.61	76.28
28	437.1	381.7	333.5	291.6	255.1	195.6	150.4	115.9	89.55	69.34
29	424.3	368.7	320.7	279.0	242.9	184.6	140.6	107.3	82.15	63.04
30	412.0	356.3	308.3	267.0	231.4	174.1	131.4	99.38	75.37	57.31
31	400.0	344.2	296.5	255.5	220.4	164.3	122.8	92.02	69.15	52.10
32	388.3	332.6	285.1	244.5	209.9	155.0	114.7	85.20	63.44	47.36
33	377.0	321.3	274.1	234.0	199.9	146.2	107.2	78.89	58.20	43.06
34	366.0	310.5	263.6	223.9	190.4	137.9	100.2	73.05	53.39	39.14
35	355.4	300.0	253.4	214.3	181.3	130.1	93.66	67.63	48.99	35.58
36	345.0	289.8	243.7	205.0	172.7	122.7	87.54	62.62	44.94	32.35
37	335.0	280.0	234.3	196.2	164.4	115.8	81.81	57.99	41.23	29.41
38	325.2	270.6	225.3	187.8	156.6	109.2	76.46	53.69	37.83	26.73
39	315.8	261.4	216.6	179.7	149.1	103.1	71.46	49.71	34.70	24.30
40	306.6	252.6	208.3	171.9	142.0	97.22	66.78	46.03	31.84	22.09
41	297.6	244.0	200.3	164.5	135.3	91.72	62.41	42.62	29.21	20.09
42	289.0	235.8	192.6	157.4	128.8	86.53	58.33	39.46	26.80	18.26
43	280.5	227.8	185.2	150.7	122.7	81.63	54.51	36.54	24.58	16.60
44	272.4	220.1	178.0	144.2	116.9	77.01	50.95	33.83	22.55	15.09
45	264.4	212.7	171.2	138.0	111.3	72.65	47.61	31.33	20.69	13.72
46	256.7	205.5	164.6	132.0	106.0	68.54	44.50	29.01	18.98	12.47
47	249.3	198.5	158.3	126.3	100.9	64.66	41.59	26.86	17.42	11.34
48	242.0	191.8	152.2	120.9	96.14	61.00	38.87	24.87	15.98	10.31
49	235.0	185.3	146.3	115.7	91.56	57.55	36.32	23.03	14.66	9.370

$$\frac{\left(1+\frac{r}{100}\right)^{n}-1}{\frac{r}{100}}$$

n	3	3½	4	4½	5	6	7	8	9	10
0	0.000	0.000	0.000	0.000	0.000	0.000	0.000	0.000	0.000	0.000
1	1.000	1.000	1.000	1.000	1.000	1.000	1.000	1.000	1.000	1.000
2	2.030	2.035	2.040	2.045	2.050	2.060	2.070	2.080	2.090	2.100
3	3.091	3.106	3.122	3.137	3.153	3.184	3.215	3.246	3.278	3.310
4	4.184	4.215	4.246	4.278	4.310	4.375	4.440	4.506	4.573	4.641
5	5.309	5.362	5.416	5.471	5.526	5.637	5.751	5.867	5.985	6.105
6	6.468	6.550	6.633	6.717	6.802	6.975	7.153	7.336	7.523	7.716
7	7.662	7.779	7.898	8.019	8.142	8.394	8.654	8.923	9.200	9.487
8	8.892	9.052	9.214	9.380	9.549	9.897	10.26	10.64	11.03	11.44
9	10.16	10.37	10.58	10.80	11.03	11.49	11.98	12.49	13.02	13.58
10	11.46	11.73	12.01	12.29	12.58	13.18	13.82	14.49	15.19	15.94
11	12.81	13.14	13.49	13.84	14.21	14.97	15.78	16.65	17.56	18.53
12	14.19	14.60	15.03	15.46	15.92	16.87	17.89	18.98	20.14	21.38
13	15.62	16.11	16.63	17.16	17.71	18.88	20.14	21.50	22.95	24.52
14	17.09	17.68	18.29	18.93	19.60	21.02	22.55	24.21	26.02	27.97
15	18.60	19.30	20.02	20.78	21.58	23.28	25.13	27.15	29.36	31.77
16	20.16	20.97	21.82	22.72	23.66	25.67	27.89	30.32	33.00	35.95
17	21.76	22.71	23.70	24.74	25.84	28.21	30.84	33.75	36.97	40.54
18	23.41	24.50	25.65	26.86	28.13	30.91	34.00	37.45	41.30	45.60
19	25.12	26.36	27.67	29.06	30.54	33.76	37.38	41.45	46.02	51.16
20	26.87	28.28	29.78	31.37	33.07	36.79	41.00	45.76	51.16	57.27
21	28.68	30.27	31.97	33.78	35.72	39.99	44.87	50.42	56.76	64.00
22	30.54	32.33	34.25	36.30	38.51	43.39	49.01	55.46	62.87	71.40
23	32.45	34.46	36.62	38.94	41.43	47.00	53.44	60.89	69.53	79.54
24	34.43	36.67	39.08	41.69	44.50	50.82	58.18	66.76	76.79	88.50
25	36.46	38.95	41.65	44.57	47.73	54.86	63.25	73.11	84.70	98.35
26	38.55	41.31	44.31	47.57	51.11	59.16	68.68	79.95	93.32	109.2
27	40.71	43.76	47.08	50.71	54.67	63.71	74.48	87.35	102.7	121.1
28	42.93	46.29	49.97	53.99	58.40	68.53	80.70	95.34	113.0	134.2
29	45.22	48.91	52.97	57.42	62.32	73.64	87.35	104.0	124.1	148.6
30	47.58	51.62	56.08	61.01	66.44	79.06	94.46	113.3	136.3	164.5
31	50.00	54.43	59.33	64.75	70.76	84.80	102.1	123.3	149.6	181.9
32	52.50	57.33	62.70	68.67	75.30	90.89	110.2	134.2	164.0	201.1
33	55.08	60.34	66.21	72.76	80.06	97.34	118.9	146.0	179.8	222.3
34	57.73	63.45	69.86	77.03	85.07	104.2	128.3	158.6	197.0	245.5
35	60.46	66.67	73.65	81.50	90.32	111.4	138.2	172.3	215.7	271.0
36	63.28	70.01	77.60	86.16	95.84	119.1	148.9	187.1	236.1	299.1
37	66.17	73.46	81.70	91.04	101.6	127.3	160.3	203.1	258.4	330.0
38	69.16	77.03	85.97	96.14	107.7	135.9	172.6	220.3	282.6	364.0
39	72.23	80.72	90.41	101.5	114.1	145.1	185.6	238.9	309.1	401.4
40	75.40	84.55	95.03	107.0	120.8	154.8	199.6	259.1	337.9	442.6
41	78.66	88.51	99.83	112.8	127.8	165.0	214.6	280.8	369.3	487.9
42	82.02	92.61	104.8	118.9	135.2	176.0	230.6	304.2	403.5	537.6
43	85.48	96.85	110.0	125.3	143.0	187.5	247.8	329.6	440.8	592.4
44	89.05	101.2	115.4	131.9	151.1	199.8	266.1	356.9	481.5	652.6
45	92.72	105.8	121.0	138.8	159.7	212.7	285.7	386.5	525.9	718.9
46	96.50	110.5	126.9	146.1	168.7	226.5	306.8	418.4	574.2	791.8
47	100.4	115.4	132.9	153.7	178.1	241.1	329.2	452.9	626.9	872.0
48	104.4	120.4	139.3	161.6	188.0	256.6	353.3	490.1	684.3	960.2
49	108.5	125.6	145.8	169.9	198.4	273.0	379.0	530.3	746.9	1057

$$\frac{\left(1+\frac{r}{100}\right)^{n}-1}{\frac{r}{100}\left(1+\frac{r}{100}\right)^{n}}$$

XXVI. PRESENT VALUE OF AN ANNUITY PAID AT THE END OF EACH YEAR.

n	3	3½	4	4½	5	6	7	8	9	10
0	0.000	0.000	0.000	0.000	0.000	0.000	0.000	0.000	0.000	0.000
1	.9709	.9662	.9615	.9569	.9524	.9434	.9346	.9259	.9174	.9091
2	1.913	1.900	1.886	1.873	1.859	1.833	1.808	1.783	1.759	1.736
3	2.829	2.802	2.775	2.749	2.723	2.673	2.624	2.577	2.531	2.487
4	3.717	3.673	3.630	3.588	3.546	3.465	3.387	3.312	3.240	3.170
5	4.580	4.515	4.452	4.390	4.329	4.212	4.100	3.993	3.890	3.791
6	5.417	5.329	5.242	5.158	5.076	4.917	4.767	4.623	4.486	4.355
7	6.230	6.115	6.002	5.893	5.786	5.582	5.389	5.206	5.033	4.868
8	7.020	6.874	6.733	6.596	6.463	6.210	5.971	5.747	5.535	5.335
9	7.786	7.608	7.435	7.269	7.108	6.802	6.515	6.247	5.995	5.759
10	8.530	8.317	8.111	7.913	7.722	7.360	7.024	6.710	6.418	6.145
11	9.253	9.002	8.760	8.529	8.306	7.887	7.499	7.139	6.805	6.495
12	9.954	9.663	9.385	9.119	8.863	8.384	7.943	7.536	7.161	6.814
13	10.63	10.30	9.986	9.683	9.394	8.853	8.358	7.904	7.487	7.103
14	11.30	10.92	10.56	10.22	9.899	9.295	8.745	8.244	7.786	7.367
15	11.94	11.52	11.12	10.74	10.38	9.712	9.108	8.559	8.061	7.606
16	12.56	12.09	11.65	11.23	10.84	10.11	9.447	8.851	8.313	7.824
17	13.17	12.65	12.17	11.71	11.27	10.48	9.763	9.122	8.544	8.022
18	13.75	13.19	12.66	12.16	11.69	10.83	10.06	9.372	8.756	8.201
19	14.32	13.71	13.13	12.59	12.09	11.16	10.34	9.604	8.950	8.365
20	14.88	14.21	13.59	13.01	12.46	11.47	10.59	9.818	9.129	8.514
21	15.42	14.70	14.03	13.40	12.82	11.76	10.84	10.02	9.292	8.649
22	15.94	15.17	14.45	13.78	13.16	12.04	11.06	10.20	9.442	8.772
23	16.44	15.62	14.86	14.15	13.49	12.30	11.27	10.37	9.580	8.883
24	16.94	16.06	15.25	14.50	13.80	12.55	11.47	10.53	9.707	8.985
25	17.41	16.48	15.62	14.83	14.09	12.78	11.65	10.67	9.823	9.077
26	17.88	16.89	15.98	15.15	14.38	13.00	11.83	10.81	9.929	9.161
27	18.33	17.29	16.33	15.45	14.64	13.21	11.99	10.94	10.03	9.237
28	18.76	17.67	16.66	15.74	14.90	13.41	12.14	11.05	10.12	9.307
29	19.19	18.04	16.98	16.02	15.14	13.59	12.28	11.16	10.20	9.370
30	19.60	18.39	17.29	16.29	15.37	13.76	12.41	11.26	10.27	9.427
31	20.00	18.74	17.59	16.54	15.59	13.93	12.53	11.35	10.34	9.479
32	20.39	19.07	17.87	16.79	15.80	14.08	12.65	11.43	10.41	9.526
33	20.77	19.39	18.15	17.02	16.00	14.23	12.75	11.51	10.46	9.569
34	21.13	19.70	18.41	17.25	16.19	14.37	12.85	11.59	10.52	9.609
35	21.49	20.00	18.66	17.46	16.37	14.50	12.95	11.65	10.57	9.644
36	21.83	20.29	18.91	17.67	16.55	14.62	13.04	11.72	10.61	9.677
37	22.17	20.57	19.14	17.86	16.71	14.74	13.12	11.78	10.65	9.706
38	22.49	20.84	19.37	18.05	16.87	14.85	13.19	11.83	10.69	9.733
39	22.81	21.10	19.58	18.23	17.02	14.95	13.26	11.88	10.73	9.757
40	23.11	21.36	19.79	18.40	17.16	15.05	13.33	11.92	10.76	9.779
41	23.41	21.60	19.99	18.57	17.29	15.14	13.39	11.97	10.79	9.799
42	23.70	21.83	20.19	18.72	17.42	15.22	13.45	12.01	10.81	9.817
43	23.98	22.06	20.37	18.87	17.55	15.31	13.51	12.04	10.84	9.834
44	24.25	22.28	20.55	19.02	17.66	15.38	13.56	12.08	10.86	9.849
45	24.52	22.50	20.72	19.16	17.77	15.46	13.61	12.11	10.88	9.863
46	24.78	22.70	20.88	19.29	17.88	15.52	13.65	12.14	10.90	9.875
47	25.02	22.90	21.04	19.41	17.98	15.59	13.69	12.16	10.92	9.887
48	25.27	23.09	21.20	19.54	18.08	15.65	13.73	12.19	10.93	9.897
49	25.50	23.28	21.34	19.65	18.17	15.71	13.77	12.21	10.95	9.906

XXVII. AMOUNT OF AN AN-
NUITY WHEN PAID AT THE
BEGINNING OF EACH YEAR.
$$\left(1+\frac{r}{100}\right)\frac{\left(1+\frac{r}{100}\right)^{n}-1}{\frac{r}{100}}$$

n	3	3½	4	4½	5	6	7	8	9	10
0	1.000	1.000	1.000	1.000	1.000	1.000	1.000	1.000	1.000	1.000
1	1.030	1.035	1.040	1.045	1.050	1.060	1.070	1.080	1.090	1.100
2	2.091	2.106	2.122	2.137	2.153	2.184	2.215	2.246	2.278	2.310
3	3.184	3.215	3.246	3.278	3.310	3.375	3.440	3.506	3.573	3.641
4	4.309	4.362	4.416	4.471	4.526	4.637	4.751	4.867	4.985	5.105
5	5.468	5.550	5.633	5.717	5.802	5.975	6.153	6.336	6.523	6.716
6	6.662	6.779	6.898	7.019	7.142	7.394	7.654	7.923	8.200	8.487
7	7.892	8.052	8.214	8.380	8.549	8.897	9.260	9.637	10.03	10.44
8	9.159	9.368	9.583	9.802	10.03	10.49	10.98	11.49	12.02	12.58
9	10.46	10.73	11.01	11.29	11.58	12.18	12.82	13.49	14.19	14.94
10	11.81	12.14	12.49	12.84	13.21	13.97	14.78	15.65	16.56	17.53
11	13.19	13.60	14.03	14.46	14.92	15.87	16.89	17.98	19.14	20.38
12	14.62	15.11	15.63	16.16	16.71	17.88	19.14	20.50	21.95	23.52
13	16.09	16.68	17.29	17.93	18.60	20.02	21.55	23.21	25.02	26.97
14	17.60	18.30	19.02	19.78	20.58	22.28	24.13	26.15	28.36	30.77
15	19.16	19.97	20.82	21.72	22.66	24.67	26.89	29.32	32.00	34.95
16	20.76	21.71	22.70	23.74	24.84	27.21	29.84	32.75	35.97	39.54
17	22.41	23.50	24.65	25.86	27.13	29.91	33.00	36.45	40.30	44.60
18	24.12	25.36	26.67	28.06	29.54	32.76	36.38	40.45	45.02	50.16
19	25.87	27.28	28.78	30.37	32.07	35.79	40.00	44.76	50.16	56.27
20	27.68	29.27	30.97	32.78	34.72	38.99	43.87	49.42	55.76	63.00
21	29.54	31.33	33.25	35.30	37.51	42.39	48.01	54.46	61.87	70.40
22	31.45	33.46	35.62	37.94	40.43	46.00	52.44	59.89	68.53	78.54
23	33.43	35.67	38.08	40.69	43.50	49.82	57.18	65.76	75.79	87.50
24	35.46	37.95	40.65	43.57	46.73	53.86	62.25	72.11	83.70	97.35
25	37.55	40.31	43.31	46.57	50.11	58.16	67.68	78.95	92.32	108.2
26	39.71	42.76	46.08	49.71	53.67	62.71	73.48	86.35	101.7	120.1
27	41.93	45.29	48.97	52.99	57.40	67.53	79.70	94.34	112.0	133.2
28	44.22	47.91	51.97	56.42	61.32	72.64	86.35	103.0	123.1	147.6
29	46.58	50.62	55.08	60.01	65.44	78.06	93.46	112.3	135.3	163.5
30	49.00	53.43	58.33	63.75	69.76	83.80	101.1	122.3	148.6	180.9
31	51.50	56.33	61.70	67.67	74.30	89.89	109.2	133.2	163.0	200.1
32	54.08	59.34	65.21	71.76	79.06	96.34	117.9	145.0	178.8	221.3
33	56.73	62.45	68.86	76.03	84.07	103.2	127.3	157.6	196.0	244.5
34	59.46	65.67	72.65	80.50	89.32	110.4	137.2	171.3	214.7	270.0
35	62.28	69.01	76.60	85.16	94.84	118.1	147.9	186.1	235.1	298.1
36	65.17	72.46	80.70	90.04	100.6	126.3	159.3	202.1	257.4	329.0
37	68.16	76.03	84.97	95.14	106.7	134.9	171.6	219.3	281.6	363.0
38	71.23	79.72	89.41	100.5	113.1	144.1	184.6	237.9	308.1	400.4
39	74.40	83.55	94.03	106.0	119.8	153.8	198.6	258.1	336.9	441.6
40	77.66	87.51	98.83	111.8	126.8	164.0	213.6	279.8	368.3	486.9
41	81.02	91.61	103.8	117.9	134.2	175.0	229.6	303.2	402.5	536.6
42	84.48	95.85	109.0	124.3	142.0	186.5	246.8	328.6	439.8	591.4
43	88.05	100.2	114.4	130.9	150.1	198.8	265.1	355.9	480.5	651.6
44	91.72	104.8	120.0	137.8	158.7	211.7	284.7	385.5	524.9	717.9
45	95.50	109.5	125.9	145.1	167.7	225.5	305.8	417.4	573.2	790.8
46	99.40	114.4	131.9	152.7	177.1	240.1	328.2	451.9	625.9	871.0
47	103.4	119.4	138.3	160.6	187.0	255.6	352.3	489.1	683.3	959.2
48	107.5	124.6	144.8	168.9	197.4	272.0	378.0	529.3	745.9	1056
49	111.8	130.0	151.7	177.5	208.3	289.3	405.5	572.8	814.1	1163

$$\frac{1000\left(1+\dfrac{r}{100}\right)^{n}\dfrac{r}{100}}{\left(1+\dfrac{r}{100}\right)^{n}-1}$$

n	3	3½	4	4½	5	6	7	8	9	10
1	1030	1035	1040	1045	1050	1060	1070	1080	1090	1100
2	522.6	526.4	530.2	534.0	537.8	545.4	553.1	560.8	568.5	576.2
3	353.5	356.9	360.3	363.8	367.2	374.1	381.1	388.0	395.1	402.1
4	269.0	272.3	275.5	278.7	282.0	288.6	295.2	301.9	308.7	315.5
5	218.4	221.5	224.6	227.8	231.0	237.4	243.9	250.5	257.1	263.8
6	184.6	187.7	190.8	193.9	197.0	203.4	209.8	216.3	222.9	229.6
7	160.5	163.5	166.6	169.7	172.8	179.1	185.6	192.1	198.7	205.4
8	142.5	145.5	148.5	151.6	154.7	161.0	167.5	174.0	180.7	187.4
9	128.4	131.4	134.5	137.6	140.7	147.0	153.5	160.1	166.8	173.6
10	117.2	120.2	123.3	126.4	129.5	135.9	142.4	149.0	155.8	162.7
11	108.1	111.1	114.1	117.2	120.4	126.8	133.4	140.1	146.9	154.0
12	100.5	103.5	106.6	109.7	112.8	119.3	125.9	132.7	139.7	146.8
13	94.03	97.06	100.1	103.3	106.5	113.0	119.7	126.5	133.6	140.8
14	88.53	91.57	94.67	97.82	101.0	107.6	114.3	121.3	128.4	135.7
15	83.77	86.83	89.94	93.11	96.34	103.0	109.8	116.8	124.1	131.5
16	79.61	82.68	85.82	89.02	92.27	98.95	105.9	113.0	120.3	127.8
17	75.95	79.04	82.20	85.42	88.70	95.44	102.4	109.6	117.0	124.7
18	72.71	75.82	78.99	82.24	85.55	92.36	99.41	106.7	114.2	121.9
19	69.81	72.94	76.14	79.41	82.75	89.62	96.75	104.1	111.7	119.5
20	67.22	70.36	73.58	76.88	80.24	87.18	94.39	101.9	109.5	117.5
21	64.87	68.04	71.28	74.60	78.00	85.00	92.29	99.83	107.6	115.6
22	62.75	65.93	69.20	72.55	75.97	83.05	90.41	98.03	105.9	114.0
23	60.81	64.02	67.31	70.68	74.14	81.28	88.71	96.42	104.4	112.6
24	59.05	62.27	65.59	68.99	72.47	79.68	87.19	94.98	103.0	111.3
25	57.43	60.67	64.01	67.44	70.95	78.23	85.81	93.68	101.8	110.2
26	55.94	59.21	62.57	66.02	69.56	76.90	84.56	92.51	100.7	109.2
27	54.56	57.85	61.24	64.72	68.29	75.70	83.43	91.45	99.73	108.3
28	53.29	56.60	60.01	63.52	67.12	74.59	82.39	90.49	98.85	107.5
29	52.11	55.45	58.88	62.41	66.05	73.58	81.45	89.62	98.06	106.7
30	51.02	54.37	57.83	61.39	65.05	72.65	80.59	88.83	97.34	106.1
31	50.00	53.37	56.86	60.44	64.13	71.79	79.80	88.11	96.69	105.5
32	49.05	52.44	55.95	59.56	63.28	71.00	79.07	87.45	96.10	105.0
33	48.16	51.57	55.10	58.74	62.49	70.27	78.41	86.85	95.56	104.5
34	47.32	50.76	54.31	57.98	61.76	69.60	77.80	86.30	95.08	104.1
35	46.54	50.00	53.58	57.27	61.07	68.97	77.23	85.80	94.64	103.7
36	45.80	49.28	52.89	56.61	60.43	68.39	76.72	85.34	94.24	103.3
37	45.11	48.61	52.24	55.98	59.84	67.86	76.24	84.92	93.87	103.0
38	44.46	47.98	51.63	55.40	59.28	67.36	75.80	84.54	93.54	102.7
39	43.84	47.39	51.06	54.86	58.76	66.89	75.39	84.19	93.24	102.5
40	43.26	46.83	50.52	54.34	58.28	66.46	75.01	83.86	92.96	102.3
41	42.71	46.30	50.02	53.86	57.82	66.06	74.66	83.56	92.71	102.0
42	42.19	45.80	49.54	53.41	57.39	65.68	74.34	83.29	92.48	101.9
43	41.70	45.33	49.09	52.98	56.99	65.33	74.04	83.03	92.27	101.7
44	41.23	44.88	48.66	52.58	56.62	65.01	73.76	82.80	92.08	101.5
45	40.79	44.45	48.26	52.20	56.26	64.70	73.50	82.59	91.90	101.4
46	40.36	44.05	47.88	51.84	55.93	64.41	73.26	82.39	91.74	101.3
47	39.96	43.67	47.52	51.51	55.61	64.15	73.04	82.21	91.60	101.1
48	39.58	43.31	47.18	51.19	55.32	63.90	72.83	82.04	91.46	101.0
49	39.21	42.96	46.86	50.89	55.04	63.66	72.64	81.89	91.34	100.9

n	0				1				2				3				4			
	1	3	7	9	1	3	7	9	1	3	7	9	1	3	7	9	1	3	7	9
0	—	—	—	3	—	—	—	—	3	—	3	—	—	3	—	3	—	—	—	7
1	—	—	—	—	3	—	3	7	11	3	—	3	—	7	—	—	3	11	3	—
2	3	7	3	11	—	3	7	3	13	—	—	—	3	—	3	—	—	3	13	3
3	7	3	—	3	—	—	—	11	3	17	3	7	—	3	—	3	11	7	—	—
4	—	13	11	—	3	7	3	—	—	3	7	3	—	—	19	—	3	—	3	—
5	3	—	3	—	7	3	11	3	—	—	17	23	3	13	3	7	—	3	—	3
6	—	3	—	3	13	—	—	—	3	7	3	17	—	3	7	3	—	—	—	11
7	—	19	7	—	3	23	3	—	7	3	—	3	17	—	11	—	3	—	3	7
8	3	11	3	—	—	3	19	3	—	—	—	—	3	7	3	—	29	3	7	3
9	17	3	—	3	—	11	7	—	3	13	3	—	7	3	—	3	—	23	—	13
10	7	17	19	—	3	—	3	—	—	3	13	3	—	—	17	—	3	7	3	—
11	3	—	3	—	11	3	—	3	19	—	7	—	3	11	3	17	7	3	31	3
12	—	3	17	3	7	—	—	23	3	—	3	—	—	3	—	3	17	11	29	—
13	—	—	—	7	3	13	3	—	—	3	—	3	11	31	7	13	3	17	3	19
14	3	23	3	—	17	3	13	3	7	—	—	—	3	—	3	—	11	3	—	3
15	19	3	11	3	—	17	37	7	3	—	3	11	—	3	29	3	23	—	7	—
16	—	7	—	—	3	—	3	—	—	3	—	3	7	23	—	11	3	31	3	17
17	3	13	3	—	29	3	17	3	—	—	11	7	3	—	3	37	—	3	—	3
18	—	3	13	3	—	7	23	17	3	—	3	31	—	3	11	3	7	19	—	43
19	—	11	—	23	3	—	3	19	17	3	41	3	—	—	13	7	3	29	3	—
20	3	—	3	7	—	3	—	3	43	7	—	—	3	19	3	—	13	3	23	3
21	11	3	7	3	—	—	29	13	3	11	3	—	—	3	—	3	—	—	19	7
22	31	—	—	47	3	—	3	7	—	3	17	3	23	7	—	—	3	—	3	13
23	3	7	3	—	—	3	7	3	11	23	13	17	3	—	3	—	—	3	—	3
24	7	3	29	3	—	19	—	41	3	—	3	7	11	3	—	3	—	7	—	31
25	41	—	23	13	3	7	3	11	—	3	7	3	—	17	43	—	3	—	3	—
26	3	19	3	—	7	3	—	3	—	43	37	11	3	—	3	7	19	3	—	3
27	37	3	—	3	—	—	11	—	3	7	3	—	—	3	7	3	—	13	41	—
28	—	—	7	53	3	29	3	—	7	3	11	3	19	—	—	17	3	—	3	7
29	3	—	3	—	41	3	—	3	23	37	—	29	3	7	3	—	17	3	7	3
30	—	3	31	3	—	23	7	—	3	—	3	13	7	3	—	3	—	17	11	—
31	7	29	13	—	3	11	3	—	—	3	53	3	31	13	—	43	3	7	3	47
32	3	—	3	—	13	3	—	3	—	11	7	—	3	53	3	41	7	3	17	3
33	—	3	—	3	7	—	31	—	3	—	3	—	—	3	47	3	13	—	—	17
34	19	41	—	7	3	—	3	13	11	3	23	3	47	—	7	19	3	11	3	—
35	3	31	3	11	—	3	—	3	7	13	—	—	3	—	3	—	—	3	—	3
36	13	3	—	3	23	—	—	7	3	—	3	19	—	3	—	3	11	—	7	41
37	—	7	11	—	3	47	3	—	61	3	—	3	7	—	37	—	3	19	3	23
38	3	—	3	13	37	3	11	3	—	—	43	7	3	—	3	11	23	3	—	3
39	47	3	—	3	—	7	—	—	3	—	3	—	—	3	31	3	7	—	—	11
40	—	—	—	19	3	—	3	—	—	3	—	3	29	37	11	7	3	13	3	—
41	3	11	3	7	—	3	23	3	13	7	—	—	—	3	—	3	41	3	11	3
42	—	3	7	3	—	11	—	—	3	41	3	—	—	3	19	3	—	—	31	7
43	11	13	59	31	3	19	3	7	29	3	—	3	61	7	—	—	3	43	3	—
44	3	7	3	—	11	3	7	3	—	—	19	43	3	11	3	23	—	3	—	3
45	7	3	—	3	13	—	—	—	3	—	3	7	23	3	13	3	19	7	—	—
46	43	—	17	11	3	7	3	31	—	3	7	3	11	41	—	—	3	—	3	—
47	3	—	3	17	7	3	53	3	—	—	29	—	3	—	3	7	11	3	47	3
48	—	3	11	3	17	—	—	61	3	7	3	11	—	3	7	3	47	29	37	13
49	13	—	7	—	3	17	3	—	7	3	13	3	—	—	—	11	3	—	3	7

n	5				6				7				8				9			
	1	3	7	9	1	3	7	9	1	3	7	9	1	3	7	9	1	3	7	9
0	3	—	3	—	—	3	—	3	—	—	7	—	3	—	3	—	7	3	—	3
1	—	3	—	3	7	—	—	13	3	—	3	—	—	3	11	3	—	—	—	—
2	—	11	—	7	3	—	3	—	—	3	—	3	—	—	7	17	3	—	3	13
3	3	—	3	—	19	3	—	3	7	—	13	—	3	—	3	—	17	3	—	3
4	11	3	—	3	—	—	—	7	3	11	3	—	13	3	—	3	—	17	7	—
5	19	7	—	13	3	—	3	—	—	3	—	3	7	11	—	19	3	—	3	—
6	3	—	3	—	—	3	23	3	11	—	—	7	3	—	3	13	—	3	17	3
7	—	3	—	3	—	7	13	—	3	—	3	19	11	3	—	3	7	13	—	17
8	23	—	—	—	3	—	3	11	13	3	—	3	—	—	—	7	3	19	3	29
9	3	—	3	7	31	3	—	3	—	7	—	11	3	—	3	23	—	3	—	3
10	—	3	7	3	—	—	11	—	3	29	3	13	23	3	—	3	—	—	—	7
11	—	—	13	19	3	—	3	7	—	3	11	3	—	7	—	29	3	—	3	11
12	3	7	3	—	13	3	7	3	31	19	—	—	3	—	3	—	—	3	—	3
13	7	3	23	3	—	29	—	37	3	—	3	7	—	3	19	3	13	7	11	—
14	—	—	31	—	3	7	3	13	—	3	7	3	—	—	—	—	3	—	3	—
15	3	—	3	—	7	3	—	3	—	11	19	—	3	—	3	7	37	3	—	3
16	13	3	—	3	11	—	—	—	3	7	3	23	41	3	7	3	19	—	—	—
17	17	—	7	—	3	41	3	29	7	3	—	3	13	—	—	—	3	11	3	7
18	3	17	3	11	—	3	—	3	—	—	—	—	3	7	3	—	31	3	7	3
19	—	3	19	3	37	13	7	11	3	—	3	—	7	3	—	3	11	—	—	—
20	7	—	11	29	3	—	3	—	19	3	31	3	—	—	—	—	3	7	3	—
21	3	—	3	17	—	3	11	3	13	41	7	—	3	37	3	11	7	3	13	3
22	—	3	37	3	7	31	—	—	3	—	3	43	—	3	—	3	29	—	—	11
23	—	13	—	7	3	17	3	23	—	3	—	3	—	—	7	—	3	—	3	—
24	3	11	3	—	23	3	—	3	7	—	—	37	3	13	3	19	47	3	11	3
25	—	3	—	3	13	11	17	7	3	31	3	—	29	3	13	3	—	—	7	23
26	11	7	—	—	3	—	3	17	—	3	—	3	7	—	—	—	3	—	3	—
27	3	—	3	31	11	3	—	3	17	47	—	7	3	11	3	—	—	3	—	3
28	—	3	—	3	—	7	47	19	3	13	3	—	43	3	—	3	7	11	—	13
29	13	—	—	11	3	—	3	—	—	3	13	3	11	19	29	7	3	41	3	—
30	3	43	3	7	—	3	—	3	37	7	17	—	3	—	3	—	11	3	19	3
31	23	3	7	3	29	—	—	—	3	19	3	11	—	3	—	3	—	31	23	7
32	—	—	—	—	3	13	3	7	—	3	29	3	17	7	19	11	3	37	3	—
33	3	7	3	—	—	3	7	3	—	—	11	31	3	17	3	—	—	3	43	3
34	7	3	—	3	—	—	—	—	3	23	3	7	59	3	11	3	—	7	13	—
35	53	11	—	—	3	7	3	43	—	3	7	3	—	—	17	37	3	—	3	59
36	3	13	3	—	7	3	19	3	—	—	—	13	3	29	3	7	—	3	—	3
37	11	3	13	3	—	53	—	—	3	7	3	—	19	3	7	3	17	—	—	29
38	—	—	7	17	3	—	3	53	7	3	—	3	—	11	13	—	3	17	3	7
39	3	59	3	37	17	3	—	3	11	29	41	23	3	7	3	—	13	3	7	3
40	—	3	—	3	31	17	7	13	3	—	3	—	7	3	61	3	—	—	17	—
41	7	—	—	—	3	23	3	11	43	3	—	3	37	47	53	59	3	7	3	13
42	3	—	3	—	—	3	17	3	—	—	7	11	3	—'	3	—	7	3	—	3
43	19	3	—	3	7	—	11	17	3	—	3	29	13	3	41	3	—	23	—	53
44	—	61	—	7	3	—	3	41	17	3	11	3	—	—	7	67	3	—	3	11
45	3	29	3	47	—	3	—	3	7	17	23	19	3	—	3	13	—	3	—	3
46	—	3	—	3	59	—	13	7	3	—	3	—	31	3	43	3	—	13	7	37
47	—	7	67	—	3	11	3	19	13	3	17	3	7	—	—	—	3	—	3	—
48	3	23	3	43	—	3	31	3	—	11	—	7	3	19	3	—	67	3	59	3
49	—	3	—	3	11	7	—	—	3	—	3	13	17	3	—	3	7	—	19	—

n	0				1				2				3				4			
	1	3	7	9	1	3	7	9	1	3	7	9	1	3	7	9	1	3	7	9
50	3	—	3	—	—	3	29	3	—	—	11	47	3	7	3	—	71	3	7	3
51	—	3	—	3	19	—	7	—	3	47	3	23	7	3	11	3	53	37	—	19
52	7	11	41	—	3	13	3	17	23	3	—	3	—	—	—	13	3	7	3	29
53	3	—	3	—	47	3	13	3	17	—	7	73	3	—	3	19	7	3	—	3
54	11	3	—	3	7	—	—	—	3	11	3	61	—	3	—	3	—	—	13	—
55	—	—	—	7	3	37	3	—	—	3	—	3	—	11	7	29	3	23	3	31
56	3	13	3	71	31	3	41	3	7	—	17	13	3	43	3	—	—	3	—	3
57	—	3	13	3	—	29	—	7	3	59	3	17	11	3	—	3	—	—	7	—
58	—	7	—	37	3	—	3	11	—	3	—	3	7	19	13	—	3	—	3	—
59	3	—	3	19	23	3	61	3	31	—	—	7	3	17	3	—	13	3	19	3
60	17	3	—	3	—	7	11	13	3	19	3	—	37	3	—	3	7	—	—	23
61	—	17	31	41	3	—	3	29	—	3	11	3	—	—	17	7	3	—	3	11
62	3	—	3	7	—	3	—	3	—	7	13	—	3	23	3	17	79	3	—	3
63	—	3	7	3	—	59	—	71	3	—	3	—	13	3	—	3	17	—	11	7
64	37	19	43	13	3	11	3	7	—	3	—	3	59	7	41	47	3	17	3	—
65	3	7	3	23	17	3	7	3	—	11	61	—	3	47	3	13	31	3	—	3
66	7	3	—	3	11	17	13	—	3	37	3	7	19	3	—	3	29	7	17	61
67	—	—	19	—	3	7	3	—	11	3	7	3	53	—	—	23	3	11	3	17
68	3	—	3	11	7	3	17	3	19	—	—	—	3	—	3	7	—	3	41	3
69	67	3	—	3	—	31	—	11	3	7	3	13	29	3	7	3	11	53	—	—
70	—	47	7	43	3	—	3	—	7	3	—	3	79	13	31	—	3	—	3	7
71	3	—	3	—	13	3	11	3	—	17	—	—	3	7	3	11	37	3	7	3
72	19	3	—	3	—	—	7	—	3	31	3	—	7	3	—	3	13	—	—	11
73	7	67	—	—	3	71	3	13	—	3	17	3	—	—	11	41	3	7	3	—
74	3	11	3	31	—	3	—	3	41	13	7	17	3	—	3	43	7	3	11	3
75	13	3	—	3	7	11	—	73	3	—	3	—	17	3	—	3	—	19	—	—
76	11	—	—	7	3	23	3	19	—	3	29	3	13	17	7	—	3	—	3	—
77	3	—	3	13	11	3	—	3	7	—	—	59	3	11	3	71	—	3	61	3
78	29	3	37	3	73	13	—	7	3	—	3	—	41	3	17	3	—	11	7	47
79	—	7	—	11	3	41	3	—	89	3	—	3	7	—	—	17	3	13	3	—
80	3	53	3	—	—	3	—	3	13	71	23	7	3	29	3	—	11	3	13	3
81	—	3	11	3	—	7	—	23	3	—	3	11	47	3	79	3	7	17	—	29
82	59	13	29	—	3	43	3	—	—	3	19	3	—	—	—	7	3	—	3	73
83	3	19	3	7	—	3	—	3	53	7	11	—	3	13	3	31	19	3	17	3
84	31	3	7	3	13	47	19	—	3	—	3	—	—	3	11	3	23	—	—	7
85	—	11	47	67	3	—	3	7	—	3	—	3	19	7	—	—	3	—	3	83
86	3	7	3	—	79	3	7	3	37	—	—	—	3	89	3	53	—	3	—	3
87	7	3	—	3	31	—	23	—	3	11	3	7	—	3	—	3	—	7	—	13
88	13	—	—	23	3	7	3	—	—	3	7	3	—	11	—	—	3	37	3	—
89	3	29	3	59	7	3	37	3	11	—	79	—	3	—	3	7	—	3	23	3
90	—	3	—	3	—	—	71	29	3	7	3	—	11	3	7	3	—	—	83	—
91	19	—	7	—	3	13	3	11	7	3	—	3	23	—	—	13	3	41	3	7
92	3	—	3	—	61	3	13	3	—	23	—	11	3	7	3	—	—	3	7	3
93	71	3	41	3	—	67	7	—	3	—	3	19	7	3	—	3	—	—	13	—
94	7	—	23	97	3	—	3	—	—	3	11	3	—	—	—	—	3	7	3	11
95	3	13	3	37	—	3	31	3	—	89	7	13	3	—	3	—	7	3	—	3
96	—	3	13	3	7	—	59	—	3	—	3	—	—	3	23	3	31	—	11	—
97	89	31	17	7	3	11	3	—	—	3	71	3	37	—	7	—	3	—	3	—
98	3	—	3	17	—	3	—	3	7	11	31	—	3	—	3	—	13	3	43	3
99	—	3	—	3	11	23	47	7	3	—	3	—	—	3	19	3	—	61	7	—

n	5				6				7				8				9			
	1	3	7	9	1	3	7	9	1	3	7	9	1	3	7	9	1	3	7	9
50	—	31	13	—	3	61	3	37	11	3	—	3	—	13	—	7	3	11	3	—
51	3	—	3	7	13	3	—	3	—	7	31	—	3	71	3	—	29	3	—	3
52	59	3	7	3	—	19	23	11	3	—	3	—	—	3	17	3	11	67	—	7
53	—	53	11	23	3	31	3	7	41	3	19	3	—	7	—	17	3	—	3	—
54	3	7	3	53	43	3	7	3	—	13	—	—	3	—	3	11	17	3	23	3
55	7	3	—	3	67	—	19	—	3	—	3	7	—	3	37	3	—	7	29	11
56	—	—	—	—	3	7	3	—	53	3	7	3	13	—	11	—	3	—	3	41
57	3	11	3	13	7	3	73	3	29	23	53	—	3	—	3	7	—	3	11	3
58	—	3	—	3	—	11	—	—	3	7	3	—	—	3	7	3	43	71	—	17
59	11	—	7	59	3	67	3	47	7	3	43	3	—	31	—	53	3	13	3	7
60	3	—	3	73	11	3	—	3	13	—	59	—	3	7	3	—	—	3	7	3
61	—	3	47	3	61	—	7	31	3	—	3	37	7	3	23	3	41	11	—	—
62	7	13	—	11	3	—	3	—	—	3	—	3	11	61	—	19	3	7	3	—
63	3	—	3	—	—	3	—	3	23	—	7	—	3	13	3	—	7	3	—	3
64	—	3	11	3	7	23	29	—	3	—	3	11	—	3	13	3	—	43	73	67
65	—	—	79	7	3	—	3	—	—	3	—	3	—	29	7	11	3	19	3	—
66	3	—	3	—	—	3	59	3	7	—	11	—	3	41	3	—	—	3	37	3
67	43	3	29	3	—	—	67	7	3	13	3	—	—	3	11	3	—	—	7	13
68	13	7	—	19	3	—	3	—	—	3	13	3	7	—	71	83	3	61	3	—
69	3	17	3	—	—	3	—	3	—	19	—	7	3	—	3	29	—	3	—	3
70	11	3	—	3	23	7	37	—	3	11	3	—	73	3	19	3	7	41	47	31
71	—	23	17	—	3	13	3	67	71	3	—	3	43	11	—	7	3	—	3	23
72	3	—	3	7	53	3	13	3	11	7	19	29	3	—	3	37	23	3	—	3
73	—	3	7	3	17	37	53	—	3	73	3	47	11	3	83	3	19	—	13	7
74	—	29	—	—	3	17	3	7	31	3	—	3	—	7	—	—	3	59	3	—
75	3	7	3	—	—	3	7	3	67	—	—	11	3	—	3	—	—	3	71	3
76	7	3	13	3	47	79	11	—	3	—	3	7	—	3	—	3	—	7	43	—
77	23	—	—	—	3	7	3	17	19	3	7	3	31	43	13	—	3	—	3	11
78	3	—	3	29	7	3	—	3	17	—	—	—	—	3	7	3	13	3	53	3
79	—	3	73	3	19	—	31	13	3	7	3	79	23	3	7	3	61	—	11	19
80	83	—	7	—	3	11	3	—	7	3	41	3	—	59	—	—	3	—	3	7
81	3	31	3	41	—	3	—	3	—	11	13	—	3	7	3	19	—	3	7	3
82	37	3	23	3	11	—	7	—	3	—	3	17	7	3	—	3	—	—	—	43
83	7	—	61	13	3	—	3	—	11	3	—	3	17	83	—	—	3	7	3	37
84	3	79	3	11	—	3	—	3	43	37	7	61	3	17	3	13	7	3	29	3
85	17	3	43	3	7	—	13	11	3	—	3	23	—	3	31	3	11	13	—	—
86	41	17	11	7	3	—	3	—	13	3	—	3	—	19	7	—	3	—	3	—
87	3	—	3	19	—	3	11	3	7	31	67	—	3	—	3	11	59	3	19	3
88	53	3	17	3	—	—	—	7	3	19	3	13	83	3	—	3	17	—	7	11
89	—	7	13	17	3	—	3	—	—	3	47	3	7	13	11	89	3	17	3	—
90	3	11	3	—	13	3	—	3	47	43	29	7	3	31	3	61	—	3	11	3
91	—	3	—	3	—	7	89	53	3	—	3	67	—	3	—	3	7	29	17	—
92	11	19	—	47	3	59	3	13	73	3	—	3	—	—	37	7	3	—	3	17
93	3	47	3	7	11	3	17	3	—	7	—	83	3	11	3	41	—	3	—	3
94	13	3	7	3	—	—	—	17	3	—	3	—	19	3	53	3	—	11	—	7
95	—	41	19	11	3	73	3	7	17	3	61	3	11	7	—	43	3	53	3	29
96	3	7	3	13	—	3	7	3	19	17	—	—	3	23	3	—	11	3	—	3
97	7	3	11	3	43	13	—	—	3	29	3	7	—	3	—	3	—	7	97	41
98	—	59	—	—	3	7	3	71	—	3	7	3	41	—	—	11	3	13	3	19
99	3	37	3	23	7	3	—	3	13	—	11	17	3	67	3	7	97	3	13	3

$$e^n$$

n	0	1	2	3	4	5	6	7	8	9
.0	1.000	1.010	1.020	1.030	1.041	1.051	1.062	1.073	1.083	1.094
.1	1.105	1.116	1.127	1.139	1.150	1.162	1.174	1.185	1.197	1.209
.2	1.221	1.234	1.246	1.259	1.271	1.284	1.297	1.310	1.323	1.336
.3	1.350	1.363	1.377	1.391	1.405	1.419	1.433	1.448	1.462	1.477
.4	1.492	1.507	1.522	1.537	1.553	1.568	1.584	1.600	1.616	1.632
.5	1.649	1.665	1.682	1.699	1.716	1.733	1.751	1.768	1.786	1.804
.6	1.822	1.840	1.859	1.878	1.896	1.916	1.935	1.954	1.974	1.994
.7	2.014	2.034	2.054	2.075	2.096	2.117	2.138	2.160	2.181	2.203
.8	2.226	2.248	2.270	2.293	2.316	2.340	2.363	2.387	2.411	2.435
.9	2.460	2.484	2.509	2.535	2.560	2.586	2.612	2.638	2.664	2.691
1.	2.718	3.004	3.320	3.669	4.055	4.482	4.953	5.474	6.050	6.686
2.	7.389	8.166	9.025	9.974	11.02	12.18	13.46	14.88	16.44	18.17
3.	20.09	22.20	24.53	27.11	29.96	33.12	36.60	40.45	44.70	49.40
4.	54.60	60.34	66.69	73.70	81.45	90.02	99.48	109.9	121.5	134.3
5.	148.4	164.0	181.3	200.3	221.4	244.7	270.4	298.9	330.3	365.0
6.	403.4	445.9	492.7	544.6	601.8	665.1	735.1	812.4	897.8	992.3
7.	1097	1212	1339	1480	1636	1808	1998	2208	2441	2697
8.	2981	3294	3641	4024	4447	4915	5432	6003	6634	7332
9.	8103	8955	9897	10938	12088	13360	14765	16318	18034	19930

$$e^{-n}$$

n	0	1	2	3	4	5	6	7	8	9
.0	1.000	*990	*980	*970	*961	*951	*942	*932	*923	*914
.1	0.905	896	887	878	869	861	852	844	835	827
.2	0.819	811	803	795	787	779	771	763	756	748
.3	0.741	733	726	719	712	705	698	691	684	677
.4	0.670	664	657	651	644	638	631	625	619	613
.5	0.607	600	595	589	583	577	571	566	560	554
.6	0.549	543	538	533	527	522	517	512	507	502
.7	0.497	492	487	482	477	472	468	463	458	454
.8	0.449	445	440	436	432	427	423	419	415	411
.9	0.407	403	399	395	391	387	383	379	375	372
1.	0.368	333	301	273	247	223	202	183	165	150
2.	0.135	122	111	100	*907	*821	*743	*672	*608	*550
3.	0.0498	450	408	369	334	302	273	247	224	202
4.	0.0183	166	150	136	123	111	101	*910	*823	*745
5.	0.00674	610	552	499	452	409	370	335	303	274
6.	0.00248	224	203	184	166	150	136	123	111	101
7.	0.000912	825	747	676	611	553	501	453	410	371
8.	0.000335	304	275	249	225	203	184	167	151	136
9.	0.000123	112	101	091	083	075	068	061	055	050

n	ne	$n\frac{1}{e}$	$e^{\frac{1}{n}}$	$e^{-\frac{1}{n}}$	$e^{\frac{n\pi}{2}}$	$e^{-\frac{n\pi}{2}}$
1	2.718282	.367879	2.718	.368	4.811	.208
2	5.436564	.735759	1.649	.607	23.14	.0432
3	8.154845	1.103638	1.396	.717	111.3	.00898
4	10.873127	1.471518	1.284	.779	535.5	.00187
5	13.591409	1.839397	1.221	.819	2576	.000388
6	16.309691	2.207277	1.181	.847	12392	.0000807
7	19.027973	2.575156	1.154	.867	59610	.0000168
8	21.746255	2.943036	1.133	.883	286752	.00000349
9	24.464536	3.310915	1.118	.895	1379406	.000000725

EXPLANATION OF TABLES.

THROUGHOUT these tables the figures of the argument are printed in thick type, the initial figures being printed in the left-hand column, and the terminal figures in the top row. The entry is found in the intersection of the row of the initial figures with the column of the terminal figure. A bar below a terminal 5 or 0 shows that the final 5 has been increased; hence, when the entry is further contracted, the terminal figure ought not to be increased by one.

I. Common Logarithms, pp. 2-5.

Pages 2 and 3 give the logarithm to four places of any sequence of three significant figures. The column headed d gives the difference between the last logarithm of the row and the first logarithm of the next row; it facilitates the finding of the difference between any two successive logarithms in the row. The small table at the bottom of page 3 gives the proportional parts of the tabular differences from 4 to 23. The tabular difference is printed in the top row, and the tenths in the left-hand column.

Pages 4 and 5 give the logarithms of any sequence of 4 figures from 1000 to 1900. The proportional parts of the tabular differences are given in the right column; only the difference is printed, the tenth being understood from the location of the proportional part.

The small table at the bottom of page 5 gives the logarithm to six places of the numbers 1.000 to 1.100 which occur in calculations of interest. The initial pair of figures are given only for the 0 entry and are understood for the remaining entries of the row; unless an asterisk is printed in front, which indicates that the initial figures are those printed in front of the next row.

Given a number to find its logarithm, or, to use the table directly.

The characteristic or integral part of the required logarithm is obtained by counting the number of places by which the first figure of the number is removed to the left or to the right of the unit's place; if to the left, the characteristic is positive; if to the right, negative. Thus the characteristic of 1234 is 3, while that of .01234 is $\bar{2}$.

The mantissa, or fractional part of the required logarithm, is obtained from the table thus. If the number has not more than two significant figures, then the mantissa is found in the column headed 0. If there are three significant figures, the mantissa is found in the intersection of the row for the first two figures with the column headed by the third figure. For example, the mantissa of 23 is .3617, that of 234 is .3692.

When the number contains four significant figures, the mantissa can be obtained directly from pages 4 and 5 provided the number is not greater than 1900. When the number is greater, the required mantissa is found from pages 2 and 3 by interpolation. Find the mantissa for the first three significant figures; find the difference between it and the next higher mantissa in the table (it will in general be nearly equal to that printed under d); find from the table at the bottom of page 3 the proportional part of this tabular difference for the fourth significant figure and add it to the lower mantissa. Thus log 2345 is .3692 plus five-tenths of 19, that is 10; hence .3702. For log 23456 we add besides six-hundredths of 19, that is 1; hence .3703. Or we multiply 19 by .56 and take the nearest integer to the value, namely, 11.

Given a logarithm to find the corresponding number; or, to use the table inversely.

When the number is wanted to not more than three significant figures, find the mantissa in the table which is nearest to the given mantissa; the corresponding argument gives three figures of the number, and the position of the decimal point is determined by the characteristic. Thus the number corresponding to 2.5015 is 317, that to $\bar{2}$.5020 is .0318.

Suppose four significant figures are wanted. If the mantissa does not exceed .2785, the nearest mantissa on pages 4–5 will point out the number to four figures. If it exceeds the above number, the fourth figure is obtained by interpolation. Find the next lower mantissa; find the difference between the said mantissa and the next higher, also the difference between said mantissa and the given mantissa, and find from the table of page 3 what proportional part the latter difference is of the former. For example, the next lower to .7370 is .7364, hence the first part of the number is 545, and the fourth figure is that part of ten which 6 is of 8: namely 7; hence 5.457.

To find the logarithm of a product.

Take the sum of the logarithms of the factors. Thus,

$$\log (123 \times 4567) = 2.0899$$
$$3.6590$$
$$\bullet \qquad \underline{6}$$
$$5.7495$$

To find the logarithm of a quotient.

Subtract the logarithm of the denominator from the logarithm of the numerator. Thus,

$$\log \tfrac{123}{4567} = 2.0899$$
$$3.6596$$
$$\overline{2}.4303$$

To find the logarithm of a power.

Multiply the logarithm of the base by the index of the power. Thus,

$$\log \ 987^2 = 2(2.9943) = 5.9886$$
$$\log (.987)^2 = 2(\overline{1}.9943) = \overline{1}.9886$$

To find the logarithm of a root.

Divide the logarithm of the base by the index of the root. Thus,

$$\log \sqrt{987} = \tfrac{1}{2}(2.9943) = 1.4972$$
$$\log \sqrt{.987} = \tfrac{1}{2}(\overline{1}.9943) = \overline{1}.9972$$

II. Antilogarithms, pp. 6-7.

This is a table of the fractional powers of 10 from $10^{.000}$ to $10^{.999}$. The first two figures of the fraction or mantissa are given in the left column, and the third in the top row.

To find the number corresponding to a logarithm.

This is given by a direct use of the table. Find the entry for the first three figures of the mantissa, take the difference between that entry and the next higher, and from the column of proportional parts find the part which requires to be added to the entry on account of the fourth figure. Insert the decimal point in the place indicated by the characteristic of the logarithm. For example, to find the antilogarithm of 2.9876. For 987 we have 9705, difference is 22; the proportional part of 22 for 6 is 13, therefore $9705 + 13 = 9718$, and inserting the decimal point, 971.8.

The direct use of a table of antilogarithms serves the same purpose as the inverse use of a table of logarithms.

III. Addition Logarithms, pp. 8-9.

The argument is $\log n$, where n is a fraction less than unity. Thus the characteristic of $\log n$ is negative; it is not printed so, but is indicated by its complement to 10. Thus the argument 9.713 means $9.713 - 10$, or $\overline{1}.713$.

Given the logarithm of each of two numbers, to find the logarithm of their sum.

Let a and b denote the two numbers, of which b is the less. Then

$$\log (a + b) = \log a + \log\left(1 + \frac{b}{a}\right), \tag{1}$$

and $$\log n = \log\frac{b}{a} = \log b - \log a. \tag{2}$$

Having found $\log n$ by means of (2), we get $\log (1 + n)$ from the table, and by adding it to $\log a$ obtain $\log (a + b)$.

Example, $\log a = 3.8060,\ \ \log b = 2.1618.$

Therefore, $\log n = \log\frac{b}{a} = 2.1618$
                               3.8060
                               $\overline{2.3558}$

therefore, from the table, $\log (1 + n) = 0.0097$
therefore, $\log (a + b) = 3.8060$
                                          0.0097
                                          $\overline{3.8157}$

To solve the same question by means of Tables I. and II. :

$$a = 6397, \quad b = 1449 + 2 = 145.1,$$
$$a + b = 6542, \quad \log(a + b) = 8156 + 1 = 3.8157.$$

IV. Subtraction Logarithms, pp. 10-13.

This table is arranged similarly to the preceding, excepting that the tenth decade is expanded on pages 12–13.

Given the logarithm of each of two numbers, to find the logarithm of their difference.

Let a and b denote the two numbers, of which b is the less. Then,

$$\log(a - b) = \log a\left(1 - \frac{b}{a}\right) = \log a + \log\left(1 - \frac{b}{a}\right)$$
$$= \log a - \log \frac{1}{1 - \frac{b}{a}}.$$

Let $\log n = \log \frac{b}{a}$, then from the table we get $\log \frac{1}{1 - n}$, which subtracted from $\log a$, gives $\log(a - b)$.

Example. Given $\log a = 1.9876$ and $\log b = 1.5432$.

Then
$$\log n = \log \frac{b}{a} = \begin{array}{c} 1.5432 \\ 1.9876 \\ \hline 1.5556 \end{array} \ i.e., \ 9.5556 - 10.$$

Now, from the table, 9.555 gives 0.1931 and 6 gives 3,

$$\therefore \ \log \frac{1}{1 - n} = 0.1934,$$

$$\therefore \ \log(a - b) = \begin{array}{c} 1.9876 \\ 0.1934 \\ \hline 1.7942 \end{array}$$

Suppose that $\log(1 + n)$ is known (n being less than unity) and its position in Table III., then $\log \frac{1}{1 - n}$ can be found in the corresponding position in Table IV., and $\log \frac{1 + n}{1 - n}$ can be found by adding these two logarithms together.

Logarithms of addition and subtraction are sometimes called Gaussian logarithms.

V. Logarithmic Sines and Cosines, pp. 14-17.

Pages 14–15 give the logarithm of the sine to every tenth of a degree, that is, every six minutes. The logarithm of the cosine is obtained by taking the right-hand argument and reading backwards. The d column gives the difference between the two last entries of a row, the last entry of one row being identical with the first of the succeeding. As the sines and cosines are all less than unity, the characteristics of the logarithms are all negative; they are indicated by their complement to 10. Pages 16–17 give the sines and cosines for the first nine degrees to every hundredth of a degree.

Given an arc, to find its log sin.

If the arc is less than 90°, its log sin is found by the direct use of the table. For example, to find log sin 17°.66. By the table log sin 17°.6 is $9.4805 - 10$, the difference is 24, and the proportional part for 6 is 14; hence, $9.4819 - 10$. If the arc is $> 90°$ but $< 180°$, find the log sin of the difference between 180° and the arc; if $> 180°$ but $< 270°$ find.that of the difference between the arc and 180°, and if $> 270°$ but $< 360°$, find that of the difference between 360° and the arc.

Given the log sin, to find the arc.

For example, to find the arc in degrees the log sin of which is 9.6669. The next lower log sin in the table is 9.6659, which corresponds to 27°.6; the tabular difference is 14, and the given difference is 10; hence, the arc is 27°.67.

At the bottom of page 17 there are two auxiliary tables. The one gives the equivalent in minutes of the fractions of a degree; thus, 0°.63 is equivalent to 37'.8. The other is called a Delambre's table; it is used to find the log sin of a small arc. On account of the table, pages 16–17, this auxiliary table is not required, except when the arc is less than 0°.4. By S is here meant the logarithm of the ratio of the number expressing the degree to the number expressing the corresponding sine.

To find the sine of a small arc.

Let n denote the number of degrees; then,

$$\log \sin n° = \log n - S.$$

Example: to find log sin 0°.123. Log .123 is 9.0899 − 10, and S is 1.7581; hence, log sin 0°.123 is 7.3318 − 10.

To find a small arc, given its˙log sin.

We have $\log n = \log \sin n° + S.$

For example, given log sin to be 7.1234 − 10. As the log sin is less than 8.2872 − 10, the value of S to add is 1.7581. Hence, 8.8815 − 10, the number corresponding to which is .0761, hence 0°.0761.

VI. Logarithmic Tangents and Cotangents, pp. 18-21.

This table is similar to the preceding. After 45° the tangent is greater than unity, the characteristic is no longer negative; hence, the true characteristic is printed.

Of the two auxiliary tables at the bottom of page 21, the one gives the equivalent in degrees of so many minutes; the other is a Delambre's table of T for the first four degrees. By T is here meant the logarithm of the ratio of the number of degrees to the number expressing the tangent. It is used in finding the log tan of a very small arc. We have,

$$\log \tan n° = \log n - T$$

and $\qquad \log n = \log \tan n° + T.$

VII. Logarithmic Sines and Cosines for Minutes, pp. 22-23.

Here the log sin is given directly to every ten minutes, and by interpolation to every minute. The same table gives log cos when read backwards. Pages 22-25 give the proportional parts for all the differences from 1 to 100.

Example: to find log cos 19° 28'. Log cos 19° 20' is 9.9748 − 10, the tabular difference is −5, the proportional part of −5 for 8 is −4; hence, 9.9744 − 10.

At the end we have a table of S for the range between 0° and 7°, where the change in the value of the tabular difference is too rapid to allow of interpolation by proportional parts. Here S is the logarithm of the ratio of the number of minutes expressing the arc to the sine of the arc. Thus, 3.5372 is the log of the ratio of 378 to .1097.

VIII. Logarithmic Tangents and Cotangents for Minutes, pp. 24–25.

This table is similar to the preceding.

By T is meant the log of the ratio of the number of minutes expressing the arc to the tangent of the arc.

IX. Natural Sines and Cosines, pp. 26–27.

The natural sine is given to each tenth of a degree; that is, to every six minutes. The equivalent minutes are printed alongside of the tenths of a degree. At the bottom of page 27 there is a table of proportional parts, the whole interval being six, to facilitate the interpolation to a minute.

What is the sine of 34° 46'? The sine of 34° 42' is .5693, the tabular difference is 14, and the pp. of 14 for 4 is 9; hence, .5702.

What is the arc whose cosine is .4326? The arc of .4321 is 64° 24', the tabular difference is 16, the difference of given cosine is 5, corresponding to a pp. of 5 for a tabular difference of 16 we have 2'; hence, the arc is 64° 22'.

X. Natural Tangents and Cotangents, pp. 28-29.

XI. Natural Secants and Cosecants, pp. 30-31.

These tables are similar to the preceding. At the end of each we have a continuation of the table of proportional parts, the interval being six.

XII. Radians, pp. 32-33.

By a radian is meant the unit of circular measure of an angle. The table gives directly the number of radians equivalent to any number of degrees expressed by not more than three significant figures. The integer figure of the entry is printed only in the 0 column. Thus, the equivalent of 67°.8 is 1.1833 radians, and the equivalent of 1 radian is 57°.3. The tabular difference is either 17 or 18; hence, to find the equivalent for 4 significant figures, we add the proper pp. of either 18 or 17, as the case may be.

The column headed $h\ m$ gives the equivalent in hours and minutes of the corresponding number of degrees in the left column; and the adjacent column headed p gives that fraction of a whole period or perigon which is equivalent to the ratio of the corresponding number of degrees to 360°.

The small table at bottom of page 33 gives the number of radians equivalent to the given number of minutes, while the column headed p gives that fraction of a period or perigon which the corresponding number of minutes bears to 360°.

When the decimal point is changed by any number of places in the argument, the decimal point is changed by an equal number of places in the entry. Thus,

$$3°.6 = .06283 \text{ and } 360° = 6.283.$$

XIII. Reciprocals, pp. 34-35.

The reciprocal is given directly for any sequence of three figures, the decimal point being after the first. When the decimal point in the argument is shifted any number of places, the decimal point in the entry is shifted an equal number of places in the opposite direction. Thus,

$$\frac{1}{7.89} = .1267, \qquad \frac{1}{78.9} = .01267,$$

$$\frac{1}{789.} = .001267, \qquad \frac{1}{.789} = 1.267.$$

At the bottom of page 35 we have the first nine multiples of the fractions $\frac{1}{2}$, $\frac{1}{3}$, etc., up to $\frac{1}{16}$. A bracket indicates that the figures included repeat themselves.

XIV. Squares, pp. 36-37.

This table gives directly to four significant figures the square of any sequence of three figures, the decimal point being after the first. When the decimal point changes in the number, the decimal point in the square changes by double the number of places in the same direction. Thus the square of 3.76 is 14.14, that of 37.6 is 1414, and that of .376 is .1414.

When the number consists of more than three figures, the square may be found by means of the table of proportional parts. For example, to find the square of 1889 to four significant figures. The square of 188 is 35,340, the pp. of 38 for 9 is 34; therefore the square of 1889 is 3,568,000. Here the zeros are not significant, but only indicate the position of the decimal point.

To find the complete square for any sequence of three figures.

The complete square of any two figures is given in the zero column. If the number of three figures is less than 317, we have to find the square of the third figure, and append the terminal figure to the entry of the table, diminishing the terminal figure of the entry by one if the number appended is equal to or greater than 5. For instance, take 234. The square of 4 is 16, hence 6 is to be appended to 5476, but the fourth figure reduces to 5 because it has been increased by one when the 6 was cut off. Hence the complete square is 54,756. When the number exceeds 316, find the square of the two terminal figures in the zero column, take the last two figures of it and append them to the entry, diminishing the terminal figure of the entry by one if the addendum equals or exceeds 50. For example, the last two figures of the square of 96 is 16, the entry for 896 is 8028, hence the complete square is 802,816.

The table at the bottom of page 37 gives the square of the reciprocal of any number of two digits. Thus the square of $\frac{1}{3.4}$ is .0865. When the decimal point is shifted in the argument, the decimal point of the entry requires to be shifted by twice the number of places in the opposite direction. Thus the square of $\frac{1}{.87}$ is 1.32.

XV. Cubes, pp. 38-39.

This table gives to four figures the cube of any number of three figures, and in the 0 column the complete cube of any number of two figures. When the decimal point is shifted in the number, the decimal point of the cube requires to be shifted thrice the number of places in the same direction. Thus the cube of 1.23 is 1.861, that of 12.3 is 1861, that of .123 is .001861.

The small table of page 39 gives the cube of the reciprocal of the number. Thus the cube of $\frac{1}{8.9}$ is .00142. When the decimal point is shifted in the number, the decimal point in the reciprocal of the cube is shifted thrice the number of places in the opposite direction.

XVI. Square Roots, pp. 40–43.

The first part of the table, pages 40–41, gives the square root of any number of three significant figures, when the decimal point is after the first figure, or is any even number of places to the right or left of that position; while the second part of the table, pages 42–43, gives the square root, when the decimal point is after the second figure or any even number of places to the right or left of that position. The square root is given to five figures, the initial figure being printed only in the 0 column.

When the decimal point of the number is shifted any even number of places from its position after either the first digit or after the second digit, the decimal point in the corresponding entry shifts by half the number of places in the same direction. Thus,

$$\sqrt{9.87} = 3.1417, \quad \sqrt{98.7} = 9.9348, \quad \sqrt{987} = 31.417,$$

$$\sqrt{9870} = 99.348, \quad \sqrt{.987} = .99348, \quad \sqrt{.0987} = .31417.$$

The small table of page 41 gives the square root of the reciprocal of any number of two figures, the decimal point being after the first figure; while the small table of page 43 gives the same when the decimal point is after the second figure. Thus,

$$\frac{1}{\sqrt{9.8}} = .319, \quad \frac{1}{\sqrt{98}} = .101, \quad \frac{1}{\sqrt{.98}} = 1.01, \quad \frac{1}{\sqrt{980}} = .0319.$$

XVII. Cube Roots, pp. 44–49.

The first part of the table gives the cube root, when the decimal point is after the first significant figure, or when displaced any multiple of three places to the right or left of that position; the second part similarly when the decimal point is after the second significant figure; and the third part when it is after the third. A displacement of three places in the number causes a displacement of one place in the same direction in the cube root. Thus,

$$\sqrt[3]{1.23} = 1.0714, \quad \sqrt[3]{12.3} = 2.3084, \quad \sqrt[3]{123} = 4.9732,$$

$$\sqrt[3]{1230} = 10.714, \quad \sqrt[3]{.0123} = .23084, \quad \sqrt[3]{.123} = .49732.$$

Similarly the three small tables give the cube root of the reciprocal of any two figures for the three distinct positions of the decimal point.

XVIII. Multiples, pp. 50-67.

This table gives the first nine multiples of any number of three figures, and the folding table at the end gives the same for any number of two figures. By means of this table and our knowledge of the ordinary multiplication table we can write down any of the nine multiples of a number of four figures, and with the help of the folding table we can do the same for any number of five figures. By a double reference to the table we obtain a multiple of six figures, and so on. Thus,

$$8 \text{ times} \quad 789 = \quad 6312$$

$$8 \text{ times} \quad 6789 = \quad \begin{array}{r} 6312 \\ 48 \\ \hline 54312 \end{array}$$

$$8 \text{ times} \quad 56789 = \quad \begin{array}{r} 6312 \\ 448 \\ \hline 454312 \end{array}$$

$$8 \text{ times} \quad 456789 = \quad \begin{array}{r} 6312 \\ 3648 \\ \hline 3654312 \end{array} \quad .$$

To multiply any two numbers together.

Consider, for example, the product of 123,456,789 and 6987. Turn up the multiples of 789, and write down the 7, 8, 9, and 6 multiples under one another in the usual manner, only space is to be left between each pair of multiples for another row of figures; then turn up the multiples of 456, write down the 7 multiple with its initial figure below the fourth figure of the 7 multiple of 789, and similarly for the other multiples; then turn up the multiples of 123, write down the 7 multiple with its first figure above the fourth figure of the 7 multiple of 456, and so on, as follows:

```
    8 6 1     5 5 2 3
          3 1 9 2
      9 8 4     6 3 1 2
          3 6 4 8
  1 1 0 7     7 1 0 1
        4 1 0 4
  7 3 8     4 7 3 4
      2 7 3 6
  ─────────────────────
  8 6 2 5 9 2 5 8 4 7 4 3
```

To divide one number by another.

For example, to divide 4,567,890 by 567.   Turn up the multiples of 567 ; find the next lower to 4567, deduct it; take down another figure, find the next lower multiple to the number so formed, and so on, as follows :

$$567)4567890(8056$$
$$\underline{4536}$$
$$3189$$
$$\underline{2835}$$
$$3540$$
$$\underline{3402}$$
$$138$$

If the divisor consist of four figures, as 5678, turn up the multiples of 567 and correct them mentally for the additional figure 8.   If there are five figures, as 56,789, correct the multiples of 567 by adding the multiples of 89 from the folding table.

XIX. Circumference of Circle, pp. 68-69.

When the decimal point is changed in the diameter, the decimal point in the circumference changes by an equal number of places in the same direction.   When n represents the radius, the circumference is obtained by doubling the entry.

The small table, page 69, gives the value, the logarithm, and the reciprocal of frequently occurring constants, which involve π.   The mantissa of the logarithm of the reciprocal is the complement to 1 of the mantissa of the logarithm of the constant.   Thus, $\log \dfrac{1}{\pi}$ is $\bar{1}.5029$.

XX. Area of Circle, pp. 70-71.

When n denotes the radius, the area is obtained by multiplying the entry by 4.   When the decimal point is changed in the diameter, the decimal point of the area changes by double the number of places in the same direction.   Thus, when the diameter is 3.96 the area is 12.32, when 39.6 then 1232, when .396 then .1232.

The diameter of a circle of given area is obtained by the inverse use of the table.

When n denotes the diameter of a sphere, the surface is

πn^2. Hence the surface of a sphere of given diameter is obtained by multiplying the entry of the table by 4.

The auxiliary table, page 71, gives the decimal equivalents of the binary divisions of the inch, and also the decimal equivalents of a number of inches as part of the foot or of the yard. Thus, the area of a circle of $3\frac{3}{8}$ inch diameter, is that of 3.375 inch; hence, 8.920 + 26, that is, 8.946 square inches.

XXI. Content of Sphere, pp. 72-73.

This table gives the content of a sphere of which n is the diameter. When the radius is given, the spherical content is obtained by multiplying the tabular entry by 8. When the decimal point is changed in the diameter, the decimal point of the content is changed thrice the number of places in the same direction.

The small table at the bottom of page 73 gives the logarithm of the product of successive integers from 1 up to n, and the logarithm of the powers of 2 up to the 29th. For example, $\log 1 \cdot 2 \cdot 3 \cdot 4 \cdot 5 \cdot 6$ is 2.8573.

XXII. Hyperbolic Logarithms, pp. 74-75.

This table gives directly the hyperbolic or natural logarithm of any sequence of three significant figures, the decimal point being after the first. When the decimal point of the sequence is shifted n places to the right from the above position, find the logarithm of 10^n in the auxiliary table and add it to the entry; and when the decimal point is shifted n places to the left, add the logarithm of 10^{-n}. Thus,

$$\log 56.7 = 1.7352 \qquad \log 567 = 1.7352$$
$$2.3026 \qquad\qquad 4.6052$$
$$\overline{4.0378} \qquad\qquad \overline{6.3404}$$

$$\log .567 = 1.7352 \qquad \log. .0567 = 1.7352$$
$$\bar{3}.6974 \qquad\qquad \bar{5}.3948$$
$$\overline{\bar{1}.4326} \qquad\qquad \overline{\bar{3}.1300}$$

By m in the auxiliary table is meant the modulus or multiplier for converting the natural or hyperbolic logarithm of a number into the common logarithm of the number, and by $\dfrac{1}{m}$ is meant the reciprocal modulus or multiplier for converting the common log of a number into the natural.

Example: To find the hyperbolic log of 1889, given the common log to be 3.2762.

$$
\begin{aligned}
\text{The equivalent of } 3 \quad &= 6.9078 \\
\text{The equivalent of } .2 \quad &= 0.4605 \\
\text{The equivalent of } .07 \quad &= 0.1612 \\
\text{The equivalent of } .006 \quad &= 0.0138 \\
\text{The equivalent of } .0002 &= 0.0005 \\
\hline
\text{Therefore hyp. log. of } 1889 &= 7.5438
\end{aligned}
$$

XXIII. Amount of One Unit of Money at the End of a Given Number of Years, p. 76.

The argument in the left-hand column is the number of years during which one unit of money (whether dollar, pound, franc, or mark) has been allowed to accumulate at compound interest, while the argument in the top row is the rate of interest expressed as so much per cent per year. The general expression for the amount of one unit in n years at r per cent per year is $\left(1 + \dfrac{r}{100}\right)^n$.

Given the principal, the number of years, and the rate, to find the amount.

Find from the table the amount of one unit of money for the given number of years and rate, and multiply that number by the principal. For example, to find the amount of $123 at the end of 25 years at 6 per cent per year. The entry for 25 years and 6 per cent is 4.292; to find the product of this number and 123, turn up the multiples of 123.

$$
\begin{aligned}
4.292 \times 123 = \quad &246 \\
&11\ 07 \\
&24\ 6 \\
&\underline{492} \\
&527.916
\end{aligned}
$$

As the fourth figure of 4.292 is inexact, the figures 1 and 6 of the product are not significant; hence the result is $527.9.

Given the amount, the number of years, and the rate, to find the principal.

Find from the table the amount of one unit for the given number of years and rate, and divide the total amount by it; the quotient is the principal.

Given the principal, the rate, and the amount, to find the number of years.

Divide the amount by the principal and compare the quotient with the entries in the column under the given rate. For example, to find the number of years in which $456 becomes $742.82 at 5 per cent per year. Dividing 742.82 by 456, we get 1.629, which is the entry in the 5 per cent column for 10 years.

Given the principal, the amount, and the number of years, to find the rate.

Divide the amount by the principal and compare the quotient with the entries in the row of the given number of years.

To find the amount of a unit of money for a number of years and a fraction of a year.

Find the difference between the entry for the number of years and the next higher entry, multiply it by the fraction of the year, and add the result to the lower entry. For example, to find it for 7 years and 3 months, the rate of interest being 8 per cent. The entry for 7 years is 1.714, and that for 8 is 1.851; the difference is 137, the fourth part of which is 34, which added to 1.714 gives 1.748.

To find the amount of a unit of money for an intermediate rate of interest.

The value may be found approximately by applying the principle of proportional parts as above. For example, the amount for 9 years at 5½ per cent is 1.551, plus one-half of 138; hence, 1.620.

To find the amount of one unit of money for a number of years greater than 49.

Break the number of years into parts each not greater than 49, multiply together the entries for the several parts; the result is the amount for the given number of years.

For example, to find the amount of one unit of money for 70 years at 10 per cent. The entry for 40 years is 45.26, and that for 30 years is 17.45. To find the product of 45.26 by 17.45, turn up the multiples of 745 and correct them for the 1; the result is 789.7870, but the last three figures are not significant; hence, 789.8. The true value is 789.747.

This problem may also be solved by means of the small table of logarithms, page 5, where the logs of the coefficients from 1.000 up to 1.100 are given to six places in order that their multiples may be obtained exact to four places. The log of 1.10 is .041393, which multiplied by 70 gives 2.8975, the antilogarithm of which is 789.8.

XXIV. Present Value of 1000 Units of Money, p. 77.

This table gives the present value of 1000 units of money due n years hence, the rate of interest having any one of the values in the top row. The entry is given, not for 1, but for 1000, in order to simplify the specification of the decimal point. When an entry is taken out, the decimal point ought to be shifted three places to the left.

The method of using this table is the same as that for Table XXIII.

XXV. Amount of an Annuity when paid at the End of Each Year, p. 78.

This table gives the amount of an annuity of one unit of money per year, when the annuity is allowed to accumulate for n years, the first payment being made at the end of one year from the time of reckoning.

The method of using Table XXIII. applies to this table, " one unit of money per year " being substituted for " one unit of money," excepting the rule at the end for extending the table. In order to extend the table, the value of $\left(1 + \dfrac{r}{100}\right)^n$ must be found by that rule, and the result substituted in the formula at the top of the table.

XXVI. Present Value of the Preceding, p. 79.

This table gives the value at the beginning of the time of reckoning of an annuity of one unit of money per year allowed to accumulate for a given number of years, the first payment being made at the end of one year from the beginning of the time of reckoning.

The method of using the table is the same as for Table XXV.

XXVII. Amount of an Annuity when paid at the Beginning of Each Year, p. 80.

This table gives the amount of an annuity of one unit of money per year, when the several payments are allowed to grow at any one of the rates of interest specified, the first payment being made at the beginning of the time of reckoning.

The method of using the table is the same as for Table XXV.

XXVIII. Annuity required to extinguish a Debt of 1000, p. 81.

This table gives the annual sum to be paid for a given number of years, the first payment being made one year from the present time, in order to extinguish a present debt of 1000 units of money. Here the 1000 is introduced for the same reason as in the case of Table XXIV.

To extend the table, the extended value of $(1 + r)^n$ must be found and substituted in the formula printed at the top.

XXIX. Least Divisors, pp. 82–85.

This table gives the least divisor of any number up to 10,000. The first two figures of the number are given in the left-hand column, the third figure in the top row and the terminal figure in the row beneath. The only terminal figures entered are 1, 3, 7, 9, because any number which terminates otherwise is evidently divisible by 2 or 5.

To find the factors of any number less than 10,000.

If it is an even number, divide out 2 until the remainder is odd; if it then ends in 5, divide out the power of 5; then enter the table with the remaining quotient to find its least divisor; divide out that divisor, and with the then remaining quotient enter the table again; and so on until the remaining quotient is a prime, which is indicated in the table by a bar.

Example: 1889 is a prime.

$$9876 = 2 \times 4938 = 2^2 \times 2469.$$

Now 2469 has least divisor 3, and quotient is 823, and 823 is a prime. Hence,

$$9876 = 2^2 \times 3 \times 823.$$

XXX. Exponentials, p. 86.

The upper part of the table contains the ascending powers of e from .00 to .99 and from 1.0 to 9.9; and the lower part the corresponding descending powers. The upper part forms a small table of hyperbolic antilogarithms.

At the bottom of the page we have the first nine multiples of e and of the reciprocal of e, the first nine fractional powers of e, both positive and negative, and the powers of e given by the first nine multiples of $\frac{\pi}{2}$, both positive and negative.

XXXI. Multiples (Folding Leaf).

This table contains the first nine multiples of the numbers from 1 to 99. It may be used as a table of proportional parts for tenths by inserting a decimal point before the last figure, and for hundredths by inserting the point before the second last figure.